DONALD CASKIE

*The Tartan
Pimpernel*

Collins

FONTANA BOOKS

First published by Oldbourne Book Co. Ltd. 1957
First issued in Fontana Books 1960
Thirteenth Impression july 1974

© Oldbourne Book Co. Ltd. 1957
Printed in Great Britain
Collins Clear-Type Press
London and Glasgow

THE TARTAN PIMPERNEL

"As exciting and eventful as the novel from which its title derives. It is an inspiring story, a testament of the power of goodness in the conflict with evil."

SCOTSMAN

"Dr Caskie recounts his adventures racily and well, without rancour and with constant humour." GLASGOW HERALD

"Told with admirable sincerity."

THE TIMES LITERARY SUPPLEMENT

CONTENTS

CHAPTER ONE

Sombre Dimanche

I PREPARED for my morning service at the Scots Kirk in the Rue Bayard, Paris, with a heavy heart. The weather was beautiful and a slight haze that seemed to promise heat hung over the bridges. It could have been drifting smoke from the battles that were being fought around the city. German soldiers were driving up the valley of the Seine and the Wehrmacht, two millions strong and at the height of its power, was engulfing France. It was June 9th, 1940—a Sunday. Under a blazing sun, in their oven-like tanks, enemy soldiers, relentless and confident, smashed through villages, reduced homes to rubble and raced towards the French capital, jubilant in the belief that Paris lay defenceless before the might of their Fuehrer. So far, Paris was untouched, except by fear. It was a day when the avenues and boulevards should have been alive with gay and chattering Parisians, making the most of the Sabbath break from work. But Paris seemed dismal and dark. The sunshine, gilding the greenery of the trees in the gardens, mocked a people who knew but could not admit that defeat was imminent.

Rumour ran like wildfire through the city, false reports and tales that startled and struck horror. The Fifth Column was active and already a great exodus had begun. Cars packed with officials, private citizens, politicians and journalists made their way out of the City. Heavy lorries carried whole families and parties of neighbours, together with the pathetic conglomeration of household and personal oddments that human beings clutch in an emergency. A Siamese cat blandly grooming its whiskers sat on some luggage piled on a truck. Strapped to the back of a bicycle, ridden by a serious-looking girl, a doll stared unseeingly into space. An old woman laboured under a heavy, anonymous bundle.

Slowly in the heat, the endless snake of assorted vehicles

moved on the jammed roads, all making for the ports, jerking
into speed for a few moments and then halting, or returning
to a sullen crawl.

Many more thousands of people, more than half the pop-
ulation, remained at home, clerks, working people, café pro-
prietors, the great mass who had no other place to go. Some
of them had been in the city in 1914 when the Boche
advanced to within thirty miles of its outskirts. Faithful
and fearless, a little obtuse and poignantly brave, they believed
that another miracle would stop the new advance, that their
Paris would not, could not, fall to the enemy. But the majority
of Parisians knew they were imperilled, that Paris must fall,
and they refused to be stampeded by Hitler's Wehrmacht.
They were prepared for temporary occupation by the enemy.
All around me that morning, as I made my way to the Scots
Kirk in Paris—that little bit of France which is for ever
Scotland—I felt the agony of France. Five years earlier in
1935, I had been called to Paris from my quiet country
parish of Gretna on the shores of the fast flowing Solway, and
I had learned to love the beautiful city to which I had
come. I remembered the last sermon I had preached in
Gretna before my departure for France. The text was prophetic
of the work that lay before me on the Continent of Europe,
and in some of its cities. It was the great Call that came
to the Apostle Paul on the Damascus Road after his con-
version: 'Arise, and go into the city, and it shall be told
thee what thou must do.' Perhaps, I thought, the purpose
of my call to France is about to be vindicated, and I prayed
with Rupert Brooke that God would match me with this
hour, and catch my youth, and waken me from sleeping.

I chose the Psalm and the hymns and the readings with
special care. As I sought out familiar faces in the congregation,
my heart was full. Old, middle-aged and young friends were
present. We needed the comfort of prayer, and we knew
that trials and tribulations awaited all of us, especially the
older members of the Kirk. But here, on that Sunday morning we felt at home—here was a happy place in this ancient
European capital. We might so easily have been in Scotland.

For centuries the Hundredth Psalm has been popular with

Scottish folk. Our Covenanting Fathers sang it before the Battle of Drumclog.

Almost exactly four years after the ' sombre Dimanche' of Paris, 1940, thousands of Scottish soldiers from the Highlands and Lowlands, from cities and crofts, would sing it again as they stood at the ready, part of the liberating invasion army of 1944. On that sunny Sabbath morning in 1940 it lifted the hearts of the Scots gathered in the Kirk on Rue Bayard.

> ' All people that on earth do dwell,
>   Sing to the Lord with cheerful voice.'

A minister of the Gospel has a very special affection for his own congregation, and I wanted my people to feel strong in God, even though the world seemed to be collapsing about them. The Old Testament reading was chosen to remind them of their unfailing support: it was from the 46th Psalm.

> ' God is our refuge and our strength,
>   A very present help in time of trouble!'

I suppose the appalling drama that was being fought out a few miles away made us tense as we worshipped. The threat was incalculable. The most fearful army of all time was marching towards us. My own heart lifted and was high when I read the New Testament lesson. Imminent peril strengthens faith and the words of the Gospel are always appropriate. I had chosen from the 24th chapter according to St. Matthew :

> ' And ye shall hear of wars, and rumours of war, see that ye be not troubled, for all these things must come to pass, but the end is not yet. For nation shall rise against nation; and kingdom against kingdom, and there shall be famines, and pestilences and earthquakes. All these are the beginning of sorrows.'

The service was nearly ending, and the walls of our little church had become like a strong hand confidently and happily holding us secure from the world. We closed with an item of praise that some have called the Scottish National Anthem. It was sung to the tune ' Salzburg.'

> ' *O god of Bethel by Whose hand,*
> *Thy people still are fed,*
> *Who through this weary pilgrimage,*
> *Hast all our fathers led.*
>
> *O spread thy covering wings around,*
> *Till all our wanderings cease,*
> *And at our Father's loved abode,*
> *Our souls arrive in peace.'*

I commended my people to God. I committed to Him the Kirk where our kinsfolk have worshipped for nearly a century and then, outside in the warm sunshine, I said *au revoir* to my congregation.

On the table in the vestibule lay a bunch of white heather I had brought from my native island of green grassy Islay the previous year. That heather gave me an odd certainty that all would still be well for Paris. In my heart I was certain that I would see her again before I went westering home. I closed our church.

I had to leave Paris immediately. Out of the rumours one fact was clear. Within a few days the city would be occupied by the Germans. The heroism and strength of the French and the British armies could not halt this new type of military leviathan created by a nation that prepared for war, while our countries concentrated upon the crafts and arts of peace. General Weygand announced in one of his despatches that the enemy was attacking under great smoke-screens, and something of the kind covered news reports in and out of the city during those fateful days. But we knew that the majority of minor Government officials were packing their bags, under orders to abandon the city. M. Paul Reynaud, we knew, was with the High Command, and it was a safe deduction that the Government soon must leave.

The British Embassy was evacuating. There was the hurry and flurry of departure around the buildings where our flag was still flying. Only neutrals remained. The U.S. Embassy flag was displayed and it was some consolation to know that a few friendly foreigners would be in Paris to remind Parisians that their city was not all German.

As I made my way to the manse in the Rue Piccini, I was thoughtful and preoccupied with plans for my own departure. Ordinarily, I suppose, a minister of religion, falling into the hands of enemy soldiers can rely upon their innate respect for the cloth. But my Scots respect for religion and human beings had prompted me to denounce Hitler, his works and absurd pomp from my pulpit. Hitler had elevated racial persecution into an expression of national and individual virtue, and corrupted the souls of his own people, especially the young. He lusted for power in a diabolical way, and his wicked pretensions and idolising of military ' might ' appalled all decent men. When news of his concentration camps and atrocities reached us in Paris, I denounced them in the Scots Kirk in more than one sermon. In my first I chose the text from the Prophecy of Hosea:

' They have sown the wind and they shall reap the whirl-
    wind.'

Like most texts the prophecy it contained was apposite, and as always, it was fulfilled in God's time. I could have chosen my texts more carefully for the Fifth Column was about, but my sermons had been delivered with no thought of flattering the master of the German ' race.' From every point of view it would be wiser to leave Paris, I decided, and make my way to the coast and from thence home to take stock of my future and render whatever service I could to my own country.

As the day went on it became apparent that I must go to Bordeaux. Our own soldiers had closed most of the roads out of Paris and stories were filtering through of enemy aircraft straffing the routes taken by escaping Parisians. There were fantastic tales of parachutists disguised in the most improbable ways landing and attacking at the least expected places. I was to discover within a few days the meaning of this new type of air warfare. In the meantime I saw the French become refugees in their own country—a country which had given refuge in former years to many victims of the Nazis and Fascists. Mussolini had declared war on us now and beset on all fronts, poignantly fleeing—as their soldiers made a last hopeless stand—the French left their homes. The refugees were oddly silent; the old men and women who trudged along behind handcarts or sat on lorries, seemed curiously, nobly reconciled, so much more reconciled than the young, who know less of life's sorrows and so are more easily overcome by disaster. The old are surprised by joy but in adversity are more content. But one was sad for them above all, and I felt that the sunshine illuminating this most beautiful city was cruel in its warmth and comfort.

The afternoon was busy with preparations for my departure. I visited the older members of the congregation who would not be able to take flight, and bade them farewell, knowing that some I would not meet again. I deposited ten years' accumulation of sermons in manuscript in the cellar where later they were found by a German patrol which searched the manse. I never saw them again. My concierge reported that the soldiers were uninterested in my silver but seemed particularly interested in the matter of my preaching. I have no doubt they were aware of my opinions before they arrived, for a young person, known humorously to the congregation as ' the chiel' among us takin' notes,' had been present at most of our services, assiduously jotting down notes in a large book on his knees. I had hoped I was providing him with edification but, alas, events were to show it was evidence he sought. Time was to play a strange and consoling trick upon both of us.

To the ordinary citizen a Fifth Column is an especially sinister force. You may be aware of its agents and almost certain that you know some of them personally, but in times of war, when the powers they are pledged to support are

victoriously advancing, one is powerless to deal with them.
The German Fifth Column was strong and active in France
before 1940. It was highly organised and efficient and like
an iceberg, by far the larger part of it was unseen and unsuspected in its true dimensions. We know now that it was more
alert than our British Intelligence. Only after Dunkirk and
with the German Army gathered in force on the cliffs above
Boulogne, with the threat of imminent invasion of Britain,
did we train our agents into the fierce intensity and disciplined
work which they carried out after the fall of France. They
girded their loins and relit their lamps.

I had locked the doors of the Scottish Kirk and to my
very faithful friend, M. Gaston the proprietor of the café
next door, given the key of the church for custody. With
a bag on my back, and with a great sadness in my heart,
I left the manse, and joined the great Exodus.

The guns at Mont Valerien, rumbling thunderously, were
the accompaniment to a Paris which seemed to be entirely
on the move. Unopposed enemy aircraft filled the sky and
one felt they were extinguishing the light of the sun. Millions
of refugees were marching, fleeing in all sorts of conveyances
into the unknown, leaving the familiar places and escaping
from the realities that had bound their lives. To get within
a mile of any of the railway stations south of the city, Lyons,
Austerlitz or Montparnasse was impossible. A rumour that
the French Government had moved to Bordeaux heightened
the tension. Alas, the rumour proved true, and within a
week Marshal Pétain had formed a new Cabinet. After that,
the military authorities were given control of the capital
and Paris was declared an open city.

The Germans marched in on the 13th, a Thursday in
June. I have been told that they came as if from all ends
of the earth, in every street, on every road, precise and correct
in their grey uniforms. There were no French men or women
on the streets to greet them. The open city was deserted,
vast, silent, impersonal and uncommitted. The sun was shining
and birds were singing as the alien soldiers marched through
the suburbs.

They mounted anti-tank guns on the bridges and posted sentries on guard at the Tuileries. Their sense of humour did not equate their sense of history. They enforced a 9 p.m. curfew and a complete blackout, and, over the graveyard hush, the trudge of the boots of sight-seeing soldiers beat like mourning drums. Most of the theatres and places of entertainment closed. Only a few restaurants were open to feed them. Above the Eiffel Tower and over the Arc de Triomphe, the swastika was flying. One procession of French civilians was visible in public. It was under the Arc de Triomphe, quite oblivious of the flying swastika.

There at the Tomb of the Unknown Soldier dozens of women wept bitterly and prayed. The passing victors gravely saluted. Behind them they had left roads littered with dead, the towns they had passed through, had been reduced to a shambles.

At twilight on the 13th, the sky was red and as the sun faded, the swastika, became enveloped in darkness and the Arc de Triomphe was outlined against a fiery sky. Trains had stopped running and the clock over St Lazare had failed and stopped.

We refugees were on the march and Paris was behind us. On that early morning as I moved through the suburbs, which are so much more characteristic of a people than the centre of any great capital, I mourned for the little streets, the homes, factories, shops and cafés and the people who must endure.

The weather changed as evening came and rain began to fall. Because, I suppose, I am a Highlander I remembered the white heather and was not too downcast. I knew that work awaited me wherever I went.

CHAPTER TWO

Last Ship from Bayonne

THE TRAIL of refugees struggled silently through the day. We wore an assortment of our most valuable or favourite clothes—summer finery and heavier winter garb, incongruously thrown on. A very few were practically and neatly dressed as for a hike in the country. None spoke to strangers such was the common fear of the Fifth Column. As evening fell thunder rumbled in the distance and rain began to fall, gathering force and soaking us. A few stragglers from the retreating army appeared; and the chastened civilians eyed them as if they were beings from another world.

The rain fell heavily, lightning flashed across the sky and I felt curiously relieved as if the violent weather somehow put the violence of nations into perspective, and brought humans nearer to human stature, small created creatures whose arrogant brutalities were being played out within their own small world. I halted late in the afternoon and gazed back towards Paris. The city was dead and silent.

The ordinary pains of life, such as being footsore and hungry I gladly accepted, they seemed to be a cross for me to bear, but I was utterly exhausted when I arrived at the village of Sceaux near Chevreuse Valley. By my side an old woman pushed an infant in a perambulator; farther ahead a youth trundled a very old peasant in a wheelbarrow; a dainty girl sat on a pavement, her back against a wall examining one of her feet, a light pair of city shoes lying by her side. In bundled ranks thousands of refugees lay on the village green trying to sleep in the deluge that poured down. I rested with them, sore and weary, but I could not sleep. Long before daybreak, only slightly less exhausted, I was on the march again. I knew the direction in which I was trudging, but the events of the past few days, the previous long day's walk and the night in the open under the rain had dazed me. Now, with the sun gathering in strength, my clothes began to steam. Many soldiers had joined us; they seemed to be sleep-marching, their eyes still seeing blazing buildings, the brutal onslaught of enemy armour, and dead comrades. They were under orders to make their way to the south, and had the right of way. Women, old and young, too tired to move out of their path, were roughly hustled aside. Many of their officers had deserted them, and there was no one in authority. Miserable, soaked in the dirt from days in the open, they struggled on, defeated and disorganised.

All through the day the dreary trek continued and at times I marched as if under hypnosis.

I covered thirty miles, and came to the town of Dourdan at nightfall. There I was slightly more fortunate than on the previous night. I found a roof for my head, in a dilapidated and half demolished school. Into its shelter I crawled and—luxury of luxuries—found a bundle of straw, spread it carefully over the floor and stretched out for a few hour's sleep. The sun was rising when I awoke, and took the road to Tours.

I had caught up with a straggling mass of people when German and Italian aircraft streaked down from the sky. Machine guns spat indiscriminate death. Bombs thudded and exploded all along the road. Men, women and children were blotted out of existence in a few moments. Some died by the roadside, some quietly, some sobbing, others shrieking. Far away I heard the rumbling of guns, and behind us smoke was rising from tiny villages. The French Army had been defeated, and it seemed that Hitler and Mussolini had given orders to ' mop up ' the French civilians.

Half conscious, but curiously alert to danger, I flung myself into ditches all through the day. It is impossible to judge the trajectory of machine-gun bullets striking from the air; sometimes when the aircraft seemed overhead they went wide, sometimes inexplicably close and once, I felt them thudding into the earth a few inches from my head.

The attacks ceased in the late afternoon and the sky was quiet again. I felt a wonderful sense of peace, I revelled in the freedom from the threat of instantaneous death. The road was under my feet and I drew deep breaths and enjoyed the air in my lungs. I was marching again.

There was no food to be found anywhere, and the days that followed were hard and hungry but I had a feeling of achievement when I reached Tours.

Before looking for a lodging for the night, I found a second-hand ironmongery shop and for a few pounds bought an aged and rickety bicycle. The shopkeeper was a kind and eager man. It was reassuring to notice how enthusiastically he subscribed to the adage—business as usual—solicitous, efficient and friendly, he was so eager to please and encourage me on my way that when I pushed the old crock into the street I felt all was well. The first bomb of the heaviest bombardment Tours was to receive landed at that moment, and I jumped on that rickety old bike and raced into nowhere. Close to the banks of the Loire I noticed people dodging into an opening in a wall. I followed them and plunging downstairs, bicycle on shoulder, came to rest in a nice dark anonymous cellar. My own kind, the refugees, were huddled about me, and in the darkness I did my best to comfort them, talking to them as the city rocked under the impact of high explosive. Not far away was a ruined castle, the scene of Sir Walter Scott's *Quentin Durward* which I had read as a boy and again as a young man. I hoped that it would not be hit. Bombs crashed all around us through the night and in the darkness we waited patiently. When the sun rose all was quiet and I left the cellar and pushed the old bike up the hill that lies on the south side of Tours and looked back at the city. It was enveloped in smoke, and in places tongues of flame curled through the shattered roofs. I turned my wheels towards Bordeaux.

The next night I slept in a byre with a pleasant old cow. A friendly creature and a perfect hostess. She did not disturb her guest, but philosophically munched the nourishment which, unfortunately, I couldn't share, and consoled me with her rhythmic champing. In the morning she awakened me with a cheerful ' moo.'

The following night I dined on grapes and had been so long without food that a fruit which might normally have made my dessert, satisfied me. Under the vines loaded with luscious fruit, I rested and felt secure. I looked up at the summer sky and considered the strange position in which the Rev. Donald Caskie was finding himself.

Like everyone, the events of the past few days had been a a shock to me. My education, hopes, aspirations, my desire to serve God—what did it mean? History does not so much play tricks upon a man, as confound him so that he is suddenly launched into the violently inexplicable. Poor chap, he must rely on a rickety bicycle. Eventually he finds that God can do more with a man on a 'rickety bike' than a tyrant can do with armoured divisions, but the immediate impact of the situation is testing. He finds a vineyard and has a good meal under a sky that only the Provider can create, and he is reassured.

That night was heavenly. On such a night one recalls the goodness of life. My mind drifted over everything that had led to this interval in a long moment of universal peril. Parents and family love, school days and friends at Bowmore on my lovely native Islay and later at Dunoon on the bonnie banks of Clyde. Student days in Edinburgh, my first degree as Master of Arts and then the absorbing study given to theology and finally my initiation as Assistant Minister at the High Church on the Mound at Edinburgh. I remembered the companionship of friends and my thoughts were happy.

Yet, as with most reminiscences, my thoughts came back to the present. I could see again the maternal gaze of my bedfellow (the cow) of the previous night. Solemnly she munched away. What, in the name of goodness, was the good lady chewing? Cows are amiable materialists, a small and blessed compensation I suppose for lack of the greater joys that are given by God to men.

I knew what had brought me to this place on that night, and I believe I was grateful. My life had been less eventful than those lived by many of my wandering race, but it had been good. I had seen many countries and worked in places where God walked.

The years at Edinburgh had been happy, filled with study

and all I strove to win. A few years before my appointment to Paris, the University of Michigan appointed me to work for a year on archæological research in the Libyan Desert, in Egypt.

I spent a Christmas night at Bethlehem. That experience made even my present predicament so much more worthwhile. If I had only one wish for men in this life it would be that, like the young minister I then was, they should at some time be close to the birth-place of God on His birthday.

My work took me to the other side of the world after that blessed season in the Holy Land, and I had the good fortune to meet men and women of the Christian religion in the U.S.A. and Canada. I had been a prairie parson in the wheatlands of Manitoba serving—and serving is the very spirit and essence of a minister's life—people so good and honourable, so God-fearing that only a minister can really know them.

I found such people again when I became the Rev. Alex Macara's assistant at St Inan's Parish Church in my own country at Irvine and during the period after my ordination and first full charge, at St Andrew's Parish Church, Gretna Green. For three years I worked on the shores of the Solway Firth until I received my call from the congregation of the Scots Kirk in Paris. Life had been kind to me and here I was in a world, apparently hurtling itself to destruction, and the Lord had fed me with grapes.

The next day I continued on my way and at nightfall I lay down behind a stone dyke and slept undisturbed.

On the following evening I arrived at a little village not far from Bordeaux, again tired and hungry. As I rode into the main street I was puzzled to hear angry shouts behind me. I halted and jumped from the bicycle and a turbulent crowd surrounded me.

' C'est un Boche. Un sale Boche. Tuez le.'

They seemed to mean it; angry hands stretched out at me and blows were aimed in my direction. I protested, shouting loudly that they were talking nonsense; I was no German! I was a Scot—an ally. Then gendarmes pushed their way through the threatening mob. I was handcuffed, and hustled off to the police station, vigorously demanding what charge was going to be brought against a friend whose country was in alliance with France.

'You are a German spy,' a gendarme said when we were inside the police headquarters. 'One of the advance guard sent by your criminal compatriots to prepare the way.'

My eyes widened.

'You carry the hateful symbol of Hitler and the Huns.'

He pointed to the bike that I was pushing awkwardly along with me, my hands constricted by the iron bracelets.

'Look on the back of it. Your identity card is there. That is proof of your mission, Boche!'

I could not turn the bicycle round but when we reached the police station and my hands were free I twisted old faithful about and peered at it. There on the rear mudguard was a miniature swastika which must have been stuck on before I bought the contraption. Furiously I ripped it off. I flung it far into the garden through the open window of the station.

Outside the mob roared and clamoured on the doorstep.

'Ask him for his identity card,' a man cried.

I handed it over. A policeman flung my bag on the table and the crowd quietened, those nearer the door standing on tip-toes, gazing in over the shoulders of their comrades.

On top of my personal effects lay two items that immediately protested my innocence—a Bible and a kilt. It was the latter, not the Bible that did it. No German would have carried a kilt; only a Scot would pack one at a time when France was falling about his ears. My *carte d'identité* was handed back and all was now well. After profuse apologies by the gendarmes I was conducted to a comfortable room above the station where I slept soundly and next morning they gave me breakfast. As I rode out of the village to Bordeaux, people rushed at me again, but this time to shake my hand, and pat my back. I wobbled through them and friendly voices chorused:

'Bon voyage!'

When I reached Bordeaux I found it a maelstrom of rumour, fear and frustration. The last ships had left the harbour and were on their way to the United Kingdom. The first, loaded with refugees packed like herrings in a box, was torpedoed as she cleared port and sailed into the Gulf of Gascony. There were few survivors. The French Government, I was told, had left for North Africa and the Wehrmacht was at La Rochelle. Bordeaux would be occupied in a few hours. I lingered by the dockside, stunned by the news and then made my way to the railway station.

I was advised to go on to Bayonne, make another attempt to take ship and if that failed I could try to escape into Spain.

My spirits sank lower, and as I cycled slowly and hopelessly away from the port, I felt spiritually and morally exhausted. During the long trek to the south, hope had buoyed me up and the thought that I'd win through to join my own kind who, I knew, would hit back at the enemy and finally defeat him. Now for the first time, I felt completely alone, isolated from all I loved, even God Himself. Fatigued beyond endurance, my journey seemed aimless and futile. I could not even find a place to sleep and as my courage ebbed away, I sat down by the side of the road and instinctively reached for my Bible.

I opened it at random and there was the twenty-third chapter of the Book of Job. The words were applicable.

'Even today is my complaint bitter. My stroke is heavier than my groaning. Oh, that I knew where I might find Him, that I might come even to His seat. I would order my cause before Him, and fill my mouth with complaints. Behold I shall go forward but He is not there, and backward, but I cannot perceive Him. . . . But He knoweth the way I take.'

I closed my eyes, feeling comforted and my lips moved in fervent prayer; I felt God close at hand. When I opened my eyes two French soldiers were gazing down at me. They, indeed, I found were the answer to my prayer.

Their faces were covered with the stubble of men who had lived in retreat from discipline for days. They looked tired beyond human endurance, but they did not complain.

'M'sieur seems very tired,' said the taller, who even when in good condition must have been a gaunt man. He knelt and peered into my face; his eyes were red-rimmed but gentle and solicitous under the raw lids.

'When we saw you sitting here we felt we ought to speak. Can we help you?'

I told them I was exhausted. My only hope was to reach Bayonne and catch the last boat to Britain. I was a Scot.

They looked at each other and smiled without speaking. They seemed to be old friends, united perhaps by the dangers they had survived.

'Rest, M'sieu,' said the smaller man, his strong provincial accent seeming even more friendly than the quiet detachment of his comrade.

They moved toward the centre of the road. I sat back and watched. They held up their hands stopping cars, gazing into each, reassuring the drivers and passengers. But the cars were all full, even the rich limousines and then, hours it seemed, but, in fact, only about thirty minutes later, I was comfortably seated in a large car and chatting to a kindly gentleman, who turned out to be the owner.

I gave my bicycle to the soldiers who thanked me as I clasped their hands and bade them Godspeed. It seemed I had fallen among Good Samaritans. The car-owner passed me a rug and made me comfortable.

Escape was imperative for him, too, he explained, but he was not an enemy alien only. He was part of an older institution in history—a racial alien, a Jew. His whole race had been condemned to death by Hitler and the Nazis. Even worse, he was a journalist who had written of freedom, that ideal shared by all men west of the Reich. The journey to Bayonne passed quickly. We confided in each other and became friends. He drove into the town and I was grateful, but not surprised when this generous refugee invited me to join him for the night at his cousin's home. Hospitality was a family trait and the Jewish household was full of refugees. I shared a room and a large bed with four other men, one of them being my friend whose name was Abraham. He smiled as I likened myself to the beggar in the Gospels who was carried by angels to Abraham's bosom.

The kindly soldiers, on the run from peril, and that gentle Jewish gentleman, self-sacrificing, uncomplaining, restored me to Christian contentment. When I set out for the harbour docks in the morning, I was reluctant to find a ship. Overwhelmingly I was aware that I should remain in France, that there would be work for me to do there for my country and countrymen.

The British Consulate was open, and I felt at home as I walked through the front door. I remember the feel of sea air on my face and the taste of salt in my mouth. I am an islander and the sea always suggests home and peace to me. I had friends in the Consulate, and they told me that the last ship for the United Kingdom would sail in a few hours' time. There was a place on board for me.

To my own surprise I told them that I had decided to remain in France. My friends were not quite as astonished as I by the refusal that had come almost spontaneously from my lips. When they urged me, frantically, even angrily, to reconsider, I am afraid my replies were not very satisfactory. I hope they did not think the poor padre had gone insane for the thought would have recurred and worried them as the war prolonged. The padre was preoccupied trying to work out the processes that had led him to this peculiar decision. For days—how many days? he did not know how many—he had walked, trotted, run, halted, meditated, prayed, starved and staggered across leagues of France. He had, in a great company of unfortunates, been bombed, for the first time in his life, shot at, even besieged by a mob of his own allies, nearly burned in a cellar on the Loire, all to reach a ship.

Here was escape and within less time than he had spent *en route* from Paris, he might be eating a good meal and listening to Scottish voices, and willy nilly, he refused to take ship.

I left the Consulate and walked through the dockside streets. The wind from the sea was kindly and consoling and the white gulls screeched as they wheeled and dipped over the harbour.

Thoughts seemed to come into my head as if from some source apart from me. I could not take ship when so many wounded men sought transport. They should have that priority which is the right of the suffering.

The last ship steamed out of Bayonne. I saw it go. Scotland had been so near and now I was cut off from it forever maybe. My heart sank, but surely I was doing the right thing? At that time I was not entirely certain but I had chosen as a Christian minister should choose in duty to his vocation. Of that I *was* certain.

Throughout that day I wandered among the distracted and nerve-torn people, clustered on corners, talking in groups and in cafés, their voices muted by fear of the unknown. Here and there a man or woman would laugh loudly and for a few moments one could sense a feeling of relief, like balm pouring over their anxiety and easing the tense atmosphere. The docks always produced a few happy-go-lucky souls, incapable of fear, jesters who refuse to be intimidated and such men when we feel that we are dropping down to hell, bring us back again to reality.

Night fell, a summer night when honest men might sit at their front doors and talk to their wives of the day's work, when wives might confide to their husbands little precious things they had done and left undone. It was the sort of night when God recompenses us for the trials we think we have endured. On such a night young people walk together and dream of the homes and families they will build. But the morrow could bring an invading army and I had to decide what to do.

My decision was to escape into Spain and I turned my back on the harbour, walked through the town, and climbed up into the hills, walking in happy exhaustion along dark winding roads until I came to a tiny Basque village called Cambo les Bains. There I prayed for further guidance. I was sure that it would be given by Him who had promised to guide all those who put their hand in His, through each preplexing path of life.

CHAPTER THREE

The Seamen's Mission

THE LITTLE village where I rested was in the Basque country
and it seemed on that summer night a perfect haven. I walked
along the main street until I found an hotel, and was shown to
a room by the night porter. Before sleeping I prayed, as I
had prayed now for hours, asking for a sign. I slept well
into the morning and awakened at a late hour.

There was a new Government in Bordeaux which had
surrendered to the Germans. The village where I stayed was
not peaceful, and there was no escape for its inhabitants.
The traditional threat of the Boche had become an imminent
reality. At any time they expected its outriders to appear
on the road.

The spokesman of the Bordeaux Government was Marshal
Pétain. His voice added the last touch of bitter irony to
France's tragedy. The Victor of Verdun, that invincible
warrior who had proclaimed 'They shall not pass' and kept
his word at a terrible price, had capitulated. He now led a
Government of refugees, and a decision to accept defeat was
made after acrimonious debate at a meeting held in a police
station. There were men present who would have died ful-
filling the promise Churchill later made—'We will fight in
the streets and on the beaches.' The French knew the Boche
in a way that the British and Americans would never know
him. In the past he had marched into France, and the taste
of defeat lingered in their mouths and they hated it.

Beyond the village backwater, Frenchmen were still fighting; companies severed from a great army, disorganised but
brave, were hopelessly struggling to keep the enemy from
final victory. Ruthlessly the Wehrmacht stamped them out.
The battle was soon to be over and all that remained, the
government realised, was to acknowledge defeat.

I lingered in the streets of the village that morning and felt a fierce and stubborn fatalism close in on me. History was being made, and the worries of ordinary men are of little account at such times.

After the first broadcast by the Marshal, the news spread rapidly, but so confused were reports, that people kept on the move, still trying to escape. We heard of German soldiers satirically showering refugees with looted foodstuffs and of the owners of marooned limousines being offered petrol, stolen from French units, by cynical Teutonic ' old soldiers.' People had taken flight in despair. They had built homes, had lived to the ritual of hour to hour, day to day, and year to year jobs and careers; and now they were adrift, not knowing where to rest, or where to go.

The new leader of the French people offered something like death. That he, Marshal Pétain, was the spokesman of defeat made their condition more appalling. The Marshal was old and senile and bearing a burden that should have been the responsibility of men half his age. Well-meaning, confused, confronted by complete problems when he was contemplating death, he was simply an old and tired soldier who thought he was saving France when he was sacrificing her. The free French were escaping to Africa and London. The fighting French had begun to rally, but the ordinary people of France, in that miserable hour, were aware only of defeat.

I was standing outside my hotel in Cambo les Bains, a few hours before the Germans marched into the village, feeling I must leave, impelled by a force that was inexplicable. The problem that perplexed me was, which way was I to go. If I went on foot towards the Free France side of the demarcation line, I would most certainly have been overtaken by the enemy. At that moment, two cars drove up and stopped outside the hotel. They both had British plates. There were two occupants in the first car, a French gentleman of Jewish extraction, and an English lady. The occupants of the second were a Russian Princess, her son, and a very old lady, the Princess's mother. I immediately recognised one of them. We had often met in Paris in social, artistic, and intellectual circles, and we both had mutual friends. While I was still staring at my friend in amazement, I heard him say, 'My God, Donald Caskie. What are you doing here, and the Germans only a few miles away? We're making for the other side of the demarcation line.' 'Then I believe you're the answer to my prayer,' I replied. 'Of course we are,' rejoined the Russian Princess from the car behind. 'Come with us. We have room for you.'

Rushing back to the hotel, I paid my bill, ran to my room, grabbed my bag, stuffed my belongings into it, and in a few minutes, I was in the company of friends in my hour of need. The cars hastened towards the demarcation line which separated Vichy France from occupied territory. We were just in time, for a few hours later Cambo les Bains was occupied by the Germans, and the bed that I had slept in the previous night was occupied by a German high-ranking officer. After a long drive we reached Marseilles.

The Mediterranean port was in turmoil. All traffic was uncontrolled and converging on the water front. The streets around the docks were crowded with British soldiers and airmen, the remnants of Dunkirk who had escaped and with incredible ingenuity and bravery made the journey south. Among them were merchant seamen who had been torpedoed in the Atlantic and escaped while on the way to prison camps in Germany. The plight of these men was pitiable. All were hungry, some weak with starvation, others wounded; and their wounds, rudely dressed, were often dirty and gave them intense pain. A number were crippled. For a variety of causes there was not a man to be seen in the crowds who should not have been in bed receiving attention. In groups on the pavement and dockside, they huddled, worn out and totally exhausted. Yet they were held up by a grim spirit of utter determination that drove them on towards survival.

France had surrendered. Public services were at a standstill. France had fallen, and there was no one to help the British soldiers. It was distressing to see them waiting around in their unrelieved misery after the hell they had come through in defence of the common cause.

I wandered around the docks, speaking to them, trying to console the wounded, but feeling helpless before their need.

Here indeed were sheep without a shepherd. I prayed for relief for their agony, for some way in which I could bring help to them.

I had said good-bye to my friends who had brought me here and now I had to find somewhere to stay. I knew of a colleague in Marseilles and I went off to see him. He was a French pastor and he found me cheap and good accommodation. My landlady was the widow of a French pastor and she was delighted to have me in her house. She had spent holidays in Scotland and spoke wistfully of the happiness of those days in our lovely warm-hearted country. Strangers are always welcome when they visit Scotland. We are interested in foreign countries, and the viewpoints and customs of foreign peoples, and try to make our guests feel perfectly at home.

I moved into her house and prayed for enlightenment as to my next move. We Highlanders have the gift of second sight which admits us to dimensions of the unseen world which are closed to races other than the Celtic. I had been moved to pray on the road to Bayonne and two weary 'poilus' had placed themselves nobly at my service. I turned my mind to God, praying for a sign and a way to help my countrymen. Several days passed and I was feeling more and more dispirited until one morning when I was at my devotions, an unmistakable call came. Immediately I knew why, when at Bayonne, 'I had essayed to go into Bithynia, and the spirit suffered me not.'

As I knelt in that house in Marseilles all things became clear. The city outside the window was remote. Its noises diminished, and I was secure in the embrace of God. My new vocation came with the clarity of crystal. The words of the Prophet Isaiah sounded in my ears. 'And thine ears shall hear a word behind thee saying: this is the way, walk ye into it; when ye turn to the right hand, and when ye turn to the left.'

In that plainly furnished and unpretentious little room, cut off from my own people and the happy normality of my life as a minister, I was alone in an alien world, but not alone in the infinitely larger world of God. Distinctly a Voice spoke from behind me in an unmistakable tone of urgency.

'Comfort ye, comfort ye my people. . . . Feed the hungry, clothe the naked; bring deliverance to the captives, and the opening of the prison to them that are bound. That is your task. Arise and go.'

Immediately I rose from my knees. Instinctively I looked around the room. I had heard the Voice so clearly that I thought I surely should see someone. Unseen but not unknown, God had shown me that I was not isolated, nor were my comrades, the soldiers on the waterfront.

The little apartment now became as impersonal as a railway waiting-room. The objects in it, the bed with its home-made quilt, the table, chair, and mirror over the dressing-table, became things that had their uses, but made no impression. I had an important job to tackle and I was aflame with its urgency.

I have only one recollection of my walk to the American Consulate. The sun was blinding; I could feel the heat penetrating the soles of my boots; and I knew my destination instinctively. I did not hesitate.

The door was open and I walked up the stairs to the office until I was restrained by a hand laid on my shoulders. I heard an English voice.

'Padre, we've been looking for you.'

I turned, and the speaker regarded me intently.

'We need you to help starving soldiers and airmen from Dunkirk,' he continued. 'My name is Dean. I'm the former British Consul from Nice.'

I did not answer for a moment. Insistently, he said. 'Can you do anything to help these chaps, Padre? I feel sure you can.'

I grasped his hand and told him that I had received my instructions. Hurriedly I blurted out my experience of that morning, and of the Voice I had heard.

He was a quiet, serious man. He looked at me with new confidence and at that moment we saw into each other's heart.

'We must go then, Padre, for God has spoken.'

We went out into the sunshine and talked as we went

through the streets. The first thing was to find accommodation for the men. We must open a House of Refuge. I decided to call upon the police and ask their aid in my search for a house. Audacity offered the only hope of a permanent solution.

I asked my friend to return to the Consulate and gingerly I approached the police station. Recent events, the atmosphere of distrust and fear, and the Fifth Column which lurked in my mind like a phantom, had made me wary. Despite the confidence I felt in my mission, I knew the task facing the British in France seemed impossible. We must trust in God and hope to make the best of every opportunity given us to save our own afflicted men and work for our country's cause.

They were polite and sympathetic at the police station, but the Gestapo, with its machine-like efficiency had already issued its instructions. The French officials directed me, reluctantly I felt, to the special branch where I made no apologies for my request for aid. After establishing my identity, I demanded accommodation for stranded British subjects.

The detectives sitting around in the office of the special branch listened carefully. I was not yet aware that these men had received more detailed and peremptory orders, than their colleagues, in the less subtle departments of the Marseilles police force. They too were under surveillance. We were being caught in the web of the functionaries of a police state, something outside our experience; something so remote from the character of French civilisation that to these policemen their world must have become something like a nightmare.

'Padre,' the senior of the men said, 'we know you are the only member of your calling now at liberty in France. We can arrange for you to go home if you wish.'

'There's nothing I'd like better,' I answered and hurriedly added, 'but that is impossible. I cannot desert my own people in such a dreadful hour of need. I am a minister. How *could* I leave them?'

'No?' Quizzically, he smiled. 'Then you stay here. You have permission and complete liberty to find accommodation and to help British civilians, but give help to one British soldier and you will be interned.'

I rose to leave, bowed and walked towards the door. As I opened it my inquisitor bent over his desk and another detective followed me. We walked downstairs together.

'Understand, m'sieur, now, alas, we must obey our new masters. Do not reproach us. . . .'

I told him I understood the position in which they found themselves. It was none of their doing.

Quietly he said: 'I advise you to take over the British Seamen's Mission at 46 Rue de Forbin. But let no soldier be found hiding there. And trust no man, m'sieur. You will be watched. I know it. You must beware of paid agents, and of sudden raids.'

He stopped, and caught my arm.

'My best wishes go with you, m'sieur.'

Before I could thank him, he had turned on his heels and raced back upstairs.

I made my way through the evening streets to the Rue de Forbin near the old harbour. The Mission was deserted. When I opened the door one glance was enough to tell me that it had already been looted. I searched around for evidence that would lead me to some of the people who had worked there. There was nothing. I wandered through the empty rooms, working out my problem but the only decision I reached was to be especially discreet. From my old lodgings I fetched my bag and after a rough-and-ready meal made my way back to the British and American Seamen's Mission near the Joliette.

Three sailors stood outside gazing at the building. Here were my first charges. Their pleasure at finding a padre was equalled by mine at finding them.

I invited them inside and we immediately set to work to get the place into order. Before I retired that night I prepared a notice. The seamen helped to pin it over the door.

'Now open to British civilians and seamen ONLY.'

My tongue was in my cheek as I hammered home the nails. I had a job to do for servicemen and already plans were formulating in my mind.

CHAPTER FOUR

Le Vieux Port

I THREW OPEN the doors of the Seamen's Mission with a flourish. Almost immediately travel-weary visitors began to arrive. Their stomachs were empty. Gaunt, sick from exposure, unshaven and ragged, many were almost unconscious on their feet. Marked men, aliens in a country to which they had come as allies a few months earlier, they were now sought by the police who would intern them like animals. To all save I, who existed to serve them in Marseilles, they were an embarrassment. They were starving. They had no documents that were of any use and no ration cards. Not that ration cards in Marseilles in 1940 guaranteed food; but they did ensure a place in food queues. I set to work to welcome the men, making them feel at home in the traditional way of the British Army by putting the able ones to work. We set out to get our house in order as an escape hatch for Allied soldiers airmen and sailors.

The old harbour district, 'le vieux port,' close to the Mission was a rather different spiritual bailiwick from the one to which I was accustomed in the Rue Bayard. It was a labyrinth of narrow winding streets where the poor of many nations, human flotsam of the Mediterranean, had settled. The majority of its inhabitants were decent, working folk who struggled to raise large families, and feed and clothe their many children. Lithe, grimy, sun-tanned boys and girls swarmed, racing, skipping and dancing, tumbling on the cobbled lanes and alleys. So congested was the district that it became an ideal place for criminals hiding from the police. There was always a substratum of crooks in the old harbour, dope pedlars, agents for the indescribable brutes whose livelihood is vice, smugglers, dealers in international currency and stolen property, in effect, all the villainy that is part of the traffic of cities.

These criminal elements had increased in Marseilles with the fall of France. From all parts of the republic, especially Paris, they had escaped with the facility of old practitioners of the art of making the quick exit. Now they coagulated in the cafés, garrets and remoter hide-outs of the district.

Rogues were safe enough in the new Vichy France. The Government, rigidly directed by the Gestapo, was urged on pain of further invasion to concentrate the police on rounding-up their former allies—much to the distaste of some members of the force The refugee evil-doers who joined their brethren in Marseilles were left in peace to establish themselves in the old harbour district, and get organised to exploit war irregularities which usually are fruitful for the wicked.

A little more than two years after the mushroom rise of Vichy, the Pétainists and the Nazis had cause to regret this myopic drive upon Allied soldiers. At the end of 1942, when the Wehrmacht marched into the city, both the maquis and the criminals were so snugly organised, so craftily hidden in ' le vieux port ' that heavy armour had to be sent in to root them out. Even then, they escaped, and at no time was it safe for a German soldier to venture into the quarter. At any moment a bullet fired from a window or roof-top might despatch him out of this world. If he was accompanied by friends, so much the better from the viewpoint of the experienced sharp-shooters. There was no safety in numbers for a man in alien uniform in the old harbour. They merely ensured that the soldier did not go alone to death, and the sniper could congratulate himself on a bigger ' bag.'

After nightfall, the maquis and the crooks (one never knew which—different in most ways, they had a common zeal for killing Germans) did their work even more efficiently and at close quarters. Silently and neatly they struck and then laid out the bodies on the pavements where the morning patrol would find them.

The old harbour became the province of the underground army and the scum of the republic. The latter especially resented Teutonic intrusions.

In August 1940 they had not yet organised the Black Market. It was still possible to purchase food if one had

T.P.   B

money and was prepared to work at the task of hunting it out.

I enlisted foraging parties. Rising at four in the morning, we paraded, in a most unmilitary way, I and about half a dozen of the men. We had contacted nearly every possible source of supply when the time came to postpone the hunt until the next morning. Everything was rationed; but we soon found friends, the best of whom were Greek and Cypriot merchants in the harbour. As I write our country is at variance with their countries, but I shall never forget the help those men gave me in the Rue de Forbin. As soon as they heard that I was a Scottish clergyman, that my companions were servicemen from the U.K., and that we sought food for a houseful of refugee soldiers, mariners and airmen, they went to extraordinary lengths to find us provisions. Without them I could not have fed the men.

With every train from the north the escapers poured into the city and quickly sought out the Mission. Many arrived foot-sore and bleary-eyed from days and nights on the road escaping from Dunkirk. So many crowded into the Rue Forbin and I was kept so busy that invariably some time passed before I questioned new arrivals, asking them how they had known, before they reached the town, that help might be waiting at the Seamen's Mission. Surprised at my ignorance, they told me they had received orders from British Intelligence operating in Northern France. Make for Marseilles, find the Seamen's Mission and ask for Donald Caskie. That was all. It seemed I had been already put on the active list by my countrymen who were engaging the enemy in the north.

Stories of my guests' adventures would fill many books. The journeys from Dunkirk in the north over the demarcation line between Occupied and so-called Free France were long and arduous. Most of these lads had accents unmistakably British. A fair cross-section of the Island's accents clamoured in the Mission hall at most times. Some of them had feigned dumbness as an essential feature of disguise while travelling.

In the general disorder some gentlemen in Northern France had
blandly awarded themselves fantastic medical degrees and were
patriotically assisting their ex-allies—the ' ex ' they refused to
recognise—with certificates of various ailments, all designed
to disguise the fact that if they spoke French at all it was with
decided accents. Certificates of dumbness naturally were most
popular. These soldiers just kept silent and they got themselves papers to prove it. The papers, accompanied by letters
from the ' accredited ' physicians requested that help and travelling facilities on priority should be given these poor creatures.
They were making their way to the south to find their families
and visit them, which in a way was perfectly true.

Some of these lads spent so many weeks pretending to
be dumb that when they entered my room over the Mission
and the door was locked behind them they gulped, panicked,
lost their breath, gulped again and got the fright of their lives
before the dormant faculty suddenly came to life again. Then
they chattered until they found it all very funny and laughed
uproariously, indescribably happy to be able to use their
honest English, Scottish or Welsh tongues again. They had
great courage and wonderful resources in themselves.

I remember, for example, a sergeant of the Seaforth Highlanders who, after his unit was destroyed, travelled by night
and lay hidden by day, until after some weeks of dodging
about, trying to find his way besides making it, he finally
won through to Moulin on the wrong side of the demarcation
line. Still wearing the tattered rags of his khaki he had one
more river to cross, the Allier, before he reached the land
of the relatively free—at least free of the Germans. But the
bridges that had spanned the river had been bombed and he
could not swim.

On reconnaissance the sergeant noted that the locals had
furnished themselves with special passes and set up in business as ferrymen. Back and forth across the wide stream
they sailed, all carrying passengers. At nightfall, he crawled out
from his hiding place and engaged in conversation a Frenchman, who was uninfluenced by Vichy. From this friend he
received a ' pass ' and a collection of garments that, ensemble,

made him look like a civilian. He then borrowed a boat. Next morning he was up bright and early, ferrying Nazi officers and men across the water. Charging the wayfarers 100 francs a passage, he continued in business until late at night, when with his pockets pleasantly lined, he abandoned his friend's boat where it would be found by the owner early next morning. He cheerfully set out for Marseilles and the Seamen's Mission.

Such stories were common during the first weeks. British soldiers show resources of courage, good humour and intelligence that surprise none more than themselves. They would chuckle at the combination of luck and ingenuity, audacity and wit that enabled them to beat the Boche and I would do my best to help them continue to defeat him.

My first task with each new arrival was to hide him. The Mission was under constant surveillance and I had to walk cannily. My only armour was the grace of God and my native gumption. Everywhere I went I was being watched and followed. In retrospect, I believe that the Gestapo must have given the Mission a high place among the priorities they listed for the Vichy police. Raids on the house began a few days after I arrived and requisitioned it. The first came at six o'clock in the morning. Fortunately the raiders caught no one in uniform or without papers. But they solemnly warned me again that I must not give aid or hospitality to soldiers or airmen. According to international law, Vichy France had a duty to intern all alien combatants. Wagging an admonitory finger, they conveyed an unmistakable impression that they would return.

I could now ' go underground' with a clear conscience and this I did. I believed that my ministry on behalf of these men was actuated by my sense of duty and was righteous.

We went to work in the house, the men making hiding places with the utmost ingenuity; finding, for example, that the extraordinarily shallow space between floor boards can contain a man, we gently prised boards up all over the building, fitted them so that they would slide out and into position without trouble, and thus created ' holes ' in which our men could shelter.

This precaution was taken quickly, and luckily we managed to utilise floors, spaces behind cupboards and under the roof. Doors, entrances and exits for these hiding places were disguised and smoothly fitted into their places before the police could notice any signs of men.

Regularly at six in the morning they raided us. There was no need for an alarm clock in the British and American Seamen's Mission on the Rue Forbin during those months. The early morning raid became routine.

We stacked garments in the cellar, behind heaps of coal. To keep the bundles clean we wrapped them in old blankets. Men, on arrival, were refitted, if necessary, with clothes, and tucked into tiny compartments until I could furnish noncombatant papers and prepare them for despatch to Spain.

Getting forged papers for the travellers presented problems which the clergyman of a few months ago would have believed impossible to solve. The minister in charge of the Seamen's Mission discovered that put to it, as they say, he found resources that hitherto he had not thought existed. The Americans, ostensibly neutral, were especially helpful. Nothing was too much to ask of their Marseilles Consul who took incredible risks, protected, of course, by his ' neutrality ' coupled with Vichy's elaborate and pompous approach to this, its sole justifying principles.

Under international law, the American Consul was now handling British affairs. He did so with an affectionate enthusiasm and a disregard for ' red tape ' that I found wholly admirable. If a British ' civilian ' had lost his papers, passport, etc., the American representative provided new ones. He had an apparently inexhaustible supply of identity cards and, most wonderful of all, a magnificently imposing American seal, red, heavily embossed and ornate. This decoration on an identity card reduced the Marseilles detective force to solemn and silent respect. Show them one of these and only the strongest self-discipline restrained them from touching their forelocks.

I should mention, perhaps, that this gentleman, the most kindly of all the generous Americans I have met, was named McFarlane. His name may, I feel, have had an influence upon his attitude to a British outpost run by a man named Caskie and a Highlander.

Identification papers were only part of our problem and it was essential that I should get pocket compasses, materials for disguise, maps that could be copied and, most important of all, guides to lead the men over the Spanish frontier at the most inconspicuous places. The task was doubly difficult to a Scottish minister with little local knowledge.

In the meantime food was becoming even more scarce. The amounts I measured out to my guests were shrinking daily. If something were not done to solve the problem of a quick ' turn-over ' in the Mission, we would become over-crowded and before long the raiders must catch me unprepared for their arrival. The shortage of food was especially worrying, for men weakened by lack of nourishment would be in no condition to dash to the border—a perilous enterprise at best.

I was racking my brains in my office one afternoon, as close to despair as I ever have been, when from the corridor outside I heard a Cockney voice raised in cheerful song. Alfred, I thought, sounds cock-a-hoop. Corporal Alfred Smith was one of that irrepressible species, the Londoners: the memory of his insouciance in the most depressing situations is quite enough to make me understand the dimensions of the task Hitler set himself when he decided to defeat the Cockney city. Nothing daunted Alf: he was as cheerful as a sparrow and as tough as a hawk. Loudly he battered upon my door. When I called out, he positively burst into the room, beaming with joy, exploding glad tidings.

' Padre, Padre, I went out in my nice new suit to look at this lovely town. And look what I found!'

One at a time, like visiting cards, he placed seven ration cards on the table before me. Grinning from ear to ear, with his chest stuck out, he must have been the happiest soldier in the world that morning, even if he was disguised as a sailor. Obviously he believed the cards were a gift from above. I was not so sure.

' They would be very welcome, Alf,' I said. ' But where

did you find them? Seven ration cards! The person who dropped them must have been an hotel-keeper or——'

'But Padre, it means seven less mouths to feed.'

I picked up the cards and read the names upon them. My gloomy suspicions were justified. The spontaneous delight quickened by Alf's news was ill-founded. These cards were owned by poor people and only one bore the signature of an adult. The name was 'Jeanne Tillois (41)' and the woman was a widow. The other six were obviously her children and Madame Tillois, I knew, would be very, very unhappy this morning.

Alf was chattering on as happy as the widow must have been sad.

'There I was, Padre, stepping out like the Brigade of Guards, not a care in the world, the sun shining, and not a Jerry in sight, nothing but the birds and the children and lots of French people and suddenly there they were—lying in the gutter, neat and comfortable-like. I grabbed them and ran home as fast as I could.'

It was nice to know that Alf felt at home in the Mission and I hated to deflate his joy.

'I'm awfully sorry, Soldier,' I said.

'What's the trouble, Padre?'

His face had fallen but I knew it would smile again very soon. He was as resilient as a rubber ball.

'We can't use these, old man.' I pointed to the names, which he had not read. To him they were just foreign documents.

'They are the property of a widow and her children. I must return them as soon as possible. Our work here would never prosper if we were to take advantage of your find.'

Alf smiled, ruefully scratched his head and looked at me.

'Of course we can't, Padre. Now, why couldn't they have been the property of some Vichyite?'

More than an hour passed before I could leave the house to take the cards to their owners. Shortly after that I climbed to the heights of a Marseilles tenement. The door was slowly opened by a small child, opened just enough to show me

a little round face with great round eyes staring up. I smiled,
the infant opened the door wide and in I walked.

Madame was kneeling by the bedside in the room and
her face was wet. Poor soul she had been weeping, broken,
I suppose, by this final misfortune. At the best of times
life must have been difficult for her and now she was at
her wits' end. A lump came in my throat as I handed over
the cards without a word. She clapped her hands and em-
braced me. She had been praying and weeping at the same
time, she said, and now the precious cards had miraculously
been returned. She was beside herself with joy, rushing hither
and thither around the room, hugging the children and saying:
' A miracle. A miracle.'

Another miracle, which was as welcome to me, emerged
from our subsequent conversation. When I had waited for
the lady to calm down and told her how I acquired her documents, she questioned me about my presence in Marseilles.

I explained that I was a pastor and now in charge of
the British Seamen's Mission in the Rue Forbin. This impressed the good soul even more than my, to her, brilliant
talent for finding other people's ration cards and genius for
returning them. She insisted on taking me to meet her own
pastor, M. Heuzy.

Without waiting for my consent, which would gladly have
been given anyway, she put on her coat and hat, admonished
' les enfants ' to be good until the return of ' maman ', and
ceremoniously ushered me out. Only M. Heuzy could
adequately give thanks to me for the service I had rendered.
Her gratitude was poignant and, God knows, the terror in
which she found herself in Marseilles 1940 with six children
and the prospect of no food, would have struck fear to the
heart of the strongest person.

When we arrived at M. Heuzy's home I found myself
confronted by a modest-looking gentleman who listened
patiently to Madame's pæans of gratitude. Before I could
intervene, he turned and thanked me in English that was, in
his lips, so quaint and touching that I nearly became as in-
coherent in my joy as Madame Tillois had been earlier.

' Ah'm verry grateful to you, sir,' said the French pastor,

in accents that would not have raised an eyebrow in Sauchie-hall Street, Glasgow. 'You would be welcome in this house at any time. You are doubly welcome in these days. The kindness you have done Madame is verry great.'

I told him that the ration books had been found by another Briton, not me. I had only returned them.

He smiled widely.

'Ah, yes. I have heard of your Mission,' he said. 'It is close to the old harbour, is it not? You are a verry busy man. We must talk for a bit. Maybe I can help you, in fact I would be verry glad of an opportunity to do so.'

I had contacted a pocket of resistance—of moral resistance. M. Heuzy had been French pastor in Glasgow for many years and that accounted for his Caledonian accent. A Glasgow man by adoption, he was a true Christian, a minister whose assessment of the new forces in Germany was detached, balanced and shrewd. 'They are wrong; they produce professional evil-doers.' His friendly eyes held mine and in a few moments we had become old friends.

'You have many enemies,' he said.

I had suspected that although I had found friends—one always knows one's friends—there might be enemies. The French pastor spoke with simple candour.

'I also loathe the Nazis.'

The room was dim. Evening was becoming night. Madame Tillois sat on the edge of a chair looking at us respectfully, unaware of the burden of our conversation which was in a tongue unknown to her. I had been so busy that the thought of 'enemies' as distinct from the enemy had not entered my head. I suppose I hesitated and he chuckled, looking me in the eyes.

'I know a lot about your work in the Rue Forbin,' he said clearly, curiously emphasizing his accent in the way of Glasgow men when they wish to make their point without ambiguity, without the possibility of confusion or misunderstanding.

'I wish to render you and your people any help that lies within my power.'

Pastor Heuzy was a working minister and he brought me

face to face with the moral strength of France. Alf had done good work when he found the ration books of the widow Tillois and her children in the gutter. The widow had led me to a congregation of French Christians. During the next few days their minister and I became close friends and he told me of the patience of his people. Each Sunday they gathered at Christian service and prayed to God to sustain them in difficult days and for guidance in combating the evil that had befallen their country.

Like all congregations they were varied, some accustomed to prosperity, others living carefully on small incomes, paying their way, finding their pleasures with their families and in their homes, strong in their faith in God. Professional men, factory workers, intellectuals, old and young, a diversity of French Christians, they had their humanity in common and the supreme gift of faith in Christianity. Believing in God, they knew that the wicked men who directed the German invasion and conquest of their country would be defeated in God's good time. They prayed and were confident.

Pastor Heuzy and his people became a vital link in the 'escape route' that was in process of being created from France in to the free world. Never, never in my life has an honest action brought such a wonderful reward as my return of Alf's treasure trove of documents to the widow. The minister discussed our task with some of the 'elder statesmen' in his congregation and arrangements were made to lodge the overflow of our guests in selected homes where they were carefully and safely hidden. The French Christians were brave people and kindly in the modest way of the truly religious. They gave shelter to our men in their own homes and all they had, not only their own lives but the lives of those they held most dear, were risked apparently without a moment's hesitation.

This hospitality was only part of their work for us. They marshalled their resources to accumulate compasses, maps and other escape materials. Regularly, neat packages of precious goods began to arrive at the Mission. The parcels were delivered unobtrusively and quickly hidden.

One problem remained; we could not find guides and Pastor

Heuzy could not help us over that difficulty. The ' underground railway ' was perilous and our men were forced to take deadly risks alone.

A couple of nocturnal callers solved my problem.

CHAPTER FIVE

Nocturnal Visitors

THE SECRET POLICE knew that the Seamen's Mission was becoming a clearing house for British soldiers in flight out of France. As yet they could not prove it. We had not been caught, but the enemy did not despair. Apart from the regular raids, suspicious-looking men hovered about the building throughout the day. By peeping from a window with heavy curtains, I often saw them keeping an eye on the Seamen's Mission from across the street. Fortunately soldiers coming to the Rue Forbin were warned to move in quickly and stealthily under cover of darkness. But we had narrow escapes, some comic, some eerie, all nerve-racking. Our task was to transform the men quickly and efficiently into civilians, and then despatch them out of France. With the help of Mr. McFarlane at the Consulate, documents were acquired without delay and M. Heuzy's congregation was accumulating a nice little stock of equipment for the travellers. But clothes and money presented a nagging difficulty.

Major X was the first official visitor who called on me, after I found myself, willy nilly, on the active list. A tall, fair-haired young man of about twenty-five, he did not so much make an entrance to the Mission as manifest himself in my room. The men were abed asleep, or impatiently lying awake thinking of home. I was bending over my desk, working under a hooded light when I heard a polite little cough from behind me. Turning my head towards the sound, I saw a tall slim figure immaculately dressed. For a moment I was a little nonplussed by the presence of my nocturnal visitor, for this was the hour when I usually pulled my private notes from their secret repository, and arranged my programme for the next day. However, a hand was held up, a quick apology uttered, and my momentary anxiety was allayed.

'Please forgive me, Padre,' said my young visitor, 'for disturbing you at this unearthly hour, and for entering your room without being announced. I hate publicity, and very specially at this time. The work in which I am presently engaged compels me to be very cautious. My name is——'

I raised my hand, and halted him peremptorily.

'Don't tell me your name now, please. What is your business?'

A visiting card was held out. I looked at it and saw a familiar signature.

'Padre,' he began, and in less than a minute gave me a detailed report of all my activities since I had first arrived in Marseilles. Quickly, but unemotionally, he gave a résumé of my ministry in Paris.

'I'm happy to meet you, Donald Caskie.'

A hand was held out, and I took it.

'The fewer names I know, the better,' I said as I shook his hand. For I knew that sooner or later, the time would come when I would be arrested in connection with my work, and questions would then be asked. 'I'll think of you as Major X. It is a name which balances theology and science in decent proportions. Now, how can I help you?' I added.

The Major grinned. 'May I be permitted to sit down?'

I apologised for my lack of hospitality, and nodded towards a chair.

'I am an Intelligence officer,' he continued. 'I collect and transmit any and all information that can help at home. Will you assist?'

'Of course I'll help. But what can I do? I am a padre. And I'm extremely busy pushing to safety as many as possible of these good lads who have come to Marseilles.'

'I know exactly what you are doing, Chaplain, but you could also use your resources to find out certain things I wish to know. Such information is vital. I'll tell you exactly what we need.'

He approached the desk, smiled at me politely as he took

up a pencil and produced a roll of very thin paper. On it he wrote a short list of words, tore off a piece and held it out to me.

'Memorise these words and whenever possible discuss the subjects they suggest to you with the men who arrive from all parts of France. You may glean something that might also bear upon these matters from the civilians you meet.'

I ran my eyes over the page. What he had written was self-explanatory. Before I could speak, he continued: 'Please memorise this material *now*, Chaplain, and then destroy the paper. Forgive me for putting it this way. It is an order.'

'I understand,' I said.

'You may or may not see me again but our representatives will call. They will be pleased to talk to you.'

His smile was slightly mischievous and he moved over to the doorway. With a wave of the hand, half-salute, half-salutation:

'No, don't get up. Thanks for offering your help. Please forgive me for disturbing you at such an hour. Good night.'

Major X was wrong about his visit disturbing me. Paradoxically, I was heartened, feeling myself part of the large force which was fighting for freedom. I memorised the writing on the scrap of paper, and then I devised my own simple method for deluding the enemy. I began my 'Book of Words' which I wrote in my native tongue. The Gaelic is a most beautiful language, but it is more than that and I was not the first Scot during the war to put it to a practical use.

I was still harried by the problems of feeding and clothing the hungry. Intelligence officers, I suppose, made history. Clergymen are obsessed by souls, but Faith solves all problems. Would it, I wondered, bring me hard cash? Money might solve most of my problems.

Money came to me at first very slowly and in small amounts and then a sum arrived which rather confounded me. To be handed money by an apparently casual caller is not an experience with which I am familiar. I needed all the money I could raise. Goods of all kinds were in short supply and illicit traders, I learned, work on the principle that a fair profit consists of all the customer has in his pocket.

One morning a dapper gentleman called to see me. He greeted me in the hallway into the Mission in quiet English:

'Good morning, Padre. I have business with you. May we talk?'

I invited him into the office where he pulled his coat about him and without ado said, 'You need money, I know. I have brought you a little contribution.'

'That is kind of you, sir, but I don't know you.' His hands spread out in a deprecating way.

'It is not my money, Padre. I am a mere messenger. I come from Monte Carlo.'

My visitor was a very charming person, but I had become a very wary clergyman and I did not allow him to leave at that moment.

'I insist, sir, before I accept money, I must know more of *you.*'

The blue eyes glittered in the dark, tanned face. His obvious amusement was slightly irritating. In one short sentence he calmed any remaining fears I had.

I handed him a cup of coffee, and between sips, he recounted his story. Thanks to the intervention and interest of business men whom I had known in Paris and were then in England, money was released to assist me in my work from French branches of British industrial concerns on the Continent. I followed his story and checked it carefully. He mentioned names that were well known to me. Some of them had been most faithful members of our church on the Rue Bayard in Paris, and still are; others were friends of mine, living then on the Riviera, who were supporting me, loyally and liberally, in my work at the Seamen's Mission in Marseilles —Lady Robinson, Col. T. and Major E.S. Lady Robinson has passed away, but the other two, true-blue Britishers, are back again in their homes, by the blue waters of the Mediterranean, and have rendered me great service in the rebuilding of our Scots Church on the Rue Bayard.

For several reasons, I will not mention the French branches of British Industrial Concerns who assisted me, but I must say that they contributed generously to the winning of the war. Another name that my friend mentioned was that of the late Sir Benjamin Guinness—of stout fame—who came to see me some weeks after the visit of the man from Monte Carlo. He said that any time we needed money for the Great Cause, I was to write to ' So-and-So,' and a given address, and that financial help would be forthcoming. Sir Benjamin also gave me the wording of the code letter I should write to this person when we needed cash. We did not need to tap this resource, but it was good to know that the money was there, if we needed it.

After my visitor from the Riviera had mentioned all these names of good friends in France and in the homeland, I felt more confident. I was greatly encouraged by the thought that my friends at home in the United Kingdom had instructed their representatives in France to ' thaw out ' some of their ' frozen assets ' to help my work in Marseilles.

' And now, Padre,' said my friend, ' I must take leave of you, as I have further business in Marseilles. I shall be leaving for England immediately, but shall return very soon. Van Gogh has been very helpful.' Van Gogh, I knew to be Arles, where the famous Dutch painter Vincent Van Gogh lived for a time. When he mentioned this name, I felt still more confident that he was altogether bona fide, for between Arles and England there was a thriving clandestine air service. ' You must excuse me now, I must be away.' As he left he paused and said:

' Ah, our little contribution to your Mission, Monsieur le Pasteur. With it comes our good wishes and prayers.' He placed an envelope upon the ragged pad of blotting paper on my desk. ' And now, au revoir.'

We shook hands, he bowed and, refusing to permit me to show him out, left. I poured another cup of coffee and sat back in my chair. These visitors were welcome, but interviews with them were exhausting. The previous night I had worked late with a squad of tired and harassed men; I had got up from bed about 5 a.m. My eyes drifted to the thick envelope. I picked it up, burst the seal of plain red wax and turned it upside down. A fold of bank notes fell out;

there was no message. Mechanically I counted the money. It was £5,000 exactly, in French currency.

This vast sum, a fortune indeed, intimidated me and I dashed around to my friend Heuzy and placed it in his safe keeping, luckily, as it turned out because that very week we were raided and the house was searched more thoroughly than usual.

Other donations of cash trickled into the Mission from good folk, retired Englishmen and women living abroad and French resistance friends who had heard of our work. It was impossible for me to exclude ordinary civilians from my activities. I did what I could to relieve the old and distressed, and I was grieved because I could not do more for them. From my friend the Rev. S. Bishop, a Methodist clergyman from Paris who had taken hiding with his wife in the city, I received more that £200 in French money. This was a pleasant transaction because it helped both of us. My friend was penniless apart from these notes which were all he had in the world, when he and his lady took flight. I gave him an I.O.U. for the cash and asked him to present it at the Church of Scotland offices in Edinburgh when he reached safety. He did so and his first weeks in England in the days of confusion that greeted his homecoming were rendered a little easier by our exchange. But despite these gifts one had to handle money carefully. Prices were high and the moral standards of merchants were not on the same inflated level.

Sister Brigid, a member of an Irish order of Roman Catholic Sisters, brought clothes. How she learned of me, I do not know, but mendicant orders, I suppose must hear gossip. Just how this healthily happy lady and her colleagues interpreted the neutrality of the Irish Republic is also a mystery that I would not care to try to elucidate. They were Christians and knowing that my men needed clothes, they naturally played their part. One cold morning she came bustling into the Mission followed by a retinue of soft-voiced Gaels, their eyes sparkling from sable headdresses. Sister Brigid did most of the talking.

'Ah, now, Chaplain, I hear you are doing grand work

for the poor sailors in this part of the world, God help the boys.'

I admitted I was doing what I could.

'I am a chaplain, a Scotsman, Sister, God knows these lads need more than a wee bit of help.'

'Ah, there, Chaplain, of course they do, poor boys. Would some old clothes help them? Sure everywhere we go they give us cast-offs and very fine some of them are—just the thing, maybe, that would help your boys.'

A fraternity of Christian men and women exists throughout history and throughout the ephemeral place we call the world. I was deeply moved, not for the first time, by the Christian spirit, nor for the last. But I was suspicious.

'Sister, where do you come from?'

One of the richest chuckles I ever have heard bubbled from the well-worn habit.

'Sure I come from Dublin, dear dirty Dublin. Wouldn't you know it and you a chaplain?'

There was a demure chorus of giggles, and I knew who I was dealing with—real Christians. All they cared about was helping people. In the department of other-help, which is quite distinct from self-help as all Christians know, Sister Brigid and her ladies joined the organisation.

They brought us clothes, and when they could they brought food. They also brought Captain Janek.

The lads who passed through my Mission on the Rue Forbin were not all of the Protestant Faith and, I suppose, with the eagerness that is an essential part of my work as a Minister of God, I was irked by the thought that the Roman Catholics should not receive what they felt were the complete consolations of their religious faith. They wished to confess their sins to a priest. Captain Janek was a priest, a Polish padre in hiding with other Polish officers and men in the city. He heard their confessions; and he gave them Holy Communion. One morning a message came by word of mouth to me that he had gone to England with his party to carry on the good fight I was trying to fight in Marseilles. His country was in chains, and mine was free. It was good to know that the men he served would find a base from which they could fight, and he could serve them.

When Janek left, a Franciscan priest took over his work. Ecclesiastically, the Mission in the Rue de Forbin presented no more than the many problems that are presented by any cross-section of any Christian community.

The refitting problem was perennial until we found our own rather sleazy Bond Street, and then we purchased most of our necessary clothing in the Arab quarter of Marseilles, a bazaar of a place where everything traded was secondhand. After nightfall I would escort my protégées in groups of five or six to the merchants where they were fitted with suits, shirts, socks and shoes. The journeys to these peculiar tailors were trying. We would keep to the darker streets, and walk close to the walls. I soon found doorways into which we would dive and linger while one man reconnoitred before the platoon moved on its way again. The return to the Mission was more leisurely. The men were usually hilarious in a very subdued manner; their new appearance in job-lot ' civvies ' invariably struck them as extremely funny.

We would go back by different routes, each man carrying a bundle of the rags of khaki or air force blue in which he had arrived at the Mission. It was necessary to dump these. The Arabs naturally feared to have them in their premises even to burn, and so long as a thread of service cloth was in the Mission it imperilled each one of us, and the whole organisation. It was the evidence the police needed. We made our way to the walls of the old harbour and dropped the outmoded wardrobes into the blue Mediterranean.

There were times, however, when we had to work too quickly to organise the refitting department as efficiently as we would have wished. We were part of a very big machine which was uninterested in our immediate problems, and an element of comedy entered our work when this happened. Two young Irish doctors were the occasion of one of these interludes. They never, I am sure, discovered the facts of their cases.

They were officers in the R.A.M.C. and they arrived late one Saturday night. They had escaped from a Paris prison attired as nurses. Now they were in tattered army denim overalls. Tired to the point of blindness, famished for lack of food, their clothes rancid on their backs, they staggered into the Mission. They could not be placed in lodgings until their rags might be changed for garb less conspicuous in the Vichy dispensation, and at such times I billeted men in my own room. It was imperative that their presence be kept secret from the guests in other parts of the house until they were more discreetly attired. If we had been raided and caught, only I could be accused of harbouring soldiers. None but I knew these men were in the house.

I gave the doctors hot drinks and they dropped off to sleep like clocks stopping. They were beyond their powers of ordinary converse. After wrapping the poor lads in blankets I settled on my couch which I had set up behind a screen.

When I wakened they were still asleep and I left them to take my morning service. After leading my congregation in prayer I looked in on the new boys and found Dr Malachy awake.

'You had a visitor, Padre,' he informed me. 'He left something on the desk. He seemed a taciturn sort of bloke.'

The something was a message, a sign that only I could read. It instructed me to have a party ready for despatch that night.

'He was a friend of mine,' I told the doctor, 'and now we must waken John and have some breakfast. You need it.'

I turned away from them to go to the kitchen for warm food, and the problem he and John were, violently presented itself to me. They were doctors; they were priority passengers. They must leave that night and I must reclothe them before nightfall. I wandered along the corridor to the kitchen, prepared their food and took it to the office. All the time I brooded on the problem of the clothing shortage. While the lads settled happily to the first decent meal they had eaten in days, I scrounged around the house assembling 'civvy' clothes. By mid-afternoon, a complete 'new' outfit was available for each man—complete except for one suit of underwear. Up to a point I had been fortunate. Malachy could put aside the stinking rags which covered his tired body; but what about

John? I felt miserable thinking of John going home without underwear.

I sat in the room and looked at those boys whose life-long task was to heal bodies. They talked cheerfully. They felt at home with me. I found that it was imperative to my peace of mind that John's undershirt and shorts should be clean. He must be refitted completely. I scrutinised Dr John intently. He was about the same size as the padre. I fear I deceived him.

'Excuse me, gentlemen,' I said suddenly. 'I must do just a wee bit of bookwork.'

Rudely leaving my guests, without more ado I darted behind the screen and bending over the desk, wriggling in a most undignified way in his efforts to make no noise the Rev. Donald Caskie did the first 'quick-change act' of his career.

A few hours later, the doctors were on their way through the Pyrenees, bathed, fed and in clean clothes. They were ready for the journey home, and I was content. Around midnight I sallied out, took their uniforms to the harbour-side and triumphantly dropped them in the sea. Next morning, they were in Spain and I, philosophically, I hope, washed my other, now my only suit of underwear. I learned that a small wardrobe is an unconscionable time a-drying.

I lived constantly on the alert; my senses attuned to danger; my racial faculty of second sight sharpened until I could read men's characters in a frightening way. The times were out of joint and, I suppose, mind and body adapted themselves. I lived by faith and prayer, and an overwhelming affection for those of my countrymen who came to the door of the Mission demanding aid. I was aware that the stream of refugee Britons would not lessen and I was ready at all times to receive them. I lived in the moment, and found satisfaction in succouring the needy. Once, indeed, time seemed to flicker, I was projected a few hours ahead of the moments in which I lived and I saw them before they came to me.

After retiring to bed one night, I lay for some time in a state of blessed ease, my mind drifting in reveries. Whether I fell sound asleep or dozed I cannot say, but suddenly I was fully conscious and wide awake. My body was heavy with perspiration, my pyjamas soaking wet. I felt cold. It was one o'clock by my watch and I was intensely aware that I must be up and preparing for a party of men who were on their way to the Mission. I had seen them in a vision; gaunt, tattered, starving, they held out their hands, stretching their arms to the fullest extent, appealing for help. The dreadful silence of their request moved me beyond words and my eyes filled with tears. I knew they were coming to us and immediately made ready for their arrival.

I rose, hurriedly dressed and went to the kitchen. At the rough catering which satisfied our guests, I had become expert, and in a very little time a meal for twenty was spread on the table. All was ready when I heard the measured knocking on the street door that told me of a new intake. Outside in the darkness there were a score of men who had escaped from a German camp in the north. They were the men I had seen. I recognised them; they had been with me earlier in the evening. As if it had all been organised like a church social I welcomed each with a hurried word as one by one, they filed into the hallway. When all were assembled I led them to the kitchen. The table laid out, the food ready, the atmosphere of an arranged thing surprised them, but they were less amazed than their host.

One man managed to overcome his astonishment.

'Padre,' he said, hesitating, stumbling. 'Were you expecting company?'

They looked at me, waiting by the table laid before them. I faltered before I answered, but the words came to me.

'Yes. I expected you.'

'Us?'

'Yes, you. The company I expected is present. Come on now, sit down and eat. You must be famished.'

They ate ravenously, clearing the table in less time than it took me to prepare it. As each man relaxed he sat back in his chair and turned his eyes towards me.

I felt compelled to tell them of my experience; but for it the meal would not have been prepared and laid out. They listened with the rapt concentration of men who had endured much and suddenly found comfort. The kitchen with its twenty-one inhabitants was quiet. We were tired, they after their forced march, I still bemused by my experience.

A Cameron Highlander from Fort William rose to his feet. ' Ach, sir,' he observed. ' We Highlanders are most uncanny.'

My recollections of those days are diverse. In retrospect the night I managed to hide the airmen seems amateurish and comic; but when it happened it was a hair-raising experience. The previous day I had received the disturbing £5,000 which I had taken to my colleague, Pasteur Heuzy. There were three airmen in the Mission and they strained our accommodation to the point where I was compelled to lodge them in my own room until they could be refitted in readiness for their turn to travel. Glad to be indoors, shelter of any kind seemed luxury to men on the run and they soon made themselves at home.

Next morning the Vichy detectives arrived rather earlier than their habit, and literally caught us napping. I glanced from a window and got the impression that there were more of them than usual. Roughly I shook the poor tired men who were my guests.

' It's those confounded Vichy detectives again,' I hissed trying to bring them to their senses.

They were on the alert as quickly as I.

' Now listen, lads,' I warned them. ' The police are earlier this morning. And they seem to be more numerous. But don't worry—we'll see they don't find you. Get your clothes on. I'll be back in a few minutes, and tell you what to do.'

When I opened the door to the police there seemed to be a regiment of men facing me, about a dozen and a half, I suppose. My heart sank when I recognised the leader, an Alsatian. During the war, the Alsatians, whose allegiance at the best of times is ambiguous, were not to be relied upon. They had affinities with the hares and the hounds. Instinctively they ran with both. This one ran very slickly in the dual capacity.

' Monsieur!' Portentously he began his speech.

' We suspect you, Monsieur le Pasteur.'

I waited. He was very formal in his approach and I expected trouble.

'We believe that you have been housing and harbouring soldiers and airmen, and we are convinced that you are engaged on clandestine activities for your country—that you are in touch with British Intelligence and are helping men to escape through Spain to Gibraltar to the United Kingdom.'

He paused and glared fiercely at me.

'We have been informed that three airmen—one a pilot—arrived here last night from the north of France, and we have been commissioned to search the house and intern any and all belligerents we find.'

'You must do your duty,' I answered. 'You can begin where you please.' Airily I indicated the entrance to the chapel.

'Let's begin here; men are sleeping on the floor.'

I had learned to simulate innocence and they followed towards the little sanctuary at the back of the building. Starting at the point farthest from the door I waved largely over the disgruntled men who were awakening.

'There are thirty British citizens here. Their papers, I believe, are in order. I am certain I am not mistaken.'

There were a few merchant seamen in the room, survivors of the *Ville de Namur* which had been torpedoed. They had escaped from the Germans while *en route* to a concentration camp in the Reich. The others, by far the majority, were soldiers or members of air crews. Methodically the men of Vichy began to examine their documents while their padre looked on sanguinely, serenely confident in the efficiency of his American Highlander collaborator, Mr McFarlane.

The police set about the task with great deliberation and soon I felt my confidence shaken slightly. They meant business this time and my three airmen were very much on my mind. It was a cold morning and I shivered. I still wore my night-attire.

'B-r-r-r,' I stuttered. 'I'm freezing; Marseilles is a cold place today. Please excuse me for a few minutes. I should like to dress properly. This is not a night for pyjamas, unless a man is in bed.'

'You may go,' the Alsatian grunted, absentmindedly nodding me towards the door.

I moved slowly back to my room, knowing that they would not overtake me. This raid was serious. They were going to examine everything in detail, and my airmen were not the only source of danger, but at least I knew where I could safely deposit *them*.

I had often joked with the proprietor of a café around the corner, who had given me a nickname of his own and he was a friend who would shelter my protégées. The password was simple.

'Go,' I ordered them, 'to Dupont's Café outside; turn left and it's the third on your right. Go right up to the proprietor and quietly say to him, " Donald le Pasteur—Donald Duck." He will hide you in his wine cellar and send you back here when the coast is clear'

One by one they moved into the semi-darkness of dawn. I hurriedly dressed and returned to our inquisitors. They were out for blood and systematically searched every man and every possible place where evidence might be secreted. My room was the last place they entered and they tore it apart, ripping up the mattress where, but for my sixth sense they might have found £5,000. Luckily they bypassed my couch, a shabby piece of furniture indeed. In it they would have found a most incriminating document, if they could have read it, my ' Book of Words.'

This had grown into an interesting volume and no doubt the exercise was good for my Gaelic prose. It was a treasure chest of information collected from the men who passed through the Mission on the Rue Forbin. Instructions had been given by Major X for me to document anything I thought might be useful and hold it until I was contacted by a person who would be made known to me by the proper authority. By this time the book was valuable and explosive material. Possessing it did not worry me paticularly. After all, in 1940 who in Marseilles but God and Donald Caskie could read the Gaelic?

Solemnly the Vichy detectives plodded through my effects nonplussed by the absence of anything they might use. Eventually confounded, they were extremely annoyed as they took their leave.

All had gone smoothly and I felt ready to collapse, such was the relief from the tension that had sustained me during the search.

The Alsatian I could see was disgusted. As he took his leave I stood by the door, escorting him out, until the bitter end the kindly host.

He turned around and looked back when he had made his exit. The voice was menacing.

'This is not good-bye, Monsieur le Pasteur,' he said, 'but just au revoir.'

For two hours I waited until the good Dupont was confident that the detectives *had* left, and not merely set a trap for their air force prey. Dupont then allowed the three men to return to the Mission. By that time I was so exhausted that I needed a strong cup of coffee to settle my nerves before going back to bed. The men, who had been through so much in the previous weeks that nothing perturbed them for more than the duration of its existence, slept as soon as they lay down.

Dressed more discreetly the following Sunday, they were present in the congregation at morning service. I announced that we would sing the second version of the 124th Psalm:

'*Now Israel may say, and that truly.*'

I can still see those men sitting in the front seats of the chapel lustily and unselfconsciously singing with heart and voice:

'*Ev'n as a bird out of the fowler's snare*
Escapes away, so is our soul set free:
Broke are their nets, and thus escaped we
Therefore our help is in the Lord's great name,
Who heav'n and earth by His great power did frame.'

A few days later the choristers were standing on British territory on the Rock of Gibralter.

CHAPTER SIX

Lines of Departure

EVEN A life of constant peril, I was beginning to find, eventually becomes routine. After the first gruelling initiation, one becomes canny by instinct; living like a hare in the heather one's ear becomes attuned to suspicious noises, and one's eyes seek out essential truth which is revealed by the tiniest, carelessly displayed detail. We ordinary people, for the most part, live civilised lives, our days dedicated to service of a Higher Good. We work and earn to purchase the material needs of those who are dependent upon us, to keep the fulfilment of our happiness, the homes in which we find the joy of loving those dear to us, secure. But how quickly we men adapt ourselves to an existence of war which is something alien to all we strive to achieve, indeed all we experience in peace. Twice in little more than forty years men like us have been plunged into the barbarism of warfare. Somehow God has protected us, and humanity has survived.

When in the busy days at the Seamen's Mission in the Rue Forbin, I cast my mind back to the equally busy days in the different setting of the church in the Rue Bayard, the present seemed unreal. The two lives of Donald Caskie had only the great and blessed fact of God, and the discipline of prayer to give them shape.

Men came and departed, but their departures were not quick enough to satisfy me. Guides remained the perennial problem. And it was never solved to my general satisfaction. Brave men risked their lives organising escape routes, and they were intensely aware at all times that many of the professional guides whom they used were dubiously faithful to their trust.

It was my friend Captain G of the Seaforth Highlanders who accelerated the development of the line of departure from the Seamen's Mission. At three o'clock one morning he called and gave his host a disturbing moment.

58

I had fallen into a deep sleep. Quick, sharp knocks on the door jerked me into consciousness. Captain G was the last soldier I expected to see in the Rue Forbin. Some time previously he had passed through the house after escaping from the Germans at St Valery. I believed he was safe, at least in Spain, and I hoped he was in England.

But this officer had a taste for in-fighting, as boxers say, and he had an interesting story to tell.

On the road to the frontier it had occurred to him that he might be more useful here in Vichy France as a British agent working with escaping servicemen. His French was perfect and he knew the country. He decided to become an escape expert and place his craft at the service of soldiers ' on the run.' His minute knowledge of Southern France helped him to make contact with the British secret service which charged him with the building of an organisation, beginning in the north with M. Wood, the English-speaking Mayor of Calais and to include John McLean, a Highlander who had lived for fifteen years in Arles; in effect to span all France.

Rapidly these intrepid men built up their ' underground railway ' establishing it link by link, until now it reached the Marseilles area. Men could be brought to the south even more quickly and much more safely than in the past. What Captain G needed now was the last link, an organisation to take his comrades on across the Pyrenees.

Would I help him? There was only one answer to his question. He then told me that he had employed a number of guides and the following night I must be prepared for company.

They arrived without a hitch and Pierre accompanied them. I did not like Pierre: not to put too fine a distinction upon it, I considered him a rascal.

Pierre's fees for his professional services ranged from £25 to £30 a party. I have no moral scruples about a man asking a fair price for his services. The road through the Pyrenees is not easy on foot, at best of times. When France was ruled from Vichy, which meant the Gestapo always overseeing the police and taking their own precautions—neutrality was a convenient fiction for the Germans as long as it lasted. Pierre was entitled to his hire, but his demeanour made his attitude plain. If something went wrong with our finances and his pay was delayed he would not hesitate to recoup himself by claiming rewards from the Germans. He had the savage, introspective loyalty to his own material security that is characteristic of the congenital traitor. In an emergency, I asked myself, could we trust this sort of man? Working out the answer to the question did not take prescience of a high order. I was unhappy about Pierre. The men passing through the Mission in the Rue Forbin were not mere units to me. I had schooled myself and been schooled by my parents and teachers to see each man I met as a soul and a body, a being who loved and was loved, precious to his Maker and to those with whom he lived. Although they passed rapidly through that extraordinary church-cum-manse on the fringe of the criminal district of Marseilles, I knew them all. Each I loved like a brother. Pierre's single principle of twenty-five to thirty pieces of paper for the preservation of 'a batch' of souls was repugnant. I pitied the poor fellow, but he was set in his ways, and I feared him on behalf of the men I could see only as a congregation of the faithful.

For the first few months of Captain G's new order all went smoothly. In those days one learned quickly and did not make mistakes twice. I hated employing Pierre, a feeling complicated by the thought that I might be doing him an injustice, but there was nothing else for it. I was nagged by a conviction that, sooner or later, he would reveal himself in his true colours and we would not like them.

I made one mistake arising out of eager pleasure at sending the men home, and the naïvity of inexperience. A few hours before the guide was due to arrive I announced that we were sending a group into Spain that night. After the party left I felt happy about them, anticipating their joy on arriving home, and I found the house clamorous with men asking me when their turn would come to follow their comrades. I hated telling them that I could give no definite news. I was a mere cog in a machine and must await the development of arrangements made elsewhere.

After that I became canny when arranging my procedure. When instructions came, I had already mentally listed the men for despatch with the next party. But I gave no hint of my intentions to anyone. Two a.m. was starting time. At midnight I wakened the travellers and whispered orders to them. They acted quickly and on their stockinged feet followed me to my room.

Each man had been told to bring his complete gear. When the party assembled I thoroughly searched them. It was essential that if captured no one should be carrying evidence that might incriminate not only the Mission, but the whole escape route. We had become the H.Q. in the South of France. I then made each pledge himself that if he were captured he would not involve the Mission in any way no matter what happened. It was a harsh instruction, I knew, but I lived with the knowledge that hundreds of men making for Marseilles, from all over France and even Germany would be mortally endangered if the enemy discovered us. The Rue Forbin was a springboard to freedom for those men, their sole hope, and must be preserved as long as possible.

These preliminaries preceded a briefing of each man. I explained the escape route in detail, and gave them knowledge that I considered a sanction on the guides.

Before the tap on the door that announced the coming of the guide, we offered a short prayer. A quick reconnaissance followed and then, if the coast was clear, I bade them Godspeed. The system functioned perfectly during those months and twenty to twenty-five men each week were sent to freedom.

The escape route was now functioning with the smoothness of a well-oiled machine. Men were moving out to the U.K., and I made arrangements that ensured their next-of-kin learning as soon as possible that they were alive.

When a man arrived at the Rue Forbin he was thoroughly interrogated. I took (1) his name, (2) the name of his next-of-kin, (3) his regiment and (4) his address in the homeland. I entered these details in a ledger, and when times became very perilous I placed this book in the hands of a heroic French friend, Henri Thebault, who guarded it carefully.

Today it is one of the most precious possessions in my manse.

After entering this information in the register I questioned the new arrival, gleaning as much information as I could about the activities and movements of the enemy in German-occupied France. All this material was passed on to my frequent nocturnal callers from the Secret Service. The men's names were sent through Lisbon to the U.K. In that first year I despatched some hundreds of pounds worth of telegrams to Britain by way of the Church of Scotland offices at 121 George Street, Edinburgh.

It was expensive work and involved much bribery as each telegram had to be visaed by the police and further difficulties were encountered among postal authorities which only 'palm oil' solved. That was the only distasteful part of a task I grew to love. I justified it by the thought of the untold comfort and relief each message brought to distressed folk at home who had been without news of their men since the fall of France.

Looking back on that strange year those telegrams are to me the most incredible part of a unique experience. I sent them to Lisbon from Marseilles, and I knew that while this part of the country was labelled 'Free France' the post office was under German control. Bribery, however, and friendship took them to Lisbon and from thence to Edinburgh. From the office in George Street the good news was despatched without delay to the waiting anxious relatives.

They were sent to the Colonial and Continental Committee of the Church. At that time the secretary of the department was Dr Donald Webster. After his death during the war the work was nobly carried on by the Rev. Alex King. Miss Janet Blake was his faithful and devoted amanuensis. Later on she was nobly assisted by Miss May Slidders. She attended to the telegrams. In a most admirable way Janet Blake carried out her 'Hush Hush' task and collaborated with the 'French office.' There must be thousands of families in the United Kingdom and in the Colonies who bless her name.

The secret war was gathering momentum and it was about this time that the comedy of Jean le Harivel took place in Scotland. Jean was a Scottish boy of French ancestry, his grandparents had settled in our country where his father was born and became principal of Marr College in Troon. I knew the family and had met the boy often before the war, in France where he was living as a student. He played the organ for us at the church in the Rue Bayard.

With his background and knowledge of the language, he was a useful man to the Army and he was sent to France with a company of men on a special mission just before I heard of him for the first time since war was declared. Almost literally he and his comrades had fallen into the hands of Vichy. Their pilot mistook his destination, misread, I suppose, his calculations and landed in the wrong place and Jean and company were marched off to gaol where they were told by another prisoner that they should get word to me as soon as possible. He instructed them in the useful art of sending messages from prison cells and a letter was brought to the Rue Forbin telling of their plight. In my next telegram to Scotland I inserted the words ' Jean Leharivel, Marr College, Troon.' Jean's friends and relatives, I felt, would thus learn that the brave lad was alive at least and likely to survive the dangerous task to which he had volunteered.

When the message came to the Church of Scotland offices, there was much head-scratching about the interpolated name. Mr Webster, the Colonial Committee Secretary, was looking over Miss Blake's shoulder as she opened the message, both eager to extract news and send it to where it could do most good.

' Jean le Harivel,' he said. ' What on earth is the woman doing in Marseilles. Jean Leharivel, Marr College. What nonsense. It must be a mistake.'

Almost as he spoke the telephone rang. It was a call from the War Office. An official voice, which sounded rather more urgent than usual spoke.

' We are told that the name Jean Leharivel occurs in the most recent telegram you have received from abroad. Is that true?'

' Yes. But it must be a mistake, surely. What would a young lady from Troon be doing in Marseilles at this time?'

' Mistake,' replied the official with a non-official guffaw.

'It's not a mistake but a very valuable piece of information. Jean Leharivel—who, by the way, is not a woman—is a brave man. We are glad to learn that he is very much alive.'

For months this telegram service and the 'underground railway' worked with routine efficiency. And then the Germans tightened the frontier guard, became more fiercely on the alert and we were endangered.

Harassed by the new conditions, cut off as we were, I was beginning to despair when one of the most remarkable men I have ever met came into my world.

He was young, cool and humorous in demeanour but almost surgically business-like in conversation. He gave me the pass-word which proved he worked for the organisation. I gave nothing away. I listened carefully and said nothing.

'You are wise to be careful, Padre,' he said in a jesting way. His accent was vaguely foreign although his English was almost pure 'B.B.C.'

'You must check on *me*. I know your work so I can trust *you*.'

I said nothing.

'The name,' he continued, a good-humoured smile playing about his face, 'is Pat, the rank, Lieutenant-Commander, Royal Navy. I bring orders from Whitehall.'

CHAPTER SEVEN

Winter in Marseilles

LIEUTENANT-COMMANDER Patrick O'Leary, R.N., was one of the bravest men I have ever known. Gay and fearless, his sense of humour led him to enjoy situations so nerve-racking they might have stopped the stoutest heart. But he was strict, kindly and protective to those under his command: fighting the enemy he was entirely ruthless. He knew the methods of the Gestapo and hated them. A cultivated man, one felt he had set everything aside, the things he enjoyed and loved in peace-time, all that makes life worth living, until victory was won.

But Pat was not languishing for peace. The O'Leary's of County Cork are a fighting family, worthy descendants of great Irish warriors. They can have no complaints about the underground warrior who bore their name in the Southern French sector of World War II.

At first sight Pat seemed slight and frail. I think the clothes he wore contributed to this impression. He was not a tall man. He moved with uncommon grace and agility. As he moved one noticed the powerful shoulders, the brawny thrust of the legs, the steady almost machine-like grasp of the muscular hands on objects such as coffee cups, pencils, documents. Pat, I suspect, could have strangled a strong man as easily as I might stick a stamp. His efficiency was awe-inspiring. All arrangements for his operations were worked out to the minutest degree. Each man knew his task thoroughly. Pat was a disciplinarian, steel under a jaunty manner, a perfect expression I thought, of the training of the Royal Navy. Pat, drolly and unmistakably, knew all. He was a man born with all the characteristics of a romantic hero. He spoke English with near-perfection, a touch of accent colouring his vowel sounds. The lilt in his voice giving an odd inflection at times which might have been a curiously musical expression of a brogue. He would talk with fine appreciation and understanding of music and the arts, but there was a hint of the bizarre in the cut of his jacket, the design of the tie, its knot and the tilt of the hat. In the most grave conversations a sudden grin would hint at civilised scepticism, which is not to say that Pat was anything but an idealist. He merely distrusted human motives when they were expressed too solemnly; self-righteousness he found ridiculous; a man did a job and he should not dramatise it. He never showed anger. In Marseilles and beyond he was a tower of strength to us. He was ' Pat,' at first an agent, and later a leader.

Among the papers that Pat showed me were letters signed by Very Important People.

' I am working,' he said after I returned his credentials, ' with Captain G. Tell me about your work, Padre.'

I told him and he listened carefully, the quick smile coming when I mentioned my Book of Words.

T.P.   C

'Alas, Padre,' with a deep chuckle, 'I do not understand the Gaelic.'

I gave Pat the most thorough report I made to any visitor in those days. He had listened carefully and said:

'I am a traveller, Padre, and shall leave town tomorrow. The branch is expanding rapidly, so rapidly that it is difficult to keep track of everyone—but do not worry.'

Captain G's organisation was increasingly efficient. Like Pat, the gallant Seaforth was a man born to this hazardous trade. They both enjoyed danger without losing sight of their objective, which was to avoid peril as much as possible, and win victories. Victory to them meant soldiers deposited in places where they could be used to fight and information sent to an H.Q., where it would be used to harass the Nazis. They were single-minded officers and the pleasure they got from their task derived from the knowledge that it was important if the values they held dearest were to survive.

Agents were coming more frequently to the Rue de Forbin and among them was a young man named Bruce Dowding with whom I struck up a very close friendship. Bruce's brother was a minister of the Presbyterian Church in Australia. This boy and I had common things to discuss. He was a Christian with the outspoken frankness that is part of the Australian national character. He had supreme faith in our cause, and was quite fearless. Bruce Dowding's friendship was a consolation to me when I was exhausted by my dual tasks of minister and agent. His visits were of necessity fleeting. I passed on the necessary information I had gleaned, and Bruce passed on my orders.

On the Christian front I had my own agents. These were old friends of my Paris days, links with the place where I had set down roots, the Church on the Rue Bayard, and the intense happiness in the social life of my people at the manse on the Rue Piccini. Henri Thebault was one of the closest of these friends. In 1938 I had married him and his wife Antoinette at the Scots Kirk. That day I gave them a Bible in which I wrote:

'Présented to Mr and Mrs Henri Thebault on the occasion of their marriage at the Scots Kirk, Paris, 17 Rue Bayard, on June 20, 1938 by their minister, Donald C. Caskie.

'Except the Lord build the house, they labour in vain that build it.'

Henri had been transferred to Marseilles by the great firm of merchants he represented. His aid became indispensable to the Mission. His company had branches in all foreign countries and he knew his colleagues abroad. Through them he could disseminate information for me. On my 'Operation Telegraph' by which I sent to Edinburgh the lists of missing soldiers whom I had found—or who had found me—Henri played a vital role. He was adviser and reconnaissance officer, testing out post office departments and police for me. He was an ally and friend. More than once he risked his life on my behalf, and my war debts to him only began at the Rue de Forbin. At a moment when my family might have despaired of my survival, Henri brought them news that I was alive.

I needed friends during that winter of 1940-41. The mistral blowing down on Marseilles from the valley of the Rhone was scorchingly cold. On its breast it bore snow and sleet. The Old Harbour froze under a white pall that thickened as the weeks passed. In this frozen cocoon our men might have sickened and died so near, but yet so far from release. An epidemic of influenza, for example, would have crippled the link which I controlled on the escape route, and men would have piled up on us but for the stealthy friends who brought us aid. They included natives of Marseilles, some of them of British ancestry, and seamen, especially Americans who, with the impulsive warm-heartedness characteristic of their race, silently and rapidly got on with the job of relieving need at the Mission.

It was named the British and American Seamen's Mission, and because of this it was well known to American as well as British seamen. My friend McFarlane the Consul gave us helpful publicity among visiting U.S. merchant marine officers and men.

They would drift into the house in the evenings in twos and threes or fours, after their ships had docked, and they had worked their shifts. Casually they would ask for a cup of coffee and place a large can or bag of the ' makings '— enough to last a large family for a month—on the table in the dining-room.

' D'ya think you can make five cups of coffee from that, Chaplain? We'd be deeply obliged.'

The total request always amounted to the exact number of men in the company, plus one cup for the padre. They'd sip my ' makings ' judiciously, nod their approval and perhaps comment.

' Could do with a little more sugar, Chaplain. Nice though. French? Eh? I never met a Scottie who could make coffee except you, and you're a French Scottie.'

I would reach for the sugar bowl and they'd halt me, winking largely.

' Oh, no, Parson. We're slimming. But your coffee is good. All it needs is something to be added—a new flavour, maybe. Must see what we can do to bring you out. You sure are a promising coffee-maker.'

They would sit talking, joining in the general conversation for an hour or more, and then respectfully bid us adieu.

When I awakened next morning, sacks of potatoes, rice, boxes of sardines, cases of tinned food, bags of sugar, boxes of butter, even bags of coal—something from such a list (dependent on ship's stores)—would be heaped inside the building. They did not wait to be thanked, and I never met any of those kind American lads again. But I shall not forget them. Today in every part of the U.K., in Ireland and in the Commonwealth there are happy, healthy men working and living with their families who might have starved and frozen but for the generosity of those American mariners. In the post-war reveries of the minister who was in charge of the Mission in the Rue Forbin, they play a warm part and they are remembered in my prayers.

Every good work, I wryly was finding, brings its own

reward. In Marseilles was a community of old people who were British citizens; cut off from their kin, unharried, because of their age by Vichy or the Gestapo, they were left in 1940 without help of any kind. Whenever I had a moment to spare I would escape from the Mission and visit these old folks. It was on one such visit that I met Henri Thebault again and I nearly broke my neck in achieving that meeting. I had taken the bus and I saw from the window, Henri Thebault. I shot up from my seat, dashed to the platform, and yelled at his vanishing figure. He did not answer and I launched myself into space. Clerical gentlemen are not trained for space travel. Luckily the good Lord took over that snowy day and I landed on the least vulnerable portion of my anatomy. Some minutes later, I overtook Henri who was striding along intent on reaching a business appointment.

I walked with him and arranged a further meeting, after I told him my task for the day.

'By the way,' he casually mentioned as we parted, 'do you know Mr Arckless, Donald? He is truly British but has never lived in his own country. Born here, I believe, but keeps in touch. He's a member of our church. He'd be glad to see you.'

Mr Arckless's house was on my way, and I cut my time carefully to ensure that I could visit him. The old gentleman, dapper in his French suit, benign in his French whiskers, was as British as steak and kidney pie. He gave me a warm welcome and instead of asking my help, begged me to let him help us. Mr Arckless, I discovered very quickly, was a retired coal merchant. He knew every coal merchant, big, medium and small in Marseilles. They were difficult times and coal was scarce. The poor of Marseilles huddled in their houses and scraped for fuel. But from that day forward we at the Rue Forbin received a share of the fuel that was available. Wood and coke were added so that we might eke out our days above survival level at least.

The men were now moving in and out of the Mission at a better rate. We might have relaxed our vigilance but for Pat and the omnipresent threat of the Gestapo which hung over the city. Captain G's representative on the road, as he called himself, appeared when he was needed, skilfully clearing up problems and good-humouredly dissolving gloom. Obviously he was a man who was enjoying life with all the hilarity of a Glasgow apprentice *en route* to Rothesay on Fair Friday. We were aware now that the Mission was under almost incessant surveillance, but we had to move doubly carefully for our first traitor had manifested himself.

He was not a very capable traitor—spy, perhaps, is the more accurate word—for I never discovered just where his allegiance truly lay. He was a Vichy detective but for many weeks he had visited the Mission. He professed to be pro-British. His accent was Irish; I gathered he had been taught the language by a relative. He called himself ' Franky.' On the surface he seemed sincere, but when discussing Germany and the Nazis, he set my teeth on edge by the extravagance of the hatred he expressed against them. Adapting Gertrude's comment on the Player Queen in *Hamlet* one might have said of him, ' Methinks the lad doth protest too much.' But he did not attempt to penetrate beyond the wall of reserve I had built around our conversations, and in ordinary times I suppose I would have accepted him eventually as pro-allied. And then by betraying a lad he thought stupid, he betrayed himself, and paid dearly for his treason.

The episode began as a comedy. One Saturday morning I had risen very early to take stock of the supplies in the Mission before settling down to preparation for my Sunday services. I had been rationing fuel very carefully and as I worked I shivered. A knock on the front door came as something of a relief, and I went down to open it. On the doorstep stood a very young woebegone-looking Cameron Highlander. I was irritated by his undisguised arrival. By this time the organisation was delivering men at more uncompromising hours.

' Come in, lad. Don't stand gawking there. God bless me, you'll have us all interned,' I almost shouted.

He shot into the house like a human cannon-ball and I roared with laughter. He was a good lad and, finding himself at home, he laughed with me.

'Let's have breakfast,' I said. 'What's your name? Where do you come from?'

For the moment he was a problem child to me, but not a 'problem' in the accepted meaning of the word. A Scotsman, his name was Angus, he reported, and he had found his way to the Mission more by good luck and a canny use of the countryside than by knowledge of escape tactics. He had not heard of the escape route. A man he met in the street sent him to the Mission. My problem was urgent, the house was crammed with men, Angus was in uniform and to use a criminal term was 'hot stuff.' He had to be hidden until nightfall and then taken to our tailor in the Arab quarter.

We finished a quick breakfast: 'Come with me, lad,' leading the way I took him to an underground cellar where our scanty heap of coal was kept.

'Lie behind the coal until I come for you and keep as quiet as a mouse.'

'All right, Padre,' said Angus. 'Maybe I'll get a wee sleep down here.'

Poor Angus; I later gathered that he could not sleep. For more than an hour he lay behind the coal, cuddling his Balmoral, and then decided to go upstairs and inhale a few breaths of fresh air. Perhaps he was more accustomed to the scent of heather, and coal disagreed with him. He mounted the stairs, and at the top was confronted by a civilian; 'Franky.'

'Are you a Tommy?' the civilian asked in a kindly way.

'Aye, ah'm a Cameron Highlander and yon wee padre hid me in that dark cellar in case a beastly detective caught me.'

'I'm a beastly detective,' came the answer, 'and we are ordered to intern all soldiers and airmen until the end of the war.'

Angus was marched upstairs and he denied that it was I who was the little padre. The man who told him to hide in the Mission was much older, bald-headed; his accent was different. Angus learned quickly. Our 'friend' was infuriated by his stubborn refusal to recognise me and led him away, resentful and angry that he had not caught bigger game. I suppose he interrogated Angus very thoroughly at headquarters but the boy must have kept silent. When interrogating, the Vichy detectives, on the whole, were humane. I heard no more of Angus except that he had been interned. But his departure did not end the episode. 'Franky' continued to visit us, profusely apologetic. Each time he was greeted by silent men and a watchful chaplain. I had warned my guests to be extra careful when he appeared. My vigilance was short-lived.

Three weeks after Angus's arrest, his betrayer was found one morning in a narrow back street of the old harbour. His body was riddled with revolver shots.

I do not know who killed 'Franky'. Perhaps it was one of our agents; perhaps it was an agent of the maquis which by that time was forming. Perhaps it was the work of a Vichy detective. One could not be certain as to the innate sympathies of even those who on the surface were enemies.

'Franky' was perhaps a foolish traitor. There were others of his kind, ordinary agents of Vichy or the Gestapo, who did not introduce themselves. We suspected we were being watched from windows on the Rue de Forbin and I was warned that on various points of the route to the Mission men had been noticed lurking at certain times. Accordingly I worked out time-tables which, while dominating our movements, were arbitrarily changed from day to day. My arrivals and departures must have seemed very haphazard to the chiels taking surreptitious notes behind window sashes and in cafés.

Our work intensified as the organisation strengthened. Pat's orders were pressing the necessity of transporting larger parties of prisoners. They fitted exactly Pat's personal inclinations. The Mission was not the only point upon the escape route where surveillance had been increased. We had information that more and more Gestapo agents had been drafted into the area. Our contacts reported that frontier guards had been trebled and the route was becoming more hazardous. O'Leary flung himself into the task of mass escapes with characteristic enthusiasm. The day-to-day work increased in efficiency and rapidity of movement. Pat elaborated schemes which were characteristic of the artist in him. One of these was to seize a ship and transport something like a battalion at one ' go '; another was to hold up the Marseilles-Perpignan train for a sort of excursion dash into ' sunny Spain.'

He knew that London would not back him on such projects. An ' outrageous ' incident might provoke further trouble with Vichy and might bring the Boche marching into the city. But it contributed to Pat's gaiety to work out such schemes.

I should add that I am not by any means sure that he would have failed on those seemingly grandiose undertakings. Pat's audacity paid high dividends when the stake was his life. He took chances with a cool head. He had established himself in many places as a citizen with roots, and the number of personalities that were Pat O'Leary, but accepted as different characters by shrewd, hard-headed and sometimes vicious men, were and still remain a mystery to me.

There was a time, for example, when a young Englishwoman, married to a French officer who was later shot by the Germans, was captured and interrogated by the Gestapo. She was one of Pat's assistants. After some four hours of questioning the poor girl was hauled into another office and confronted by O'Leary. Blandly smug, he was in apparently chuckling conversation with a Gestapo agent. He looked at her intently and jumped to his feet shouting angrily.

' Just as I said. It's my Maria. What has happened to you, my dear?'

Maria gawked at him and muttered that she was under arrest as a resistance worker.

' Gentlemen, this is nonsense,' and with a coy smirk, ' Maria is my mistress. The poor girl would never dream of joining the resistance.'

An hour later he was dictating to her orders that on the surface seemed to be dealing with a dull mercantile project. He had hastily apologised for slandering her. He chuckled at the folly of the Gestapo.

It was that audacity plus the divided allegiance of the French that might have resulted in one of his big schemes being successful. Those who gave token support to Vichy were people stunned by the defeat of their country; others listened avidly for news from England; a tough minority was organising the French underground, the maquis, to wage its own war upon the hated Boche. Pat would have found native sympathisers with his big schemes and, as he said himself:

'You never know, we may be forced into adopting one of them in the future. We might as well work out details now.'

He loved his work. The demands made upon him had become greater as Captain G and he expanded the organisation. My own tasks now included prison visiting and in consequence my life became more hazardous. The prisons in Southern France had become internment camps. We knew that if war continued for long enough the Germans would find Vichy insupportable and would occupy all France. Internment then would become something worse. I brought such news as I could to the men in the camps and I smuggled tools that might help them to escape. It was thus that I met a man with whom I shall always be proud to have been associated— Lieut.-Colonel Richard Broad of the Seaforth Highlanders. Dicky Broad is one of the legendary officers of the Seaforths. His exploits will be discussed by the officers and men of the regiment so long as Highlanders go to war.

I had a small share in one of his greatest exploits which was carried out with the help of the organisation. It began late one night when a very shabbily dressed Frenchman came to see me at the Mission. I fear I penetrated the disguise with disheartening ease. I had met the gentleman in the past, at a distinguished social gathering in Paris. He was a French prince and now he was living in Lyons.

Over coffee we discussed the times in a detached way, as if we had many hours to spare and nothing to do but enjoy our own company. All the time I wondered just what had impelled His Excellency to visit the Mission. Then he asked:

'By the way, is it possible for you to give me a full list of the Seaforths in hiding or in prison camps around here?'

He was a loyal friend to Britain, I knew, but I considered him quizzically for a moment.

'Yes, I could supply you with such a list if you tell me

why you want it. What possible use can *you* find for a
selective list of men in hiding or in gaol?'

'Oh, I only want it for a friend who happens to be interested.'

I couldn't resist pulling his leg.

'Richard Broad, by any chance?' I innocently enquired.

The poor prince nearly fell off the chair with astonishment.
How did I know? he demanded. It was supposed to be a
complete secret that Dicky Broad was in Vichy France. This
was most serious.

I reassured him.

'I just keep my ears to the ground. But I assure you I
have told no one. And the Seaforths who know don't blab
either.'

The saga of Dicky Broad and his seven Seaforths should
be commemorated in an epic poem and sung to the music
of the Seaforth pipers. When, years later, I asked him how
it all had been accomplished, he dismissed the matter by
saying with a smile, 'The easiest thing in the world, Padre.'
But it happened like this.

When the Wehrmacht closed in on the Seaforths at St
Valery, the Highlanders held on until surrender seemed the
only way out. As the end approached Lieut.-Colonel Broad
gave orders that formations had to split up. Every man must
try to break through the German cordon and make for the
south.

He gave an example by gathering seven soldiers, one of
them Sergeant James Chalmers, and quickly eluding the converging armour the small party took to the country. Moving
by night they covered many miles until on the third day a
German bomber crash-landed within thirty yards of their
hide-out. Within minutes scores of Germans from a nearby
camp were swarming close to them, over-running the ground
in the vicinity. But the Seaforth luck held. The bomber
caught fire and the Germans, fearful that its cargo of bombs
would detonate, took to their heels. Dicky and his men
silently slipped away.

Living as best they could, Broad and his men continued
their journey until they reached the Seine where, work-

ing like beavers through the night they constructed a large raft. Good as their ship-building was by intention, it proved inadequate when put to the test. The Seaforths arrived on the other side of the river wet and weary. A German patrol sighted them. To an accompaniment of bullets they plunged into a forest where they were hunted for days.

Farmers, foresters and labourers helped the party to evade their pursuers on the way through the forest and beyond. They were brought to the town of Honfleur. There they met Raymond Lecesne of the Resistance, a young student, who housed them in a convent.

By this time the men were exhausted, with the aching bone-breaking tiredness that comes from days in the open, living like hunted beasts but with only the resources of civilised intelligence which is not so readily adaptable to beastly living. The nuns gave them gentle hospitality, food, beds, hot water —they were intensely pro-British. Their Mother Superior, a charming old lady, was English. For more than forty years she had been in Holy Orders in France but she was fervently patriotic and ready to take risks for the Allied Cause. She must have had a remarkable spirit for, concerned as she was, worried about the peril in which these boys found themselves, their spirit amused her. She joked with them. It was she who nicknamed Dicky Broad and his fugitives, Snow White and the Seven Dwarfs and the name stuck. The party that, led by Raymond Lecesne, who had adopted them, struck out for Paris from the convent one night, was refreshed in body and spirit. Nothing could stop them now, they felt. The Mother Superior was confident they would win through.

The youth brought them closer to Paris, knowing every turn on the roads. He was a skilful guide. Late at night they found themselves in a farm-house. The farmer's wife was ready to smuggle them on the last stage of the journey into the city. This intrepid woman secreted them in pairs in the boot of a battered old car and thus on five journeys they were smuggled past Wehrmacht road blocks. They assembled at a hide-out in the suburbs and when mustered they waited for nightfall. Raymond had fixed an appointment with the maquis. In the darkness he brought them to the foot of the Eiffel Tower.

The little party arrived by night and hid in bushes, scarcely breathing; German patrols moved close to them, so close that they could have reached through the foliage and touched the enemy. The long night passed slowly. Their man was due at 3 a.m. He was late and their hearts sank, but they waited. Just before dawn he arrived and took command.

Stealthily, familiar with the route, he darted through the German lines, the Highlanders following until they found themselves in a back-street. There the maquis brought them to a man-trap, opened it and they plunged into the sewers of Paris. Fetid water rushed past them. The tunnel was cold, clammy and nauseatingly filthy. In the darkness rats by the thousand squirmed, squeaking, jumping, sprawling. The atmosphere was indescribably foul. For more than three miles the Highlanders followed the course of the water, and then they surfaced and were brought to workers' flats in the suburbs.

In humble French homes, much like their own, they rested. Food was brought to them and clothes for disguise. They were given faked papers. Afterwards Dicky separated them into pairs and they set off by various routes towards the broad river that sealed off Vichy France. The Seaforths had received orders to assemble there and on arrival they made up a band of twenty-one men and one officer.

As they crossed the river, they were detected and a running battle took place. All save one, Private Turner, reached the other side in safety. Turner was wounded.

Once in Vichy territory the company again divided and Broad made his way to Lyons, to the home of the prince. The others were nearly all picked up by Vichy. Unaware that special passes and travel visas had now become the order of the day in Vichy territory they walked into road-traps. Raymond was handed over to the Germans and sent to Belsen. He did not survive the brutalities which were the normal routine of that outpost of hell.

The internment of these gallant men was made known to us within hours of their capture. Some of them were taken to St Jean where, on my first visit after their arrival, I was contacted with a view to reconnoitring the escape position for them. We were determined to get them out and their escape into Marseilles was our first objective. That accomplished, we could hide the lads until their Colonel was ready to make his plunge into freedom. I smuggled various gadgets, tools of escape into St Jean and put brakes on my impatience and theirs. They had made their plans and would move when the time was opportune.

That time did not come in St Jean. To our disgust the Seaforths were transferred to St Hippolyte du Fort where, by that time, forty-seven of the regiment were interned. I could still help in a small way. Pat took over the hazardous and tricky work of escape from the tougher gaol. It was beyond my powers and resources. All I could do was arrange that the usual necessities, food, clothes, papers, etc., be supplied to the commanding officer. We became anxious. We had to work quickly for a message had reached me from Dicky. To his regret, he said, he could not handle more than a dozen of the company. His situation was becoming 'rather trying.' He had 'knocked off' a truck from the enemy and built up a reserve of petrol—goodness knows how that miracle was accomplished in those petrol-starved days. He dare not steal another lorry. A dozen men was the maximum number he could take with him.

Pat went to work with machine-like rapidity, blandly controlling his gleeful zest and his disappointment. He would have liked to snatch the forty-seven 'blokes' from Vichy and send them all home, with souvenirs of Marseilles if possible, but the dozen would be released.

We soon collected our dozen. After one of my visits to St Hippolyte two took flight; I left a rope ladder with them. We had provided the prisoners with maps of the 'hotels' in which they were receiving French hospitality of the New Order and these they put to good use. One bright lad crawled into the prison laundry van and made his escape as it halted at a dark crossing on its road. Clothes which we had brought in over a period of weeks were assembled, and a further Seaforth emerged at dusk as a very shabbily-dressed workman.

Four were thus accounted for when O'Leary presented me
with a neat box of pills which, he said, had been specially
blended by his physician to relieve the pains of men suffering from the tedium of incarceration. His physician was a
young doctor, part of the organisation, who was employed
in the Marseilles hospital which the prison used for serious
cases. The men must take the pills at an appointed time,
said Pat. They would become very sick, 'dangerously sick,
poor blokes.' Their infection would 'scare the pants off the
guards.' They would be rushed to hospital, he continued, and
his physician would take over from that point. I confess my
hair was standing to attention on my scalp as he unfolded
his scheme. He, I am sure, was gleeful. It was characteristic
of O'Leary and it proved successful. But not before I was
subjected to further nerve-strain.

Next day I delivered the pills and the orders. The first
part of the operation was smoothly effected. The pills apparently brought on the most violent effects, and symptoms of
food poisoning. The Seaforths roared with pain and writhed
in agony because they *were* in agony and, perhaps, with added
zest because, for once in their lives they found it a joke, part
of the battle, and enjoyed it. Within an hour of their swallow-
ing the pills they were being examined by a grave young doctor
who, after writing an innocuous prescription, asserted that
these men must be given a route march the following afternoon. Prison life had made them flabby; they must walk off
the effects of the poison. He also solemnly informed the guards
that he would be compelled to place a report on the quality
of the food being served in St Hippolyte before his senior
physician.

Two men were examined even more thoroughly than their
comrades. They were given further orders.

I have never discovered just how the guards were persuaded
to halt their column of convalescents next day for a cup of
tea at the Seamen's Mission. Perhaps they were bribed; perhaps
the men, made hungry by the enforced diet of their 'con-
valescence' prevailed upon them. But midway through the
afternoon fifteen men and four guards filed into the Mission.
A few minutes later O'Leary, neat and sportily dressed, arrived

with bottles of rather fiery spirits. I gave the men tea; Pat entertained the guards. He was a wonderful host. The party grew more and more hilarious; Pat became more and more generous. It was, I suppose, disgraceful for a man of my cloth to stand by and watch this alcoholic jamboree, but I was under orders. I grew more and more unhappy. The guards became ecstatically silly. The party ended suddenly and they staggered out supported by only eleven of their charges. Pat courteously showed them the door. The other four men must have escaped on the way back to St Hippolyte.

By devious means, none quite so eccentric, we soon assembled the remainder of Dicky Broad's party and the time was set for their departure. The men would meet at a fixed hour in the suburbs and the O.C. would take over. But before his departure Dicky arrived at the Mission to thank me for the care I had given his lads, and to ask a further favour. He had two cherished possessions, he said, and he feared he might lose them on the last stage of the journey home. Would I hide them for him and we would meet after the war ended and I might return them. I said I would. They were his Balmoral and the compass he used throughout his sojourn in France. We parted.

' Au revoir, Donald, and good luck,' he whispered as he disappeared into the darkness. I went back to the office to brew coffee.

Henri hid Dicky's Balmoral and compass for me in the cellar of a French friend.

That night the truck set off with each man carrying faked papers. They posed as a party of workers *en route* to a destination where they would strengthen coastal defences. Many hours later they safely crossed the border. I am uncertain of their adventures in Spain. They experienced difficulties, I know, but eventually they arrived in Gibraltar.

The effect of their successful adventure upon the morale of the men who remained behind was incalculable. The Sea-forths were dazzled by the Colonel's daring, and they never missed an opportunity to try to follow his example. Among prison commandants the regiment became a by-word. They would glower when a Seaforth was delivered to them and mutter:

'Another week and this man will be trying to get away.'

Dicky Broad and his now twelve dwarfs, left our hearts high. They left, too, someone whose memory will live as long as the Seaforth Highlanders parade, a French youth, their comrade of the maquis and a townsman of Honfleur, Raymond Lecesne, the lad who guided them on their way to freedom and, for his salary, died under the whips of the fiends of Belsen.

Raymond was twenty-four when he died for freedom. They sent him home to die in Honfleur. After the war Lieut.-Colonel Broad heard of the boy's ending and suggested to his old comrades that they raise a stone over the grave. The men agreed. Today in the cemetery of his native place a noble slab covers the ground under which Raymond lies. On it, above his breast, is carved a crucifix. At his head a stone stands erect with these words inscribed on it: 'Ici Repose Raymond Lecesne. Resistant du 18 juin 1940.' The details of his birth and death follow and then a sentence stating his work for Snow White and the Dwarfs, the names and ranks of the Scottish comrades who shared his last adventure against the Nazis.

They have carved Binyon's lines beneath the crucifix, beginning,

'He shall not grow old ...'

So one Frenchman, one of many, is remembered. His life and death are a testimony to a very ancient friendship, the Auld Alliance, which bound Scotland to France and which has endured through many centuries and wars.

CHAPTER EIGHT

Death and a Traitor

I HAD AN appointment to meet one of our agents, known as
'Le Patron,' outside Jean's Café on the waterfront near the
old harbour of Marseilles. As I walked from the Mission
in the early afternoon I felt winter waning and spring stirring.
The sun was high in a clear sky and a shabby little sparrow
hopped in the gutter; I stopped to watch it. I thought of
Edinburgh, the city of my student days. On such a day, Auld
Reekie, loveliest of towns, is at its best. The lads and lassies
from the University come running helter-skelter down the
braes, scarves flying behind them, books uncertainly held
under their arms. They would be laughing. Another two
weeks and March would come to Edinburgh, and I allowed
myself to feel nostalgic. There would be holidays soon. A
lad might go home to Islay and be, for a few days, the centre
of a happy home. This, however, was Marseilles and I had an
appointment with an agent. I sighed. Tomorrow night would
be an 'operation' to the frontier.

I was soon outside the café and I pulled my wintry coat
around me as I sat down. The day was chilly. A man sitting
near to me, came to my table.

'Coffee, Donald? Nice and hot.'

I nodded and smiled. My mind was still in pleasanter
places.

The waiter brought coffee and my companion sipped his
drink slowly I remember the red wine in his big glass; I
watched it tilt and find its level again as he put it down on the
cold marble-topped little table for two.

'Cigarette?' The paper packet came at me. I took one
and lit it feeling curiously withdrawn from my friend and
ruefully thought, 'This must be a spring mood. Come alive,'
I urged myself, 'forget it.'

'Donald, nine men will arrive tomorrow night. Be ready for them at 22 hours. They are coming from the north by train.'

'By train?'

'Yes, by train. They have nice clean papers. It's all sweetly laid on. They have an escort too.'

'An escort? Who?'

'Fellow named Cole. An N.C.O. with a good mob. Old Scotland Yard man.'

'How old is he?' I asked. 'And he's an N.C.O. on active service? Sounds fishy to me.'

'Oh, he's not decrepit. He bailed out of the police to join up.'

'How do you know?'

'Look, Donald, you're becoming very suspicious in your old age. Cheer up, this isn't a funeral service.'

He went on to explain the whole operation.

'All right. All right. But this job seems to be too well-organised for my liking. What's this man going to do after he delivers the men? Go out with them?'

'He's too useful for that, old man. He's for the north again and more visitors for you. Now, don't worry, Donald!'

We parted then and we were not to meet again. A few months later the Gestapo shot him. He was Bruce Dowding my young Australian friend.

I had a premonition about 'Cole.' It was strengthened by his demeanour when we met. In meetings with agents, one was always aware that there was, of necessity, a missing dimension to their personalities, something withdrawn. We did not talk about our private lives. The less we knew of each other, the less could be extracted, under torture, by the experts of the Gestapo. But we were not on our guard against each other. The suppressed dimension had become an instinct. Cole lacked that instinct and to me he was insincere. The missing dimension worried him. He was always on the defensive, the difficulties of the journey he had made were as nothing, he proclaimed. That was untrue, as I well knew. Lounging into the Mission at the appointed time, he delivered the nine men and then went off to contact one of our agents.

I prayed that the lad would not talk too much to him and I wondered if I were doing him an injustice.

I could not free my mind of these suspicions. Cole was, I felt, a half man and when the unresolved half was defined he might be a traitor. I spoke to Pat and told him of my fears, but he would not listen. He laughed and, very reasonably, said:

'My dear Padre, we have no evidence that the chap is a risk. On the contrary his first job was an extremely profitable one. Nine blokes at one "go" is pretty good you'll admit. I know he's not the sort of chap one takes to—he's a bit of a loud-mouth. But he doesn't shoot anything that matters out of the cavity.'

I could not disagree with Pat. He was right and just. He took the line that, as a good officer, he was compelled to take. The man did his duty. But I was still unhappy.

In retrospect I believe that my Celtic gift was the source of my uneasiness. It enabled me to 'see through' Cole. Essentially, 'the second sight' is a spiritual faculty. Highlanders of my generation, those who went before us, and to a great extent the present generation, live simple lives, close to God and nature. We are a strictly God-fearing people. We find our intellectual pleasures in social gatherings with our own people. We are not great ones for mechanical pleasures or pastimes, good enough in themselves, but when omnipresent surely they tend to blunt the faculties. Our culture is traditional. Much of our literature comes to us by word of mouth; old tales of the clans and the Covenanting martyrs of our church mingle and interweave in the conversations of the older folk. We love music, and we have the pipes which are our own. I think our views of other folks are uninhibited by the extraneous matter that flows almost incessantly into the minds of the city dwellers from radio, television and cinema. Our vision remains fresh, undistorted by channels of mass entertainment. We live in the open more than most of the other inhabitants of the British islands. All men are a mixture of good and bad. A wicked man has an existence, secreted among his other lives, that is evil and egotistical. In this way I sought to analyse the conflict I

sensed in Cole. The evil he did pushed itself through the
surface of his disguise, betrayed itself in small indefinable
things, and I felt it. But there was nothing I could do. As
Pat said, the man seemed honest enough. I pushed my worries
into the background of my life and plunged into work, trying
to make the good soldiers happy during their stay at the Rue
Forbin and bringing help and the solace of religion to the men
in the internment camps.

Suffering, adventure, bravery were part of one's day-to-
day experience in the Rue Forbin and in the prisons. One
reached that state of mind where nothing was astonishing.

My nagging suspicions of Cole, and the possible infiltration
of the organisation by a traitor still worried me. I was feeling
very despondent but one evening my heart was lifted by a very
simple gift from God.

About nine o'clock I was reading for my next service,
feeling the contentment that comes after a busy day when
a young pilot, highly qualified as an R.A.F. officer, arrived
at the Mission.

I interviewed him and gathered that he must be given
high priority as an escapee. He was worth his weight in gold
to his service. But his clothes were in rags and so filthy he
might have been sleeping in sewers since his escape from a
plane shot down by anti-aircraft fire. I told the lad to plunge
himself in a hot bath; as I walked the floors frantically
puzzling about his departure I could hear him splashing about,
enjoying his new luxury. My problem was clothes. Two
men were going out in that next morning and I had spent
the previous day working on their ' case.' He could join them,
but he must have clothes and I had none in the house. In
daylight he could not have travelled a mile in the rags which
were burning in the dining-room fireplace. I could not go
to the Arabs; no appointment had been made and to take,
as it were, suit-luck with them was too dangerous. My guest
was tall and lanky. I am short and uncommonly broad-shoul-
dered. I could think of nothing and so I turned the matter
over to God. ' Dear God,' I prayed, ' You think this one
out for me. Please. I'm beaten.'

I dropped on to my knees and prayed intently, pouring

out my heart to Him. I was interrupted, in a most irritating
way, by a loud knock at the door. I jumped impatiently to
my feet and heard a female voice coming upstairs with one
of the lads in attendance.

I opened the door.

'Good-day, Madam Hamel. Are you in trouble? A visit
so early.'

'No, no, Monsieur le Pasteur. I have been thinking of
you all night and I have come to see you.'

She carried a large flat cardboard box, tied with string.
Dropping it on my table she continued.

'I had a feeling that you need clothes for some poor
Tommee so I brought these. Please forgive me for disturbing
you, Monsieur le Pasteur. It is very foolish.'

'Foolish. My dear lady you are an angel, sent by the
good God Himself. You are a direct answer to prayer. Please
take a seat. Coffee?'

Madam Hamel was one of Pastor Heuzy's parishioners. The
dear soul was ecstatic.

'Ah, you do need clothes. I knew it, Monsieur le Pasteur
I knew it. But I must go now.'

She grasped my hand and bade me good-bye.

I approached the box as fearfully as if it had contained
dynamite. A gift from God must not be taken lightly. Its
contents took my breath away. The suit and overcoat were
beautifully cut. Madam Hamel's husband was a rich Marseilles business man. Her eldest son was something of a
dandy. The shoes were hand-made, the shirt and tie of silk
and the underwear new. All that was missing was a hat.

Allan, the R.A.F. boy, walked in on me at that moment
a towel wrapped around his naked waist.

'Hello there, Padre. Just about choked the old pipes I
fear. I feel a ton lighter and want to go to bed. I am
beastly tired.'

I turned to him.

'Try this lot on first.'

The boy scrambled into the clothes and then stood contemplating himself in a rather short mirror in my corner

'By George, Padre. I've never been as well dressed in all my life. They won't know me when I get home, I'm such a toff. Must say, your service in these parts is pretty good. I'll recommend you to all my friends.'

I gazed at him happily marvelling.

'I am so sorry, Allan,' I said, 'I cannot supply you with a hat. We're all out of them and our outfitter did not send one for you.'

'Oh,' he said, 'don't worry about that, Padre. I wouldn't have used it if he had sent one. I've never worn a civvy hat in my life.'

Quietly I packed Allan off to bed and, on his behalf and my own, thanked the One, ever above all, who protects us in His own infinitely loving and omniscient way. Early the next morning Allan and two new friends whom he had just met set off for the frontier.

There were other soldiers whose departure from Marseilles was unhappy. Spring was coming to the old harbour; the sun was kindlier and the snow had disappeared from the gutters. But my days were darkened by the thought of one of the most sorry tragedies I had experienced. David was one of the unhappy ones, one of the heart-breaking minority.

I shall not forget those lads. A war ends and the men who fought in it and survived remember its comradeship, its dangers and its escapes, its victories and the self-sacrifice it inspired. It reveals saints and heroes. But when one examines the manifold tragedies that merge into the great tragedy of decent people organised to kill one another, for-saking all they love to butcher those they might have loved, but did not know, war is sombre. It is wrong. Alone and thinking of his service, a man will smile and maybe chuckle ocasionally, but in the ending of his reverie the thought of the stricken will return, and he will pray for all men. The sad ones are justified before God and men. They are eternal witnesses to the beastliness of modern warfare.

David came to me while snow was still lying on the Rue Forbin. Late at night I met him at the door of the Mission.

Another exhausted soldier, another staggering silhouette against the darkness and the whiteness of winter, he was one item in a party that fell into the house. We gave no immediate consideration to the men's more complex problems at such times. They were hungry and filth was engrained in their poor, sore bodies. They were bodies to be brought back to life.

We concentrated on these things. Released from the need of food, drink and hot water, David was helped to bed and he tumbled into sleep. Next day I made friends with all the members of the new intake, save him. He was not a surly lad but nervous and edgy and busy as I was, he disturbed me. I had many shock cases on my hands, men who had been tried too much. I was preparing for a visit to a prison out of town and there was a party to be prepared for the road. I was too much occupied to give David the immediate attention I felt he needed.

Throughout the next night the Mission was quiet. The early morning was free of police raids and I settled down to bookwork. About ten o'clock an N.C.O. interrupted me. With the business-like efficiency I found characteristic of old soldiers, he stood to attention and snapped out a request, his eyes staring into a corner where ceiling met walls.

'Stand easy, Corporal, I said. 'Something wrong?'

He stood easy and gazed down at me.

'I don't know, Padre. I just don't know, but I'm worried about the lad Davie. He seems to be in a very bad way.'

'You're all in a bad way, Corporal. Why are you specially worried about Davie? We'll send him home—with God's help we'll send all of you home, in time.'

'Yes, Padre,' he answered. 'I know what you'll do and I'm not worried a bit. But after lights-out this poor lad keeps talking and moaning all the time and crying out for his mother. I think he's a good one Padre, and I don't like it. It went on until about three this mornin'. The other lads didn't hear him. But they're young and they sleep sounder than me.'

'Tell me what you know of the boy, Corporal.'

The corporal, in a matter-of-fact way, told a story of the sort of endurance that is common enough in warfare. David was a working man, not long out of his apprenticeship at a mill, and a native of a village in the North of England. At Dunkirk he was taken prisoner. Herded into a train and removed to Germany, he made a break when the party was imprisoned in a stalag near the frontier. Before reaching Marseilles, he had walked 600 miles, living as he could on the roads and fields, sleeping in ditches, by the sides of country roads and, when he was lucky, in barns.

. 'I know that's bad,' continued the corporal, 'but he's a healthy lad and he should have begun to pull round as soon as you gave him a cup o' char, the broth and his grub. He should be well on the mend like the other lads. But I'm tellin' ya, Padre, this one is in a very bad way.'

The corporal knew the men and he was obviously extremely worried about the sick one.

'You've done well to tell me of this, Corporal,' I told him. 'I'll have a word with David and try to find out what is troubling him. You try to bring him out of himself. Go easy with the boy but bring him into things. Don't leave him entirely on his own, whatever happens. And don't you worry. We'll fix the lad up fine.'

The corporal worked hard and discreetly on David. Unobtrusively he made it difficult for the boy to evade company too much. I joked with the lad, asked him questions and discovered enough to make me want to help him to the uttermost. His problem, I felt sure, was spiritual. He had no obvious serious problems.

He was an ordinary sort of chap from Yorkshire, just one of millions of lads like himself, and he had worked in the mill before being called to arms in 1939. His accents reminded me of dialogue in North Country novels. A member of a small Christian sect, his life in the village was bound by the circumferences of ' t'chapel ' and ' t'mill.' At morning service Bible Class and evening service, Sunday was given to God. He was young, an only child and his widowed mother was the great human influence on his life. She must have been a gentle soul; his life had been happy. It might have continued on its placid industrious way. But for war, David would have married a girl in the congregation and raised a family. He loved football and cricket and his work. He loved his home. His faith in his religion was simple, unquestioning and absolute.

We became friends and I invited him to do a little work for me. He seemed pleased by his tasks. One evening I offered him a cup of cocoa before lights-out. He sat back in his chair and began to talk of the village, and the mill. That night he talked of his mother and burst into tears, sobbing bitterly.

'David,' I asked him. 'What is troubling you? There is nothing I can think of to bring you such unhappiness. I tell you, son, we'll send you home. Come on, now, cheer up. In a few weeks, you'll be sitting by the fire with the one you love.'

'I must tell *her*, Padre,' was all he said. 'And no one else.'

I did not press him to talk further but sent him off to bed and before I slept I prayed for him. About one a.m., I was awakened by panic-stricken screams. It was David. Bathed in sweat, he struggled in the corporal's arms, madly weeping until he came out of the dream and then stiffening into apathy. Next day I was preoccupied with arrangements for the next excursion to Spain. David, the corporal reported, sat apart from his comrades.

Two nights later, I broke my own self-imposed rule and told David he would cross the frontier the next night. He stared into space when I broke this good news.

'You must not speak of this, David,' firmly I cautioned him. 'I want you to know that in a few weeks, maybe less, you'll be at home, safe with your own folk. You'll be with your mother. On Sunday evening you can go to chapel with the other boys and girls.'

His face twitched, he gasped, and then he doubled up. I rushed round my desk and put my arms around his shoulders which were convulsively jerking.

'What *is* it, my dear lad? What is this trouble that is

killing the heart in you? Can't I help? Please help *me*, boy, to do something to make life easier for you.'

David caught one of my hands and held it tightly and while he sobbed, I waited. The paroxysm passed; he asked for more cocoa. During our earlier conversations, he would not have done that. He knew how short we were. I poured out a mugful strong and brown, added plenty of sugar and passed it over without a word. He caught my hand again and stared into space and then he drank a mouthful of the hot drink.

'I will never go home,' he said. 'Something tells me— I'll never get home, sir.'

I smiled and held up an admonitory finger, wagging it gently.

'David, of course you'll get home. Tomorrow night you'll be all aboard, and *en route* for the old place. Just think of it.'

He was more self-possessed by this time and I could see my raillery was helping him. Still he was determined that he would not get home. He apologised for his behaviour.

'I'm sorry, Padre.'

He pulled himself together and continued: 'I won't get home, Padre. You have been very good to me. No one but my mother has been as kind to me. I have a confession I wanted to make to Mother. May I make it to you?'

'David,' I replied, after a moment of meditation. 'God is your Father and mine and He knows what you are going to say and so much more about it than you will ever know. I work for God. That's a padre's job in life. I lead His people in prayer and worship and it is part of my job to help those God loves. He loves all His children; He loves you. Tell me what you wish, lad.'

The boy listened carefully. He was now in complete control of himself. The story emerged in bits and pieces.

When the prisoners were marched into the German train in France, David felt ready to die. He was worn out; the battle had been long and he was starved. All through the long journey, the train was sealed off from daylight. It halted for periods and then, shunting on its way, wakened him and his comrades from uneasy slumbers. He lay awake thinking of his mother and her agonising worry without him. He was not a great one for writing and two weeks had passed since he sent his last postcard.

When they brought him to the stalag, he lay sleepless all through the first night thinking of the England he knew. Reared in the tiny, ever familiar community of the chapel, all the world beyond the village was alien to him. He had nothing in common with the other prisoners. But next morning he found a friend, a German N.C.O. who spoke some English and was in charge of the men who distributed bread. The German was a much older man than David, 'easily over thirty,' and they talked in the halting way of simple soldiers. A few days passed and then the boy found that the friendly guard was a member of his own religious sect. Their friendship was cemented. They liked each other as men and the German, who was in charge of work parties, arranged that David should be employed on plumbing in new huts that were being built just beyond the barricades. It was a nice, dry, 'cushy' job, indoors.

David liked it and saw almost immediately that it offered him an opportunity to escape.

Before the outside parties were rounded-up into their bunk-houses each evening a roll was called. David waited until one night when the roll was hurriedly taken outside the huts on which they had been working. He answered his name and before the column left he dropped out quietly and secreted himself in the hut where he had been working. When night fell he struck out for freedom.

'It was a very dark night,' he said, 'but I could see the road and the hedge, so I kept them in sight.'

He walked in the fields, skirting the wide roadway that ran through them to the frontier. He could not tell how far he had marched, a mile, maybe two, before he saw the lamp of a bicycle coming towards him. Holding his breath, he stood behind a tree praying the cyclist would pass. Beyond the tree, there was a pile of building materials. Thinking it might give better cover the lad dropped to his stomach and crawled behind it. The cyclist passed and David relaxed. He felt safe. Then the bicycle braked and stopped. Panic-stricken, David raised his head. Coming towards him he saw a German soldier with a hand on his pistol holster. Involuntarily the boy's grip tightened on a limb from a fence that lay under him on the roadside pile. It was a long, heavy, slim iron stanchion, part of the building materials. The German loomed blindly over him and the lad stood straight up and brought his weapon down on the man's head. He must have gone insane. The blows followed in quick succession raining on the back of the bowed head. The German crumpled to his knees and then toppled forward and writhed on to his shoulders. He was dead, the back of his head smashed. David looked down at the face. It was his friend, the N.C.O., whose kindness unwittingly had opened the door of escape.

'I did not mean to kill him, Padre. I don't want to kill anyone. He was very kind to me. I liked him.'

I sat holding the boy's hands firmly in mine. We talked a little. I prayed with him and told him that while there was bitter sorrow in his friend's death, he was innocent. God knew that; the kind German was with God and he too would know.

Next night David was shot dead crossing the Pyrenees, betrayed to the very end. A traitor struck and the ring closed in, shooting down the helpless before it reached those of us who could fight back.

I shall not forget David. Always I pray for him. Like so many of the innocent, he was a victim of the world's hatred.

CHAPTER NINE

Dark Springtime

THE GUIDE returned to the Mission ten days after the party that included David had departed for Spain. He told me that the boy had been shot and was dead. One other soldier, he said, had been severely wounded. The remainder of the party were in prison. Only his experience of the district, and his realisation that the game was up, had saved him.

'Monsieur le Pasteur,' said the guide, 'all would have been well if we had followed your original plan. But I received your letter at Perpignan; and we walked right into a trap.'

'My letter? What are you talking about? I sent no letter,' I said. 'I rarely write letters these days. If I have an important message, I usually send it by word of mouth. You *must* know that. Experience has taught me to be cautious.'

The man insisted, and he was telling the truth. A letter ostensibly sent by me from the Mission had altered the route he was following. He had destroyed it, according to orders, but it was a fact. It was now evident that there was a traitor among us, conversant with our activities, and our escape route.

My mind focused on Cole. Obviously we had been tricked by someone inside the organisation, someone who was aware of the original route and had diverted our guide and his party to a point where the frontier guards would be certain to intercept them. He knew where and when the enemy patrolled. He must have known the inn at Perpignan where the party would halt; he must have been well-briefed in the methods of both sides.

That evening, I reported my suspicions to another agent and he pointed out that Cole had an alibi. On the night of the captured party's departure the ex-Scotland Yard man was *en route* for Paris and Lille. He could not possibly have known of our operation.

'One of your chaps must have talked out of turn, Padre,

before leaving. It takes only a word in the wrong place and you know what happens.'

'That is extremely unlikely and you know it. Cole might easily have discovered the operation before he left Marseilles. If he is, as I suspect, a Gestapo agent, a traitor, *he would make it his business to find out if there were parties ready for escape.*'

'Look, Padre, Cole is bringing down a party of R.A.F. men, everyone of them worth his weight in gold. It was not him, I know.'

I accepted the agent's judgment. I was a padre, after all, and not the man to fight a superior's orders, but I never have ceased to regret that I was persuaded against my will. Had we relied on my instinct, we would have been spared the most shameful betrayal of our experience.

A few days after David's departure and death, I had a meeting with friends of our escape route in a little village on the outskirts of a forest, thirty miles or so from Marseilles, not far from Auban. After the interview was over, I wanted a breath of the country, and I walked in the nearby forest. As I strolled aimlessly among the trees, I felt that I was being followed. Turning quickly round, I caught sight of Cole, watching me from behind a clump of bushes. I continued my walk as if nothing had happened, but now I was perfectly sure that my instinct or second sight had not led me astray. At that moment, from information I had received from our agents, Cole was supposed to be at Roubaix near Lille in the north of France. Yet here he was following me through this forest, like a detective on the track of his quarry.

Signs began to multiply that we were betrayed. It soon became apparent that I was not alone in my suspicions of the efficient agent who moved so freely between the north and the south. Other members of the organisation became edgy and harassed. The weather changed as spring came, and I moved freely as ever but under increased surveillance. In April I was taken to Vichy Headquarters for interrogation. Complaints had been received that I was 'an agitator against the State.' I was warned in a friendly, but firm way that I was in danger. That night I told the men in the house that I was suspected of being 'an undesirable alien.' They, God bless them, thought it a marvellous joke. When a padre establishes himself with servicemen, he can do no wrong. The thought that even the enemy might suspect me of being anything other than their chaplain struck the lads as funny. The padre saw their point of view. Their affection was one of the consolations that kept him going. But his sense of humour failed to see the joke.

I began to set aside more time, parsimoniously saved from my duties, to spend with Pastor Heuzy, Henri Thebault and another friend Jacques Monod, a teacher in one of the colleges in the city. We would snatch hours to talk together and plan church work. Jacques was something more than a hero. He was, I believe, a saint, and his friendship meant much to me. Jacques was a member of the great Monod family of France—of Huguenot extraction.

It was the evil of the Nazi war-machine, and his love for human beings that compelled him into an active share in the fight against Hitlerism. He was an intellectual in France, a country where words and thought are meaningless unless they are wed to action. Because of his belief, as a Christian thinker, that war in itself was bad, Jacques was a pacifist when his country was invaded. When he saw the sufferings that Germany inflicted on his countrymen and their conscienceless use of torture as an instrument of policy, he joined the resistance. He gave his life for his beliefs, one of the many Christian martyrs of all denominations whose guide was their conscience, and who died humble before God; unmoved by the power of the enemy.

Jacques, like Henri Thebault and Pastor Heuzy had links with Scotland. They were men of my own way of thinking. We were inspired by the same Christian ideal. They were towers of strength to me and I hope I contributed something to their well-being in those agonising days for France. Already Pastor Heuzy was under suspicion. The gentle good-humoured voice, which I knew and loved, speaking its odd Franco-Scottish English, when it preached in beautiful French from the pulpit in his church, excoriated the evil-doers who had ravished France. He was warned to be more discreet but, serenely believing in God and the impossibility of a pastor telling anything but the truth as he saw it under God, he continued.

Jacques sustained me practically, spiritually and intellectually. We spent many happy evenings together in his home on the Roucas Blanc in Marseilles. I learned of his death long after he had joined the maquis and taken to the hills. Finally he was caught, tortured and killed by the Gestapo. His going from us was mysterious. He just disappeared without fuss or drama to take up his task. But we knew what he had undertaken, and we prayed for him.

Long after his disappearance, I received a letter from his cousin Pastor Alfred Monod in which he wrote:

I believe that the motives that prompted Jacques to take up arms and throw in his lot with the Maquis are similar to those which inspired the Scottish Covenanters—those martyrs of the moors whose monument stands in the old churchyard of Greyfriars in Edinburgh.

The bond between Jacques and Edinburgh was strong. Throughout the war, a member of his family served the Allied Cause in the Scottish capital. He is now in the Foreign Office in Paris—Philippe Monod. His grandmother was a MacGregor.

I did not see my friend after his disappearance, but I have a message from him which I should like to set down in these pages. Before he died he sent a letter to his wife and family and friends. Characteristically, he begs our forgiveness for leaving us ' in the night.' In the following excerpt, one can see the type of man that Jacques Monod was. This is a translation from the French:

At this moment, when I am about to leave this world, I ask your pardon for having so poorly repaid the trust which you placed in me. My wife will tell you the circumstances which compelled me to cancel our intended meeting and impose those long months of silence and separation.

At this moment when the ramparts of silence are about to sunder us from one another, we know that nothing can separate us from the love of Christ.

T.P.   D

I pray God to grant each of you the peace of His pardon and the power of the Faith at a time when our hearts are so heavy from our own suffering, and the sufferings of others.

I beseech Him also to pardon my faults, for I know that the deliberate recourse to violence needs to be forgiven.

I leave the world without hate in my heart. Nevertheless, we Christians should never allow pagans alone to offer their lives in the name of a purely political ideal, in a fight in which we are involved with the fate of the State, the fate of the Church and the spiritual destiny of our children.

Remain united. Remember the Church. Cherish and guard, in the midst of a world that will be hard, those human and Christian treasures which have so much enriched our friendship and fellowship.

And finally, let us give thanks to God together for having transformed Life and Death, through His Son, Jesus Christ, the saviour of the World.

Jacques was one of the many friends I lost in the dark springtime of 1941. It ended in a blood-bath. Only a handful survives of the brave band who lived in peril, their lives dedicated to their Faith, their God and their countries.

The forged letter which brought David to his death was quickly followed by two more betrayals. First Captain G was arrested and taken to the Reich, and Pat became the officer in total command. Then our top contacts inside Spain were arrested and imprisoned. One of our men brought the bad news to me from the Pyrenees. I had not spoken to him of my suspicions of Cole.

'It's treachery,' he told me. 'It must be. I have been told you are uneasy. Tell me, Donald, whom do you suspect?'

I hesitated to answer. I had been told so often, and God knows with truth, that I was 'an unworldly minister,' and that I had no proof that my fears of Cole were justified. Yet I felt from the beginning that the man was not to be trusted. He was, as we say in Scotland, ' Aye speirin' '—trying to work information from me. The tales he told of his resource and daring were supported by the dozen or so escapes from the north he had organised but why, I asked myself, tell them. There was not an agent in the organisation who had not risked his life often. It was their war work. They did not talk of it.

The man from the Pyrenees watched me.

'I think,' he said bluntly, 'it is No. 11.'

No. 11 was Cole.

'Our wonderful No. 11,' he continued, 'spends too much money on his girl friends for my liking, and they are all aiding and abetting him in his double dealing.'

'Then there's only one thing you can do,' I told him. 'Report your suspicions to Pat. I don't know what to think. Pat will have a special investigation made into No. 11 and his off-duty behaviour and contacts. We cannot go on like this, suspecting each other. We'll never prosper without mutual trust.'

The report was made to Pat, but he would not listen. For reasons which were entirely sound, Cole had his full confidence and we were moved only by our suspicions. Cole had been thoroughly checked again and again. Escaped soldiers sang his praises; so did the Secret Service. London had complete confidence in him and Pat was not alone in his faith in the man's loyalty. I was silenced because I had been constantly harried by the knowledge that it is evil to speak ill of anyone without absolute proof, and we who suspected, had no proof, only our instinct and that might be at fault. Confirmation of Cole's baseness was to come from an unsuspected source.

A few days after the report was made to Pat, security officers circled the Mission and entered to search the house. Every man in the place was interrogated and his papers thoroughly checked; the walls, floor and cupboards were tapped in search of hiding places. Nothing was uncovered that compromised us, and it was with a feeling of relief that I showed the officers to the door. But before they departed, one drew me aside. One of the many French detectives who had shown goodwill to me, his sympathies were with the Allies.

'I want to ask you a question about Monsieur——' he said, using the name Cole had chosen as his alias. 'I know you have met him several times.'

Immediately I went on the defensive.

'I have met the man, but I know nothing of him.'

'Has he a wife and children in England?'

'Why do you ask?'

'Because, mon cher Pasteur, he is very much too friendly with a certain pretty little Parisienne, and she is in league with the Gestapo. And I am friendly with a certain Scottish pastor which is my reason for asking questions.

'You will understand, M. le Pasteur,' he went on, 'that to trust such a man is to invite disaster. In your case, my dear friend, the danger is very, very great.'

He took my hand and shook it warmly, bowed and departed.

The heart sank in me. This was confirmation of our suspicions with a vengeance. It might mean the end of all our good work. Already the organisation, without G and the Spanish agents, had been weakened. Pat and his lieutenants were working at full stretch. Time was needed to replace the gaps made in our ranks. Cole could ruin everything—if he had not already done so.

After dark, I slipped out of the Mission and, by a devious route, made my way to Pat and placed my report before him. He acted promptly.

Cole was due in Marseilles two days later, bringing down airmen from Belgium. As soon as he arrived, he was invited to a room and there confronted by Pat and three other agents, Dowding, Prassinos and Duprez. Pat immediately challenged him, throwing the accusations clearly and unambiguously in his face.

To my knowledge, O'Leary had decided to kill him that night. Pat and his lieutenants were certain that the case against Cole was complete. His movements in certain areas coincided with betrayals or were close enough to make it likely that he had been more than a possible traitor. All other members of the organisation had been checked. Only Cole remained ambiguous. The friendly man from Vichy Headquarters had put his finger on the suspect—Cole, he

revealed in his oblique way, was the Gestapo agent. O'Leary
decided to strangle him.

Heatedly he denied his guilt. Pat, losing patience with
his self-righteous indignation, beat him into a condition of
stupidity. But still he asserted he was innocent. True, he
admitted friendship with a girl in Paris; but when he heard
she was consorting with Germans he refused to meet her again.
He demanded an investigation at the Northern Headquarters
of the resistance. He demanded an apology. By this time
O'Leary was again undecided and was reluctant to kill the
man.

He agreed to ask Paris for a report. He ordered Cole to
proceed to Madrid, pending its arrival. England, he reasoned
could be radioed, and Cole arrested by our agents in Spain
and smuggled home by plane. There the matter could be
finally and justly decided.

That night Cole was despatched through the Pyrenees with
the R.A.F. men and the wretched creature led them into a
Nazi trap. Afterwards he fled north and joined the Gestapo.
We did not see him again in Marseilles.

The news of his final treachery reached us on the day
we heard from Paris, that their investigation of his mistress
proved beyond all doubt that he was an enemy agent, a
professional betrayer of his country and countrymen. Now
it was clear that we were all in the gravest danger. Pat
contacted me without delay and gave orders to burn all papers
in the Mission that might incriminate me. All activities which
might place me in any danger whatsoever were to be discon-
tinued. I must take cover and function only in my vocation
as a chaplain to the men in the Mission. He and his three
chief lieutenants would leave immediately to warn all other
agents in the organisation. Alas, it was too late.

Cole's report had been thorough. The four British agents
walked into separate gangs which were lying in wait upon their
routes. Only O'Leary escaped to carry on the battle and later
in the war to endure torture most horrible. He became, as a
prisoner, a centre of hope and bravery in a concentration
camp. Bruce Dowding was shot by the Gestapo; Prassinos was
beheaded; Duprez was taken to a concentration camp and

there, after indescribable suffering, was shot by enemies who were without reverence for brave men.

Pat's escape was due to the heroism of a schoolgirl who cycled for many miles through a long night to intercept him before he moved on the final stage of his journey. He went into hiding. The great enemy round-up continued, with him as the prize object of the search. Over 100 of our more than 150 agents were arrested and within a few days thirty of these were shot out of hand. The rest, including housewives and nuns who were moved by charity for the hunted men they had helped, and young French members of the resistance were sent to the gas chambers in Germany from which there was no escape.

The tale of Cole's treachery does not end with the deaths and imprisonment of these heroic men and women. More than 500 of his own countrymen, British soldiers, were secreted along the escape route. They too were captured. Some were shot as spies because they were wearing civilian clothes.

Among all these heroes let me tell the story of one man who lives in my memory. He was a priest, another clergyman who was not of my Church, but of the same Christian Faith, the Abbé Carpentier, a gentle little curé whose parish was in Abbeville.

Like so many French priests and nuns the Abbé thought little of his life when he balanced it against the liberty of La France, which is more than a country to its sons and daughters. It is a personality, mother, father and ancestor, the great reality which surrounds their humble lives.

Like the Apostle Paul, who sat at the feet of Gamiliel, the Abbé was a craftsman. Paul was a tent-maker; the Abbé in the days of peace had made himself a fine printer. Whenever he was free of the manifold duties that are part of a clergyman's day he retired to his little printing press. He became an artist in that gracious craft. He printed and bound rare copies of the classics. He became an expert in photogravure. And then the Boche came and the Abbé ached for his youth so that he, priest as he was, might take up arms for France. But France was defeated, and he was old so he carried on with the holy tasks of the day and waited for God to call him. His prayers were answered. The resistance was organised and, before long, the Abbé received an appeal from its leaders.

They had learned of his craftsmanship, they said, and they appealed to him to use it for the cause. Would he set up a press for the printing of passports, ration cards and identity cards for soldiers of the British ally who were trying to make their way across France so that they might rejoin their army and prepare for the Liberation? It was the moment for which the good little man had waited. He set up his press, and through the night hours worked with patient, meticulous skill carrying out the orders of the patriots. The papers he prepared were perfect down to the smallest detail, and were prized by the man in control. But, like his senior officers, the modest little man was known to Judas. There is something classical in the history of Christianity in his ending.

Cole brought him three exhausted R.A.F. men one night. The priest was alone in his study when they arrived, and he gave them food. The agent told him that his guests were part of the air-crew of a British bomber that had been shot down over the coast. For ten days the lads had been on the run. Would the Abbé help them? They wished to reach Marseilles and there strike out for Spain, but they needed papers issued by the occupied zone of France. The three men produced proof of their identity. One even showed burn marks he had received when the plane went on fire. The Abbé was convinced.

He took them to his secret workroom and assembled his press. After testing it, he brought out fresh cards and was about to start on the first job when he heard a noise behind him and turned. Three revolvers were pointed at him. He was in the hands of the Gestapo. He made only one comment, and we know what it was; turning to Cole sorrowfully, he said:

'In all my life I have met many Englishmen. You are the first I have known who would sell his country, for gold, I suppose. I am not likely, thank God, in the short time I have to live to meet another.'

The Abbé was taken to Paris, secretly tried and sentenced

to be beheaded. Like many of his countrymen he met friends in prison among the gaolers, and it is to one of these, who smuggled out a letter telling the story of his arrest, that we are indebted for the facts I have set down. The priest-printer was taken out early one morning and modestly as he lived, he died.

From that moment, the Resistance took oath to seek Cole out and kill him. He became a marked man and fled to Berlin to work there for his German masters. Before he died as squalidly as he lived, they were driven from France.

Meanwhile in Marseilles I carried out Pat's orders. Most of the men in the house were scattered through friendly homes in the city, quickly, surreptitiously and, I suspect, under the blind eyes of certain friendly Vichyites. I burned all incriminating papers apart from my books of names which Henri Thebault took from me and planted, as I later discovered, at the bottom of a disused well. I bade farewell to my friends. I was never to see Pastor Heuzy again. He too was arrested.

They silenced his pulpit and the Gestapo shot him. So his life ended, but not his witness which is remembered by his congregation and told to their children in Marseilles.

They came for me one morning about 8 a.m. I was taken from the Rue de Forbin in a Black Maria.

I was angry as the Black Maria left the door. There is something unreal about being arrested by the police; one is irrationally indignant. Most of my life I had been a law-abiding man; the laws I could not abide in 1941 were wicked and stupid. I thought of the men left in the Mission and became more angry. What was going to become of them now? Not one of the poor lads knew his way about the town. The journey was very short, but by the time we arrived at Fort St Nicholas, which lies at the mouth of the old harbour, I was in no mood to be trifled.

I was given a seat before a long table in the Salle de Tribunal in the old fort, and the Vichy Military Tribunal studied me. I bowed before taking my seat. The Juge d'Instruction leaned forward, rested his elbows on the table, pursed his lips and said:

'You are English?'

'No, sir,' I answered sharply, 'I am Scottish.'

The lips flickered. My reply seemed to amuse the old gentleman. He sounded more friendly as he proceeded.

'We have arrested you,' he announced, 'because we have proof that you are agitating against the interests of unoccupied France. You are in touch with the British Intelligence Service. You are helping soldiers, airmen and civilians to escape from France, across the Spanish frontier. You are spreading pro-British propaganda among our own people, and urging them to join the Resistance.'

He paused and looked at me.

'I have no counsel,' I replied. 'This, I take it, is a Court of Law.'

He shrugged and held up his hands.

'May I take it that I must act as my own counsel. If so I should like to hear the witnesses for the prosecution.'

He smiled and went into a long vague dissertation on my work in Marseilles; nothing definite emerged from the story. No witnesses were presented and again I challenged the court on that point. The interrogation began, and I answered questions without incriminating myself. The farce irritated me more and more. It was much later that I realised that the Court was more embarrassed by it than I.

They were in a difficult position. They must have known of my liaison with Edinburgh. I was a clergyman. My work in Marseilles was known to all the priests in the city. The nuns were among my friends and helpers and, God knows, they must have been aware that Sister Brigid's neutrality was of a distinctly Hibernian type. She was a neutral, enthusiastically against Hitlerism. If I were handed over to the Gestapo and shot, Vichy would be in extremely hot water. Every Christian church and convent in Marseilles had contact with foreign countries, foreign missions, and any violence to me could not have been kept secret. The French, God bless them, had not acquired the diabolic skill of the Germans in covering their misdeeds, nor did they aspire to it.

For five hours the interrogation continued. I became very hungry. Hunger reminded me of the poor lads in the Rue de Forbin. What would they do for dinner? My anger became insupportable and for a moment the quiet hum of the court was upset.

'I have told you,' I snapped, 'that I am a Scot and you say that I am an enemy of France. My record in France proves that accusation is nonsense. The history of our two countries shows it to be demonstrable rubbish.

'I love France next to my own country, which is France's ally now as ever.'

Then the balloon went up. The court was in an uproar when I shouted across the table:

'When our troops liberate France from its present undignified position, with the help of honest Frenchmen who are, thank the good God, by far the greatest number of Frenchmen, you will discover again how much we love this land.'

The Juge d'Instruction remained cool and withdrawn. With a smile he watched me, and then thumped on the table. The court came to order.

'Will you explain to us, Monsieur le Pasteur, how it is that many of the men who have been arrested on the frontier had passed through the British Seamen's Mission?'

'Sir,' I answered, 'those men had identity papers which were checked by members of the Sûreté Nationale, experienced security officers who expressed themselves satisfied that they were in order. I am a pastor. Can I be expected to detect something that professional police officers have missed in their systematic investigations?'

I was becoming very tired. The events of the past weeks had placed an agonising burden upon all of us. Comrades whom I had loved might be dying as this trial proceeded. Hope was draining out of me. The court withdrew and I waited. About an hour passed and then they filed in again.

'We find the prisoner guilty.'

The Judge paused, and I watched him assemble his papers.

'You are sentenced to two years' imprisonment. But '—I wondered what was coming next—' your sentence will be *avec sursis*.'

'Pardon me, sir,' I said, 'what does that mean?'

'It means,' he replied drily, 'that you will be temporarily released—put on probation. You will close the British Seamen's Mission within ten days. You will leave Marseilles and go to another place. I suggest Grenoble And I warn you that if you are caught again, engaged on any clandestine activity whatsoever, you will be arrested and thrown into gaol without further trial. You are, I repeat, sentenced to two years' imprisonment and are released on probation.'

They escorted me back to the Rue Forbin, with great courtesy, in the Black Maria. I found a house full of disgruntled men who came to life when I entered the front door. I could hear them spreading the word through the house, and from all parts they ran to meet me. The poor lads thought that I would never return to them. Already, I was told, they thought I had been shot.

We had a celebration dinner that night. Not even the news that the Mission must be closed in ten days worried them. It was a pleasant dinner, but my thoughts were elsewhere. Where would I go now to carry on the work which I had pledged myself to do nearly a year ago when France was falling?

A few days after my trial at the Fort St Nicholas, a young Englishman arrived at the Mission. 'Padre,' he said, 'we know all about your trial, and condemnation, and we feel sure that your life will from now on, be in danger. A plane will take off from an airfield near Arles in a day or two, and I have been commissioned to offer you an air flight to England.' 'Thank you,' I said, 'it's most kind of you, but I feel that wherever I go from here, I must continue my war work. I have been called to this work, and I feel confident that all will be well with me.'

CHAPTER TEN

Second Stop Grenoble

THE HOUSE had quietened into the silence which a marauding mouse can shatter, and to me the future seemed as empty as enigmatic, as the dark noiseless night beyond the Mission walls. I lit a cigarette, tried to read but could not settle to my book. Restlessly I wandered through the rooms of the Mission and then I lay down in my room and tried to sleep. But my mind would not rest. It careered over immediate problems. More than sixty men were still at various addresses in Marseilles, soldiers and airmen whom I had vowed to succour. Only ten days remained to me. If they were left here they would be defenceless. I was exhausted physically. What more could I do? Soon my thoughts were pursuing each other in circles until I reached a fruitless stage of worry but, before oblivion came, I stilled my soul with a prayer for the dead and fleeing comrades whose plight was the true cause of my agony. It is not easy for a man to live when those he has served with are in danger, and he is in comparative safety. It is a sorrowful experience to see the good work of many men who have risked their lives brought to nothing by a traitor.

The bright sunshine of the early summer morning instilled courage in me. I heard the birds singing outside my window and I prayed for help and contemplated the problem that faced me. The men must be cleared out of the city without delay. The stores in the Mission must be placed in the hands of Christians who would put them to good use.

The days that followed were happy. I found golden loyalty among my friends in the southern port. Guides seemed to spring from nowhere, men who had already escaped death only because their professional services were occasionally rather than regularly employed by us. My French comrades were embittered by our betrayal. My contacts among the

108

Christians spread the news of the difficulties at the Mission and the battered remains of the escape route were inspired to heroic action. I suspect that during those ten days the Sûreté winked, knowing that my work in Marseilles was ending. They were content to be rid of me. As I have recorded I had friends in the police, French Christians who did their duty to Vichy and were ashamed of it.

I visited the men in their hiding places and I made arrangements with guides to escort parties through the mountains as soon as the frontier hysteria quietened and the guards slackened their attention. We had little time for farewells, but the old routines were maintained. I briefed each man on the hazards of the journey that faced him; counselled each to give absolutely no information to the enemy if captured; and prayed that they would find a way home to work and fight for our country.

The Quaker Mission in Marseilles solved the problem of liquidating the material resources of the Seamen's Mission. Donald Lowrie, an American who was attached to this centre of Christian endeavour, had helped me enormously with food and francs for my work. A fellow student at New College, Edinburgh, Donald Stevenson, was another of the Quaker officials. I gave all that was of value in the house on the Rue Forbin to these good people when my work was completed and the next day I took train for Avignon which, I thought, was far enough from Marseilles to satisfy the Sûreté that I would be immobilised there, and near enough to the city to enable me to establish communications and continue my work.

The journey was long and tediously uneventful. The French train service had not been improved by war conditions. On arrival at the City of the Popes I was bedraggled. I hoped that the Pontiffs found more hospitality there than the twentieth-century padre who made his way to a police station to report his presence. I must go in the morning, I was told, to Central Headquarters. My case would then be considered.

I found an hotel and tumbled into bed in a room I cannot remember. Next morning I made my way to the Sûreté where polite and deferential officials received me. They were kind but slightly embarrassed. Perfunctorily they scanned my papers, which were in order. I became aware that they knew all about me and I was still an ' undesirable alien.'

'Alas, M. le Pasteur, you cannot remain in this city.'

'But why not?' I asked, hopelessly. 'My papers are in order. I complied with the Marseilles Sûreté's instructions and left the town. You will appreciate, gentlemen, that I am a clergyman and I cannot continue to wander over France. Much as I love your country, I need some place where I can live.'

The inspector smiled with sincere regret and spread out his hands.

'Please forgive us, M. le Pasteur and let us hope that sometime we in Avignon will atone for our apparent lack of hospitality. But,' his voice became intensely serious, 'we have had orders. Avignon is not far enough from the city where you have been found guilty and sentenced. You understand.'

'I understand, my friend,' I answered. 'But where am I to go?'

The inspector smiled very broadly and I began to like him more than I had done until that moment.

'I suggest Grenoble, Monsieur, a congenial city I assure you, with a fine university. You are a pasteur, a man of learning. You will be at home there, I assure you. There you will find compatriots in need of you and colleagues in scholarship.'

He arose from the desk upon which my papers lay. Very smartly his assistants followed his example. The inspector offered me his right hand and I shook it.

'You will escort M. le Pasteur to his hotel,' he instructed, 'give him the courtesy due to him, and see he suffers no inconvenience before his departure.'

He bowed gravely, shrugged impatiently, threw out his arms in the traditional gesture of Gallic irritation.

'Forgive us, M. le Pasteur,' he muttered, and with a quick turn on his heel left us.

The subordinates stood looking at me. I held out my right hand to one of them and they relaxed. They were good lads, doing a duty as distasteful to them as it was to their superior officer. As we walked out on the broad boulevards to the hotel I felt happily elated. Avignon could not offer the Scottish outcast hospitality, but it revealed friendship.

I settled into the train with a parcel of food, fell asleep and wakened from time to time as we steamed through the night. The carriage was dimly lit and crowded with uneasily slumbering figures. Bending towards the light I took out my scriptures, and lost myself in the story of the Master and His disciples until sleep came again. After many halts and intervals we pulled into Grenoble. I walked from the station to face a new phase in my adventures, wondering what awaited me there.

In the Sûreté in the University City I found the police as agreeable as their colleagues in Avignon and more accommodating. My papers were scrutinised and I was directed to the University where I might find counsel and assistance. There I was sent to the Hôtel de l'Europe where I settled down to my first war-time night in the city I came to love next to Edinburgh and Paris.

There was a place for my vocation in Grenoble. I had arrived in the Gaullist country. It is a source of some amusement that I was sent to such a place by the police. What motivated certain officials in the Vichy Sûreté in sending me there? For Grenoble was the capital of the intellectual world of the Resistance. The most popular and brilliant student at the University was Pierre, nephew of Charles de Gaulle and his uncle had no better soldier. The surrounding country was alive with maquis. Planes were landing by night in nearby valleys, escapes were being made into Switzerland, information was flooding out of France and here the young heroes of the maquis were preparing for battle.

There was great need for a British Protestant pastor in Grenoble. The city had become a refuge for aged British citizens who were eking out their meagre existence on miserable allowances. Tired, sick, hungry, bereft of spiritual guidance, they dragged out their days. I realised as my first day winged away that I would not be unemployed in Grenoble. There was a job here for me, I thought, but I was modest in my estimate of the possibilities. There were many tasks waiting for my hands.

I spent nearly two years in Grenoble; they are among the happiest years of my mission as a clergyman. At the University I was greeted with warm kindliness and generosity and met old acquaintances and friends of my friends at Edinburgh University. From medieval times European Universities have been linked by travelling scholars; professors, lecturers and dons keep in touch with colleagues they have met abroad; war divides these men. They yearn for peace so that they may interchange knowledge with scholars in other countries. They think wistfully of the days when they may spend their 'sabbaticals' in the colleges of their choice and when they can invite professors from abroad to instruct their students. Fortunately for me, Grenoble decided almost as soon as I contacted the Senate that a visiting Professor of English was required as an attachment to the Faculty.

To a man the Senate was Gaullist. Many had taught at Edinburgh University. A few professors were neutral; they were old and tired, with memories of 1914-18. It would be foolish to condemn them self-righteously. Like the sad old Marshal, they had been valiant in youth and middle-age; the wickedness of the new world in which they lived defeated them. Had they felt strong enough to choose they would have chosen to support their old ally, but they believed the cause hopeless and had capitulated in their hearts. They were a minority. The university hummed with democratic discussion and the senators and students knew just what democracy meant.

I settled in to the Hôtel de l'Europe to prepare my lectures and found in English and Scottish literature a source of relief from more exhausting duties. We Highlanders are natural born bookmen. I always think with pleasure of Barrie's Highland ghilly in *Mary Rose* who, discovered reading Sophocles by a visiting British officer, was congratulated on his ability to read Latin. 'It is good of you to say so, sir' he answered, 'but in these parts we call it Greek.' Of course the ghilly became a minister as the play developed.

Modern life handicaps a scholar. There are so many subjects he wishes to study and his limitations irk him. Theology is the blessed discipline, but how often had I wished at college and as a young minister in Edinburgh, Canada, Egypt and Paris that I had two more lives to live simultaneously. I could work with my flocks, the greatest life of all; I could pursue my studies of the imperishable writers in English and read a little Gaelic too; and as an archæologist I might study the past, examine, as it were, the fingerprints of history.

I lived three lives in Grenoble: at Divine Service, in the university and in history, but it was not history's finger-prints I examined. I watched its fist strike; I dodged and helped others to dodge its impact.

My English lectures were simplified into the historical-cum-literary. I built up lectures on Shakespeare's plays, a life-time's study in themselves and on the novels of Sir Walter Scott which were familiar to all Scots boys of my generation. In my talks with students in the evenings I discussed Stevenson, Dickens, Thackeray, Jane Austen, using my knowledge of the country in which the Scottish writers of the various periods set their tales to bring the printed page to life for my listeners. My knowledge of English history is more bookish, but in dealing with the writers from the south I tried to set each in the context of his or her period, and all I set against the timeless truths of my religion.

The students came from all parts of France, and among them were youths from Luxembourg, these latter even more enthusiastically pro-Allied than their comrades. I made friends with them without delay, having discovered during my life in Marseilles the perfect drink to loosen men's tongues and keep them contented. I made them tea. I pride myself on brewing tea, not perfect tea—that is something I hope to achieve in my old age—but tea that one can roll on the palate and savour. They enjoyed my tea. It melted the ice between us, so much so that one lad shouted from the throng:

'Teach us to make English tea, M. le Pasteur.'

'I'll teach you to make Scottish tea, my lad,' I answered. 'The sort of tea we make in Bowmore, Islay, where I come from.'

I had to tell them about Islay before we settled to the practical task, and then, with kettle and teapot, the former bubbling on its fixed perch, the latter under escort, I inducted them into the ceremony of tea-brewing. Carefully I measured out the exact, as I then thought, amount of leaves. They watched solemnly while I heated the pot, added the carefully balanced spoonfuls of tea, let it brew, then dexterously poured.

'Tea, gentlemen, is an acquired taste. You may add, if you are a beginner, sugar, but I warn you, it is not advisable. Cultivate a palate, my dear friends. You will not regret it.'

They drank. We discussed the nature of tea and its wonderful properties. My tea-making classes began that night. They became hilarious interludes in the sessions in which I lived again my boyhood, prowling through Cheapside with Falstaff, through the Western Highlands with Allan Breck and David Balfour, listing with Baillie Nicol Jarvie in Glasgow for 'thae Hielan diels.' We became friends.

My work as a clergyman with the British in the city was more difficult, but it was infinitely rewarding. Old and infirm, tired and friendless, they needed someone to write letters for them to the authorities in Geneva, explaining their hardships and asking for material assistance. Some died without the benefits of the Church, some indeed of starvation, for their doles were small, prices were rising and, in the past, they had learned nothing of how to buy in the market place and spend their money so that they might get value for it. They hung on to life grimly, sometimes it slipped from them, and their friendless corpses were buried almost anonymously.

In the morning queues began to gather outside my room at the Hôtel de l'Europe and, at first, I was a little perturbed by them. I did not wish to become a conspicuous person; already the Resistance had contacted me. But I was aware that the authorities were pleased by my work as a chaplain to the aged. As it piled up they assumed that it kept me out of mischief. My heart lightened and I plunged into the work, finding ready helpers among the younger British ladies in forced residence. The lot of the old and often infirm was made easier, but tragedy still lurked where we could not find it in time. Sometimes too late it came to my hotel room. One Monday morning, for example, I opened the door and noticed, about third in the queue, a tall, pleasant-faced, emaciated French curé, a Catholic priest. Hastily I apologised to my other guests and drew him into my room.

'M. le Curé,' I asked, 'you wish to see me? Can I help you?'

He sat down, wiped dust and sweat from his face, and told me his story. He was parish priest in a village farther south, a small community of shop-keepers who served the local peasantry. Soon after the German invasion of France an old lady, *une Anglais,* he said, had arrived and taken a room in the local inn. She had no servants. She did her own meagre shopping and he called upon her. A gentle old soul, she welcomed him and apologised because she had no tea to offer.

'I am not of your religion, Father,' she said, 'I am Scottish and a member of the Scottish Church, but I am most happy to meet you and grateful for your visit.'

They became friends and Père Raoul visited her on his normal round of parochial visits, once triumphantly bringing her a few ounces of tea he had managed to scrape up somewhere.

'You understand, M. Caskie. It was nothing. We do not drink tea.'

She was delighted with the gift and insisted he share it with her which he did. The weeks passed until a few days before his visit to me he was interrupted in the confessional by a frantic woman of the village. The English lady was dying. Would the Curé come to her? Raoul rushed out of the church to his friend, but she was dead when he arrived. In Grenoble he had heard there was a Scottish priest of her religion. Would I bury madame? Would I officiate at her interment the next day? He must leave very soon; he was getting a lift on a lorry. Could I accompany him?

I told him to wait and then I explained to my parishioners in the hotel hallway why I must leave them for a day. They should return on Wednesday and I would continue my work for them. They almost thrust me back into the room to my colleague.

The lorry was waiting near the hotel. Crouched on the floor Raoul and I were driven deep into the country, discussing the tiresome problems war had brought to our people, comparing methods of dealing with them and our mutual experiences of the 'authorities.' I remember we talked of mission work abroad and wondered how our brothers among the heathen were faring in these days, cut off from their home directors; laughing aloud as we thought that they were safer and more secure in the twentieth century than clergymen in more 'civilised' lands. So much for the dreams of our youth when we wished to work in perilous places for our faith. Raoul and I became comrades in Christ that day for we were serving Him; with our sins upon us, we knew that we had one Master.

Early next morning, with the sun warmly rising, I read the burial service of our people over the poor coffin and grave of the English lady who was Scottish. Raoul stood by in his shabby black cassock, his eyes cast downwards, his hands clasped in prayer when he was not handing me the requisites for the office of burial.

When the last shovelful of earth was smoothed on the grave we walked back to the village square, for the lorry left early and I had to hurry back to the city. The Christian faith, love of God, our God, binds men into warm friendship with an ease that, in this world of ours, seems miraculous. Love is the enduring miracle of our God. Raoul was my friend. I stood looking down at him from the floor of the lorry that morning and he smiled that wise, happy smile, as he clasped my hand.

'Dear Donald,' he said. 'Remember in Grenoble, wherever you are, if I can help you, I am ready. Send for me; I am at your service.'

The tasks God sends us bring their own rewards. On that rolling lorry during the dusty three-hours' journey back to the city, I was happy and I prayed for my friend and the exile we had laid to rest. All three of us were in the Hands of God.

When I arrived at Grenoble about midday I did not go straight to the hotel but made my way to the church which was mine to use when my two staunch friends, M. Westphal and M. Cook, Protestant pastors in the city, were not using it for their own services. There I recollected myself and offered a prayer of thanksgiving for the work that had been entrusted to me and the kindness of Raoul who had brought me news of the dead woman to whose grave I had brought the prayers of the church to which she had been loyal. I felt wonderfully happy. I must have been in the building for nearly an hour and a half. When I walked into the blinding sunshine with a smile on my face, I was confronted by M. Brachon, the beadle.

'Good afternoon, M. le Pasteur,' he greeted me. 'You look very happy today.'

'I am very happy,' I answered. 'I've just been to a funeral in the country.'

The poor man's jaw dropped inside his long beard. I suppose he judged me just as mad as the other Britishers; I patted his shoulder and went back to the hotel to eat.

M. Brachon was a true friend and was always on duty on Sunday afternoon when I held divine service for the British. He was to prove himself an ally in the more hazardous cause of assisting our boys to escape.

I had been restricted from prison-visiting during the first few months of my stay in Grenoble, but within a few days of my arrival, I received a charming visitor.

She was a lady from the south who called at the hotel where I received her in the dining-room. Over coffee, she leaned forward and whispered to me that the Intelligence knew I was in the city. I must establish myself as a member of the community and as soon as my permit came through I must resume my visits to the men imprisoned in Vichy France. After coffee she left and I did not see her again.

My work in the university and for the folk in forced residence filled my days. I appealed to the Red Cross in Geneva for food and other necessities for the old people. They had neither the means nor the craft to use the 'Black Market.'

Shortly after the day Raoul and I buried the Scottish lady, I returned to the hotel to find that eleven large cases of food had arrived. That night with help from British ladies, willing assistants, I broke it up into fair parcels for all the people I knew who were in need. Some of it we delivered by hand, trudging through the streets to people so old they could not help themselves. The others called at the hotel and I distributed the precious food to them. The hall became more thronged. Soon we became unpopular with the *patron* of the establishment, a dubious personality, who was to prove a villain in the end. A member of the dread and obscenely cruel *milice*, those French who had sold their souls to Nazism, he was afraid, in those first days, to move against me. The Resistance was stronger than I knew at this time and the pro-Nazis were careful. I believe he kept me under observation throughout my stay. I gave him nothing to report back to the Gestapo.

The cases of food began a slight improvement in conditions for the old people. With these had come promises of regular deliveries and I organised a service with our consul in Geneva who helped the needy with money and transmitted letters for them to their relatives and friends at home. On Sunday afternoons the British Protestant colony gathered at the church and in that friendly atmosphere of dedication to God, I lived again as I had done in the Rue Bayard, leading the faithful in prayer.

The long summer passed happily. All around me in the university I found kindred spirits and the sustenance of loyal friendship. No university in Britain or the U.S.A., in war-time, could have inspired the same intense love for the freedom we western peoples love and cherish as Grenoble warmed it in the hearts of her sons. For we were threatened. We had experienced what freedom means and what men suffer when it is lost. My friends, Bruce Dowding, the French agents, even Pat, I thought dead and while I mourned them the atmosphere of the colleges in the venerable city stirred courage in me and I knew that all was not lost.

The academic year ended and Pierre de Gaulle was chosen the best student of the year which gave his colleagues a heaven-sent opportunity to express their sympathies.

The University gathered in the vast hall for the presentation of prizes. The speeches of the senators were learnedly witty, quietly droll. Laughter rippled through the crowd and then there was silence as the President of the college spoke. He announced that M. Pierre de Gaulle had attained the highest honour possible for a student scholar at Grenoble and was prize student of the year. Thunderous applause roared through the building. Those of us in the secret sat back and waited, chuckling in anticipation.

The hall suddenly was silent. Then they began chanting at first quietly and then more loudly until the rhythm of their words must have been heard far beyond the building.

'Vive de Gaulle! Vive de Gaulle! Vive de Gaulle!'

With extreme precision the noise intensified until all the students and more than one professor were shouting at the top of their voices. Some clapped hands to the rhythm of the words. Others waved the tricolour. Many waved white papers. The audience was a whirl of movement and a chaos of sounds which yet thundered between long and short pauses.

Vive de Gaulle! Vive la France! Vive de Gaulle! Vive la France! Vive de Gaulle!

It went on for about a quarter of an hour and then we sat gazing at the slimly-built, tough youth who smiled down at us.

A venerable figure arose, one of those old gentlemen who had capitulated under the burden of years and much suffering. He raised his hand and began to speak. His words were of the sorrow of *la France* and its weakness and as he spoke we heard whispers:

'Vive de Gaulle!'

The volume grew and this time there was something pathetic and terrifying in its effect for soon the old man's words were drowned by it, and he grew angry. His mouth sagged. He gazed down on those youths who must have seemed merciless children to him. Then he left the platform and cheers broke out as the undergraduates turned their eyes towards the living symbol of the leader of Fighting France.

That night the University was festive, and scholars, graduates and undergraduates dined well, sang and talked far into the night.

Pierre de Gaulle was an audacious youth, cool-headed, tenacious and, while he took chances, he calculated to a fine degree a margin in which he would achieve the end he set himself, and escape. While still in residence at the University, he was in touch with the maquis in the hills which surround Grenoble, passing information to the base where his uncle was in command of the French who were at war. With his friend Ike Feigelsen, who is now a successful surgeon in Paris, he built a formidable organisation. His family lived in Grenoble and Pierre's friendship meant much to me. He would call at the hotel and we would stroll together while he conveyed minutely detailed information about the movements of the enemy which I memorised in the hope of passing it back to Marseilles, for by this time, as I shall tell, again I was *engagé*.

After the demonstration at the university his days there were numbered. A few weeks passed and he and Ike were arrested. They had been seen moving in the vicinity of an escape route and indeed, they more than once had guided escapers over the frontier. Accused of having associated with me in organising escapes, they laughed and denied it. Subjected to torture until blood ran out of their ears, they stuck to their story until the brutes who had taken them in custody were forced to release them. They were too well-known in the town to be killed out of hand, and their arrests had been witnessed.

The youths immediately took to the hills where they intensified their work for the maquis. By means of a radio transmission set they contacted the United Kingdom, using the code with which they were already familiar. Planes bringing food, arms and ammunition began a regular night service to their forces. From the heights which surrounded the town they waged war on the common foe and his allies.

While these young men worked out in the darkness, I too had been plunged into the old routine. Granted permission to visit prison camps as a chaplain, I set off one day for St Hippolyte du Fort and the secret agents once more conscripted me. It was the early autumn of 1941 and I felt very fit.

CHAPTER ELEVEN

The Visiting Padre

WE MADE our Communion Table from beer boxes covered with a white cloth, and the Union Jack. I set up a picture of the King, His late Majesty, and the Queen, now Queen Elizabeth the Queen Mother, and led the officers and men in prayer. I preached a short sermon and we sang hymns. The relative peace of Grenoble, with its familiar undertones of scholarship, study and services in a proper church seemed somehow unreal.

My days again became balanced between the rounds of a chaplain and study, and the perilous deliberations of the Intelligence Service. In La Turbie, St Hippolyte and at Chambarran, evidence of the great battle that was spreading across the whole globe confronted one. There were the happy-go-lucky men who studied their guards and the means of escape at their disposal. To them escape was a game they would play to win. The sensitive and brave who had suffered in themselves and in watching their comrades die waited with fanatic intentness, tensely living for the day they would take the road to freedom. And there were the sick in mind and body, the unhappy ones who worried about families, often with very real cause. The 'old soldiers' sang and baited the Germans, the students, thinkers, the innocently guileless, all talked the many dialects of home. Those prisons were cross-sections of the best in British manhood. I was glad to get back to them.

Once each month I visited the camp at St Hippolyte du Fort near Nimes. Before each of my journeys, which took seventeen hours by train, I had to procure a pass from the Sûreté in Grenoble. I had no difficulty. *M. le Pasteur Ecossais* was established. I would travel through the night and as my destination approached my mood would lighten for the men gave me a wonderful welcome and I was curiously cheered by the thought that I was in the country where my beloved compatriot, R. L. Stevenson, had travelled with his donkey. It amused me to meditate upon R.L.S., the difference between his times and ours, his journey and mine and his business in the Cevenne mountains and mine in the camp which lay at the foot of them. I rather envied him and his donkey. Their era in history, with all its faults, was more amiable.

I carried the tools of escape. On my first visits the guards passed me into the prison after carefully scrutinising my papers. No attempts had been made to search me and I had received instructions to co-operate with the officers inside all the camps I visited and do all I could to assist them. Stowed about my person, I carried strong scissors for the cutting of barbed wire, files which, properly used, would sever iron bars, forged papers to further the British 'tourist' on his way and concentrated rations, all of which I passed to the officers in control of escape committees. To a great extent at the beginning of my prison visits I worked in the dark. Security, I knew, had been intensified. Pat I thought dead with the others and, with the recollection of the traitor Cole burdening me, I was glad to work with as little knowledge as possible in my head. All I needed to know for this job were the elements of the escaper's craft and the most useful type of information I could assemble to pass back along the intelligence routes. The less I knew of the organisation the better. I had become a true professional.

The phase of determined ignorance did not last for many weeks. A message came that Pat was alive and was rebuilding the organisation with characteristic speed. All who might help were conscripted to the service, life for me again became exciting.

At the prison I conducted two communion services. A special dispensation had been granted me by the Bishop of Gibraltar to dispense Communion to the men of the English Church. Afterwards I gave Communion in our simple Scottish fashion, with six of our soldiers, three on each side of me acting as elders.

Even in the chapel we were under surveillance. A French or German officer, who had a smattering of English, was always in attendance, to ensure that I did not convey information to my flock. Fortunately, they did not understand the Doric, so by quoting our national poet, Robert Burns, I was able to tell the lads all I wished, pleading against the supervisor's angry protests that I was quoting their national poet. This, alas, particularly angered one Frenchman and, I believe, he was seen by one of our officers after an especially irate altercation, brooding over a copy of Rabbie's works in a corridor. I wondered what he made of:

> But fare you weel, auld Nickie-ben!
> O wad ye tak a thought an' men
> Ye aiblins might—I dinna ken—
>   Still hae a stake....

The 'quotations' were necessary. I was compelled to find a language in which to talk privately to the men assembled in the chapel for in many of the prisons morale was low. Until the escape route was reorganised, men breaking out of military gaols had not got far before they were arrested. I had been instructed to hearten the inmates for the task ahead of them—return to the U.K. The contents of my pockets helped to rebuild morale and soon a trickle of men began to move out.

Suffering, adventure, bravery, were part of one's day-to-day experience in the prisons. One reached that state of mind where nothing was astonishing. I met men who had wandered out of the social register into the maelstrom of war and found them tough, inspiring and as careless of their own safety as the heroes in boys' adventure fiction.

Under orders I sought out in the camps 'important personalities' and officers and men of special qualifications and training. It was thus that I met a man, then an American and now a British subject, named Whitney Straight. Had the Germans managed to penetrate his true identity, they would have considered him a first-class prize. But Mr Straight, an officer in the Royal Air Force, was not the type who gave anything away to the enemy.

A member of the best society in London and a friend of

the Royal Family, Whitney Straight was famous as a motor racing driver and an airman. During the Battle of Britain he became an ace flyer in the service to which he had volunteered. His disappearance on a sortie over Le Havre had created a sensation in England. Reported missing, no further news of his fate had come to the authorities. All that was known of his ' end' was that suddenly he had ordered his flight to return to base and then, very quickly, before his crash :

' I have been hit. I am going to land here.'

His capture by the Germans had not been reported. I met him at St Hippolyte du Fort, in the country of the Gard.

There were over a thousand men at St Hippolyte du Fort, near Nimes. I always anticipated my visits to them with pleasure. I held a service, brought them whatever comforts I could find and among the hymn books smuggled in compasses, files and ropes. St Hippolyte was run efficiently. It was not easy to escape from it, but it had happened in the past and would happen again. My visits opened with a service and after that I got the men to open their hearts in song. I had reason to believe that even the irreligious enjoyed the break from the soul-deadening routine of ordinary prison life. I enjoyed being with them and, I confess, loved the welcome they gave. I talked with the officers and received news of fresh arrivals which, in due course, I passed on to Pat.

On this visit I was introduced to an officer in the R.A.S.C., a crisp, business-like gentleman, whose face was familiar. I was sure I had seen him somewhere. His name, I was told, was Captain Whitney. I knew no Whitney but I found myself puzzling over the feeling of having met this officer when I was once with one of our trusted contacts.

' On no account let this secret out to anyone but the officers in charge of the route, Padre,' the contact explained. ' Captain Whitney is Whitney Straight.'

I whistled softly to myself. Of course, I had seen Whitney Straight's photograph in magazines, at social gatherings and in the overalls of a contender for car racing honours.

' Jerry hasn't a clue to his identity,' my confidante continued. 'If he did know, Straight would be whisked to Germany before you could say Jack Robinson.'

Straight, he continued, was an extremely brave and resourceful man, 'quite a fellow.' When his plane 'hit the deck,' he scrambled from it and escaped the Germans in the simple classical way. He took to his heels. Straight took shelter in a barn, a building used as a dormitory by German troops who remained out for the rest of the day, searching for their secret lodger. When they returned for their night's rest, Straight lay hidden for hours within reach of a dozen and more snoring Nazis. The night passed uncomfortably. Before dawn, he slipped out and keeping to the fields met a friendly farmer who rigged him out in civilian clothes. After bluffing his way through checkpoints, he reached Paris by train.

He found the city hostile. Immediately he set out for the American Embassy but when he arrived there he was told that it had closed. All enquiries must be sent to Berlin. To his horror he noticed, when ringing the bell, that the Hôtel Grillon opposite had been taken over by the Wehrmacht and been made into Command Headquarters. Wasting no time, by instinct as much as good sense, Straight sought out an hotel he knew in the Rue de Rivoli and found it swarming with German officers. The streets were alive with the field-grey of the Wehrmacht. Everywhere he turned Hitler's warriors were in evidence. And the civilian clothes he was wearing were, to say the least, in a shabby condition; they were worth a rather old aspidistra. Far from being his idea of proper wear for the city, they were conspicuously odd even in wartime Paris. Eyebrows were raised whenever he appeared. But quickly he got a room and retired to it to think out his next line of escape. He knew he could not move without assistance.

Straight, like O'Leary, was, I believe, a man who took to adventure as a swallow takes to the night air. Audacity was an instinct in him, something which I had to learn. It pays when a man is in a desperate position. Straight telephoned a friend and asked him to rendezvous at a certain place. When they met he asked for a loan of 10,000 francs and, when his friend agreed, arranged that it be handed over in an hotel lavatory as soon as his creditor could return. He was certain he was being investigated, so he locked himself in the meeting place until his ally arrived, timorously knocked and was admitted. The money was handed over. Assisted by a hotel worker, Straight escaped through the back of the building, hurried to a railway station and took a train to Pau, where he swam the river into Vichy France.

Drying out, as it were, on the heel, he made his way to a nearby village and there through ill-luck gave himself away to a German agent. Unaware that ration cards were required in Vichy, he ordered a meal. He was immediately interrogated and the game was up. But he kept his identity secret. He was a captain in the R.A.S.C. he claimed and was taken to St Hippolyte where he passed unrecognised by all save the senior British officer in the prison. Straight occupied his time in gaol by thinking out plans for escape.

As soon as I reported to the Organisation that Whitney Straight was in the prison they set out to release him. He was a valuable property and it was decided that he should be ' invalided out ' with the assistance of a Polish pastor. A series of tiresome misadventures began. The Polish chaplain brought the prisoner aspirin tablets in sufficiently large quantities to make him sick. Once in hospital he could escape more easily. As I have already explained, ' the medical swindle,' given a certain amount of luck, was a useful device. But at first, it seemed, luck was against Whitney Straight. On the night of the planned escape, his comrades of the R.A.F. carried out a bombing mission that was so successful, it aroused antagonism in the authorities and the invalids were marched back from hospital to gaol, presumably to punish the airmen who by that time were back in England. During the following weeks Straight made various attempts to escape and then he was transferred to La Turbie prison. Here I again met him and our luck improved. This time we were successful. We again chose the ' medical swindle ' and dope was brought to him. He swallowed it. The symptoms looked very bad and he was moved out to hospital for treatment and this time he got clean away. I shall never forget his courtesy and thoughtfulness. Immediately he was free he sent me a charming message giving the news of his success and inviting me to visit his home after the war.

Naturally, his arrival in England leaked out, but no one, apart from the proper authorities, ever learned how it had been accomplished. Whitney Straight knew, better than most men, just how many others remained behind whose hopes of escape would be wrecked if the Boche got on the track of the escape organisation.

His departure enraged the commandant at La Turbie and the whole prison came under intensified surveillance. A number of men working upon an escape came under observation and search revealed that they had tools in their possession. Fortunately I was dramatically warned or I might have joined them in a dungeon.

It was a bright morning and I was exhausted after my night's journey from Grenoble, as I came to La Turbie behind Monte Carlo. Borne down by a sack containing Communion vessels, hymn books, cigarettes, files, chocolate, forged ration books and passports, and a few small crowbars, I felt like Atlas bearing the world on his shoulders as I climbed a hill on the road to the gaol. But I was not apprehensive. The entrance to La Turbie, I still thought ' a piece of cake.'

As I staggered up the narrow climbing lane I heard a goose cackling and turning around saw a lad of about fourteen years of age struggling with a very bad-tempered bird. Having experienced in my boyhood something similar, I knew how he felt, so I put down the sack and made towards him to help. He was about twenty yards away. As I approached he seemed to let the bird go half-loose from him and I hurried. It cackled like a fiend, louder, shriller and louder. I reached the lad under cover of the goose's sinister warblings. He whispered:

' Keep walking, M. le Pasteur. I beg of you.'

I grasped the bird firmly by its threshing feet, regretting, not for the first time, that the skull of a goose is constructed in such a way that a man cannot give it a healthy slap on the ear, while its anatomy in general precludes a lusty clout on the place where it sits down. The lad grasped her firmly. I went back to the sack and set out on my way. He followed.

We moved between low hedges, he padding in the rear, until the lane dipped in a way that cut us off from possible viewers in the prison.

'You are the Scottish chaplain?'

His eyes were eager. He was breathless.

'Yes.'

'I knew it. You are M. le Canard.'

The words shook me. Only Pat O'Leary called me Donald le Canard—Donald Duck. His sense of security disliked the label Donald le Pasteur, his sense of humour dictated a name linked in sound if not sense with the earlier label. He used a nickname given me by an old friend—Le Canard.

I had become more security-conscious, more obsessed by my remembrance that I had suspected Cole and yet, even under orders, stilled my suspicion and left him exploiting his treason until my friends died, killed by it. The use of this nickname irked me. It was known to this boy yet the Gestapo had not pounced on me. I looked at the village boy who, apparently in innocence, used it. I wondered if a new threat was hanging over us.

'What do you want of me, my boy?' I asked.

'I have a message from M. Wood,' he answered.

A bright lad, he smiled up at me. I remained silent, looking, I suppose, like a tiresome schoolmaster. Wood was a friend, the interpreter for the prisoners at St Hippolyte du Fort, an agent on the escape route and the organist at divine service in the gaol. He was one of O'Leary's most trusted accomplices.

'Well?'

'M. Wood,' the boy went on, 'says you must be careful what you bring in the sack today. You will be searched. He says to tell you it is an order from M. Pat.'

'How do you know M. Wood?'

'My name,' he said, 'is Jean Morel. My father is a patriot and so am I. He sent me. He says we always will help Le Canard. There is much trouble in the camp, he says, and the commandant believes you are bringing tools in the sack. Now I must go or the guards up there, if they have been watching, will wonder what delays you.'

Dragging the goose, the little Jean turned back a little way and watched me for a few moments. Then I reconnoitred. Below me, over the hedge a burn rippled along the hillside. Quickly I pulled the bag after me through the leaves and down I plunged until the water was at my feet. In a matter of seconds I hid the incriminating goods in the undergrowth. Then, puffing and panting, I began a zigzag climb back to the lane.

The move was lucky for suddenly before my eyes I saw what might be a way of escape from inside Fort de la Revere La Turbie. Almost hidden by a large overhanging bush, the exit to a sewer was to be seen overlooking the burn. I gazed into the fetid aperture, shone my torch and recognised its obvious route. It must come from the camp. In a flash of joy I saw its possiblities. We might run an excursion from this exit, if my delay in the dip in the lane had not been noticed by the guards. I had been out of sight about ten minutes. Apprehensively I approached the gates of the Fort.

I was out of breath when I entered, still staggering under the load in the sack. The guards were smiling and I noticed one brash blond youth wink at his comrade. The mouse, I thought, seems to have walked into the trap.

An N.C.O. took my papers and shouted an order. I found myself surrounded.

' You will follow me to the commandant,' said the sergeant.

Under escort I was led to an office where a short man, in the uniform of a colonel, open at the neck so that his jowl protruded, sat at a desk, his boots propped on a blotting pad, a short thick cigar slobbering in his mouth.

' Ah,' he sneered. ' The man of God.'

I remained silent.

' Turn around,' he yelled.

I obeyed. He came to my side, hands on hips, looking both brutish and ridiculous. The guards stood by at rigid attention, holding their breath in an idiotic way. This was one of the Vichy prisons where Nazi methods were used. One of the weaknesses in the German military machine derives from an imbecile vulgarity that raises officers to the level of godlings. This Vichy commandant might have studied under Himmler. I stood respectfully awaiting the next move.

' The sack,' he shouted. ' Where is the sack? Ah, yes.

Let us see what the man of God has brought his children this time. Empty it out. Let us see what he has brought.'

The blond youth stepped smartly forward, grasped the sack by its ears on its lower end and cascaded the contents out before 'Simon Legree' as I was beginning to think of this absurd officer.

Bibles, hymn books, a couple of cans of beef, cigarettes, chocolates, some safety razor sets and paper-back thrillers lay in a heap at the toes of the glistening boots. All were recognisably innocent. His consternation was comical.

'Let me see,' he yelled and down he went on his knees to scramble through my kit and the gifts for the men. But there was no evidence that suited his purpose.

'Put these things back in the pastor's sack,' he snapped to the sergeant. 'And get out of here, all of you, except the prisoner.'

They left and I waited until we were alone.

'The prisoner, M. le Commandant?' I said.

'Yes, the prisoner, until you leave here. Men have been tunnelling from this camp. Maps, compasses and ration books have been found in their cells. You smuggled them in.'

This was ridiculous. If he had evidence against me, I should have been arrested at Grenoble. The comedy of the search would have been superfluous.

'You will have no further communication with the British prisoners in this camp, he snarled. 'I know your reputation.'

'M. le Commandant,' I answered, 'if you handicap me in my duty I shall insist upon an investigation of conditions in this prison. I cannot tolerate your manners nor your interference with me in bringing relief to these men. I have the authority of France, I must remind you, and I have international authority. Has there been inefficiency among your staff? Are you trying to make me the scape-goat? If so, I demand immediate release and I shall report you to the Sûreté in Grenoble.'

His bluff was called. He composed himself quickly. The boots which had resumed their place upon the table-top came back to the floor. He sat straight up, the thick fingers adjusting his uniform collar.

'You may take the service today,' he said slowly, 'but I warn you, M. le Pasteur, I believe you to be responsible for the unrest among the men. I shall investigate you thoroughly before your next visit.'

I bowed and a few minutes later, flanked by two English-speaking officers, one German, one French, I greeted my parishioners. I had been given two minutes to speak with the senior officer, Squadron-Leader Higginson, my escort kept within earshot and I had to confine myself to social enquiries.

Mr. Wood, esconced at the harmonium, gave me what is called an 'old-fashioned look.' I kept my eyes averted. I pulled the Union Jack over the beer crates and as I brought out the picture of Their Majesties, an idea came to me. I could irritate the enemy, I decided, even if they handicapped me in my job.

They were hard-working lads those interpreters. They did not give me a chance of even the most stealthy word. Wood even faked a breakdown in the harmonium and I dashed to his assistance. The officers moving on each side of me, forestalled us at every point and grew more irritated by our pranks. When the service ended the moment for revenge came.

'Gentlemen,' I instructed the congregation, 'we will close this service by singing the National Anthem, which is a prayer for our beloved Sovereign and our country. It is a hymn of supplication to our God and in praise of Him for his good-ness to us in making our country great and enabling us to defend the good.'

The men stood quietly to attention. Our overseers lounged half-deferentially. I turned to them.

'You, sirs,' I snapped, 'have insisted upon intruding upon divine service fully participating, to use your own phrase. Now I must insist that you stand to attention when we sing directly to our God who is, presumably, your God too. If you do not join in, after honouring us so far, I shall construe it as a deliberate insult to our religion, my office, which is above wars, and to international agreements.'

The long ferret face of the Frenchman on my right grew longer and I thought his eyes would pop out of his hatchet head. To my left I heard furious spluttering noises. Their heels clicked as they stood to attention. The harmonium began and the men joined in, some of them, alas, smiling, others looking too serious to be convincing. I turned my head and noted our nurse-maids; their lips were moving soundlessly. Their agony was gratifying. The English service ended and the Scotsmen moved in to take their places for the second, Presbyterian service.

I forgot about the spies as it progressed. I remember recalling to our men places we all knew, telling them that in little kirks, in the Govan Road, off Leith Walk, in towns and villages, in the sunshine and the rain, their wives, children, friends, were being led in prayer by their ministers for them. That God remembered them and in Scotland those who loved them clamoured to Him to protect and bring them safely home. I came to the end of my talk:

' And now, lads, we'll sing our national anthem, asking God to protect our earthly ruler's graciousness.'

There was an angry grunt on my left. The German snarled at his French comrade and strode from the room, the latter following. We sang alone. Wood played loudly on the harmonium and I passed on the news to him.

' The prison sewer leads out on the hillside. It is a perfect escape route. Check on its position inside. This will be followed up and outside arrangements made. Higginson must not let many men into this confidence.'

My departure from La Turbie was made under formal escort to the gates. The guards were stiff and no winks passed between them. When I came to the dip in the lane, I halted, looked about me in the dusk and plunged through the hedge, down the hillside to the burn, collected the tools and papers and quickly stowed them about me. A few lines on a sheet of paper fixed the point where the sewer emerged and I scrambled back to my road. That night I descended the hill to Monte Carlo. Next morning, at a meeting with men of the French resistance, I asked them to arrange an appointment with O'Leary and to plan refuges for the men who would, I knew, escape from the camp.

Within the façade of my formal work which I had erected to take me around the country, I moved carefully until a

message came for me to go to a certain café. Pat was waiting;
the reunion was brief. I told him of my discovery and when
I concluded he smiled, shot to his feet and nearly danced
with joy.

'We'll run an excursion to the U.K., Padre,' he gloated.
'You carry on with your job. I'll check on the route taken
by the smelly tunnel and pass back routes for the men to
follow when they get out. Next time you go to La Turbie,
bring tools as usual, but linger in the "dip" for a few
moments. If there is danger, you will be warned there.'

We planned to take 150 men out of the prison fort behind
La Turbie on that operation. It was the most magnificent
opportunity that ever came to us and Pat planned it nobly.
By radio he contacted England and asked how many men could
be picked up at the coast and taken home by submarine. His
one worry hinged not on the escape but on the number of
lodgings the French could arrange in which we might hide
the tourists. This problem was solved by radio messages from
England which dashed his immediate hopes. Only thirty-six
men could be accepted by submarine. But his plans were
only halted by this discouraging report.

'You will tell Higginson,' he ordered me, 'the exact truth.
He must choose the thirty-six lucky ones. But he will instruct
the others that if they are prepared to take a chance upon
reaching the frontier under their own steam, we will provide
maps and places where they can find food and shelter.' He
continued, 'Donald, after you see Higginson, meet me at the
inn in the village. It will be safe for you to report to me there.'

It proved extremely unsafe. When I passed through the
village on arrival, I found Morel's brother walking by my
side.

'Beware of the inn, M. le Canard,' he whispered. 'The
Boche is too interested in it. Many Boche are in the prison,
Monsieur. You must be careful.'

I asked for a light for my cigarette and as he bent towards
me I whispered, 'I have an appointment at the inn with a
fellow-countryman. Watch for him and warn him. It is
important.'

Inside La Turbie the escape was organised. The sewer

had been penetrated with the help of Jean Morel, father of the goose-boy, who under orders from Pat had drawn a map of the sewer showing exactly where it ran under La Turbie, in fact beneath the gaol's boiler-house. He passed this map to Wood who brought it to Higginson and work was soon under way Labouring in relays, prisoners made contact with their singularly noxious 'Jacob's Ladder.'

It was my task to convey to Higginson the good news that the escape had been fixed for a few days after my visit and the bad news that only thirty-six men could be accepted for submarine excursion.

When I entered La Turbie all seemed normal and I was brought to Higginson immediately. The place, he told me quickly, was alive with Germans but he did not know the purpose of their visit. He was disappointed by my news, but he had chosen his party. The men who would not find places on the submarine would be given an opportunity to try to escape on their own account. Connection with the sewer had been made. Given reasonable luck—and the absence of the Boche—the escape operation would be successful.

I wished him good luck and afterwards led the men in prayer edgily wondering if Morel's brother was on the watch. The gates of the prison were clearly visible from the village and I had told him I would signal with a white handkerchief if there was danger when I emerged. I prayed the man was vigilant.

As I left La Turbie I found myself surrounded by five courteous Germans who volunteered to help me with my bag down to the inn. They said they would like to drink a glass of wine and wished me to accompany them. Scared out of my wits I had the handkerchief out in a jiffy. It was seen by Morel's brother who dashed to the inn and told O'Leary. When we arrived he had gone. After a rather nervous session of conversation with the Germans I took leave of La Turbie's environs with relief.

The zero hour came and the escape plan went into operation. Eight men went to the boiler-house and quickly overpowered a French worker in charge of the boiler. Six of them opened the tunnel and made their escape into the sewer. Two remained to take control of the traffic. In parties of six the men moved out until, within ninety minutes, the chosen thirty-six had gone into the night, met their guides and were on the way into Monte Carlo and their hide-outs.

Another twenty-two men followed them, each ready to take his chance on making a solo getaway. Still more would have escaped but for a tragi-comic miscalculation involving a fat man, a squadron-leader from the R.A.F. who stuck in the tunnel.

The poor man struggled furiously to get through the aperture. He succeeded only in becoming more tightly wedged. His comrades sent down a small fellow in the role of human ferret to try to dig him out but the task was beyond him. Infuriated by the delay, the men in the boiler-house began to whisper instructions and then to call louder and louder until at last the French were disturbed. Within a few minutes the boiler-house was surrounded and the would-be escapers were escorted back to their quarters. The alarm went out for those who had gone. But the organisation had arranged their departure efficiently. Fourteen of the solo escapers were re-captured, eight got clean away. Not one of the submarine passengers was lost; all returned to England to continue the fight.

Within a few days of the operation I was placed under arrest and interrogated by the Security Police. There was no evidence against me. Again I was released.

CHAPTER TWELVE

Returning an M.P.

WINTER CLOSED in and travelling became more arduous.
Grenoble was an enclave in which learning, espionage, and
death were strange companions. We were cut off from the
great movement of the allies that was taking place all over the
world. At home, soldiers from the British countries were
gathering and Britain had become an armed camp. Confidently
the British leaders were concentrating industries for the final
battle and, I know now, that our people were sustained by
faith in its outcome. Sir Winston Churchill's massive oratory
and bronze-like honesty had created an atmosphere of expec-
tancy in Britain besieged. Out there our nerves were tautened
by the perils of each passing hour; we had become accustomed
to living as citizens of the underworld which the Germans
had made the only place where a man might honourably exist.
An opaque curtain of secrecy cut us off from the free world
and news of home.

Christmas came and I brought food and the little seasonable
oddments men cherish at such times. I even managed to obtain
more than one goose for my interned compatriots to be
roasted and eaten on the Christmas day. They made paper hats
and they played games. When tired of that they relaxed and
talked of home. I led them in prayer and loved watching them
lose thought of themselves as they remembered and celebrated
the birth of the Child. Christmas is a time when all men
remember God.

Winter passed and 1942 emerged from its icy grip into the
gentle season of spring. Summer came with life dragging on
in the camps. August brought word of the landing at Dieppe
and there was a resurgence of confidence through the camps.
Guards looked at us more grimly. Dieppe seemed to us, the
turning point. Our armies were at the ready. We knew they

would strike when the moment was propitious and soon we would be free.

Our escape organisation was moving smoothly but slowly. We lost men, it is true, but we expected that death might come to any one of us. The important thing was that the traffic of information and escaping prisoners should be maintained and that the disaster Cole had brought upon the escape route should not be repeated. In Grenoble I had my problems but I was surrounded by friends. The manager of my hotel, I knew to be an enemy but I did not wish to move out because I could watch him while he thought he was checking up on me. My old friend M. Brachon, the beadle, was one of my great consolations. His assistance in the church and his practical approach to his duties were a perpetual reminder of the normal work of a pastor in peace-time, work that must continue in war. He was heart and soul in ' La Grande Cause.'

Brachon was quite fearless and his detached assistance in my more dangerous work was given as if it were part of the ordinary duties of a beadle. As befits the office, he moved with imposing dignity; he addressed everyone with measured courtesy. The great beard which spread over his chest slightly intimidated me. Our Scottish beadles too are dignified men but in my generation the beard had gone out of fashion, and the French language always sounds more ceremonious than my own homely Scottish tongue. When Brachon escorted me one morning to a very dark cellar which, unknown to me, lay beneath the sanctuary of the church and formally confronted me, I was not quite prepared for the little speech that followed.

' Voila, Monsieur le Pasteur. Consider this excellent 'cellar. Surely here is a safe hiding-place for your men. Here you can conceal them in an emergency. Have confidence in me. This place is secure.'

I was startled at first and then began to thank him. Majestically, he raised his hand.

' It is a privilege, Monsieur le Pasteur. And it is one of the few ways in which I, Brachon, who am too old to fight, can serve. Please do not thank me.'

Obediently I followed him without another word, my

emotions stirred to that embarrassing point where a man does not know whether to laugh or weep.

Within a few weeks I was compelled, much against my instincts, to make use of the cellar and Brachon's suggestion. The thought of endangering the church where my people had been given divine hospitality terrified me. But prisoners-of-war on the run are men in danger of death. Two entered my room one evening and I had no other place to secrete them.

They were tough cheerful lads and I did not doubt that we could get them through to freedom. I led them to the church cellar where they settled down for the night.

Next morning, which was Sunday, I brought them food. We sat talking while they exercised healthy appetites, washing down great mouthfuls of bread and sausage with draughts of vin blanc. When they had finished they rested, opening the tops of their trousers to let their stomachs expand because they had eaten, I suspected, rather more than their fill. As I got up to leave I told them that service would begin in less than a half-hour and they must keep quiet. I did not want my flock to be worried by mysterious noises coming from the floor under their knees.

'But we want to come to church, Padre,' one of them protested. 'Don't we, Johnnie?'

Johnnie agreed that he was as eager as his friend and reluctantly I took a chance. I led them to the church gallery, told them to lie on their stomachs throughout the service and promised no one would intrude upon them. Outside I found Brachon and asked him to stand guard at the stairway and forbid anyone to enter the gallery.

The service proceeded in the ordinary way. Not a sound was heard from my stowaways. At lesson-time I chose, as is my frequent custom, at random the Old Testament lesson. The large pulpit Bible opened at the 27th Psalm and I began to read:

'The Lord is my light and my salvation, whom shall I fear? The Lord is the strength of my life, of whom shall I be afraid?' I continued until I came to a passage that was a veritable word in season for the soldiers prostrate on the floor of the gallery.

'For in the time of trouble, He will hide me in His pavilion, in the secret of His tabernacle shall He hide me.'

I glanced for a second at the gallery. They had raised their heads. Two pairs of sparkling eyes gazed down at me, two ruddy faces were grinning. Two weeks later those lads who heard the service in hiding in the French church were strolling down Piccadilly in brand new battle dress blouses and uniforms, on the way to their homes for leave before rejoining their units.

My second winter in Grenoble began and the grip of the Germans upon France grew more cruel. The landing at Dieppe had alarmed them and too many men were escaping from French prisons. The Nazis knew that a large number of French guards were divided in their allegiance and that their sympathies were with the British. They issued new and brutal orders that all men on duty at the time of an escape would be transferred to forced labour camps in Germany. We knew then we could expect no quarter. Even the most friendly official would not accept the suicidal consequences of turning a blind eye upon our activities in gaol. I was banned from visiting. I protested, sent letters to Geneva, stating my case, knowing these would be opened and read on the way. I said all I could—and I had comprehensively learned the methods of embarrassing the authorities—to make things awkward for our persecutors. Eventually I was reinstated, in time to help one of the most heroic men I met and worked with during those years. He was Commander Redvers Prior, the officer who served as beachmaster at Dieppe during that valiant action in which so many of our men, Canadians and U.K. troops, died.

As I was smoothing the white cloth a shabby figure entered the improvised chapel with the rest of the prisoners and sat close to the Communion table. He looked desperately ill, his eyes sunk deep in their sockets, the face skeletal, the figure a drooping bundle of bones. Instinctively I moved towards him. Another officer introduced us. The man was Commander Prior, I was told, he had been captured at Dieppe.

'He's in a shocking state, Padre. He has lost four stones in weight and he is cracking up.'

'No private conversation.' A harsh voice rapped out the command.

'But this officer is extremely ill,' I protested.

'No private conversation.'

Commander Prior raised a hand and signalled to me to be quiet.

After the service I was given some time with the senior British officer in the prison and I heard Commander Prior's story.

With a small party of men he had fought a desperate and bloody rearguard action at Dieppe to cover the retreat of survivors of the raid. Most of his party were killed but it was not until all ammunition was exhausted that Prior surrendered. Sorely wounded he was placed on an hospital train and sent to Germany. But ill as he was, near the Belgian border he flung himself from a carriage and escaped. A sensitive and good man he found himself submerged in a nightmare world of pain and cruelty, but he did not forget that he was a serving officer. For weeks he wandered behind the enemy lines and then he made his way to the coast where he stumbled on the West Wall, the great fortification the Germans were raising against the possibility of invasion. Miraculously, in his weakened condition, he escaped capture time and time again and, in search of information, stumbled on installations for V weapons.

Loaded with vital information, Prior decided that he must escape to England where it could be used. He set out for Paris and on the journey saw some of the most soul-sickening sights of the war. The Germans were taking reprisals against the French in revenge for the deeds of the maquis who, by this time, had gathered strength and were waging ceaseless war against their oppressors. Prior saw train-loads of innocent French workers who were being transported to the slave factories of the Reich. He passed through villages where whole populations had been ruthlessly punished for protecting the patriot forces. In one place he was given information of a wholesale massacre of the perennial victims of the Nazis, the Jews. The maquis brought to him people whose eyes had been put out by the torturers of the Gestapo.

To complete the nightmare when he reached Paris he found the city given over to hysterical pleasure. With German troops under orders for posting to the Russian front behaving as if driven crazy by fear, something like an obscene saturnalia had broken out.

In the capital Prior contacted maquis leaders who told him a second front would soon be opened. The British, they said, were preparing to invade France. Prior by this time was desperately ill and his urge to return to England became an obsession. A patriot advised him to make for Marseilles; there he should contact the escape route at the Seamen's Mission, which at that time had in fact been closed for more than a year and a half. Courageously he set out on the journey. Despite his physical condition he almost reached the southern city before he ran into a patrol. Weakness prevented him escaping and he was brought a prisoner to Chambarran near Grenoble to which place our men were transferred from La Turbie.

'He needs two things,' said the senior officer, 'one of which you can easily give him, Padre, spiritual comfort. The other is maybe impossible. It is escape to England. Anxiety about the invasion and the information he has in his keeping is eating the mind out of him.'

'I will do all I can,' I promised.

But it was not easy. The Gestapo had taken up residence at the Hôtel de l'Europe during the past week. Every move I made was being reported by their agents. Of necessity I was playing safe. Any message sent or any contact made with other members of the organisation might imperil all my comrades. Every morning my room was being searched. It was a dangerous time. It seemed I could do nothing for the Commander.

When I made my next visit to the prison, it seemed he was mortally ill. The commandant astonished me by inviting me to his room where he said:

'Will M. le Pasteur do something for Commander Prior? He is very sick—mentally sick. He is beyond our help.'

'I shall be happy to do what I can for him,' I said, and agreed to speak to this officer. After service I found myself alone with the spectre—for that is what Prior now seemed to be.

I took his right hand and asked if I could help him. Almost mechanically he began to speak. Suffering from intense anxiety neuroses, he described the dreadful carnage of Dieppe, saying his men had been mown down to their deaths. He broke down completely. I remained silent, waiting. He went on. He had failed in the task he set himself of escaping home. His failure, as he saw it, must be made good without any further delay. I interrupted, suggesting that information might be sent home with trusted contacts but he halted me. The facts he had gathered were too important. He would not take the smallest chance of his knowledge going amiss.

'Padre,' he pleaded, 'you must help me escape. I know the strength and the weakness of the Wall defences. I am needed for the big landings in France.

'If I break from here can you get me over the frontier?' he asked.

'I can.'

'Where can I contact you when I am free?'

The question, in present conditions, was a poser. I thought about it for a minute. The only answer I could find was one that, to anyone else, might have seemed insanely audacious. But Commander Prior had been through so much that nothing could seem extraordinary to him. He accepted my suggestion without demur.

I think you must come to my room at the Hôtel de l'Europe. But come only between the hours of six and seven in the evening. Do not ask your way. If you are challenged say that you have to go to the Scottish pastor to ask him for bread.'

'You will expect me, Padre?'

The voice had changed. There was a note of command in it. The sentence was partly a question, but more an order. I glanced at him; he was gazing steadily at me.

'I will expect you, sir,' I answered. 'But do exactly as I say and now listen carefully.'

All the tenseness had gone from the yellow, worn face. He was relaxed as I explained to him, with extreme precision, the approach to the hotel, the entrance he must use and the way from there to my room. When I stood up to leave he rose with me, the weariness still apparent, but now under control. His shoulders had squared. As we shook hands he smiled. The Royal Navy, one supposes, is trained, in the last analysis, for action; and to a prospect of action officers and ratings respond.

Two days later I returned to Grenoble and on my first evening visited a friend of the organisation, Colonel Julius, a Polish officer residing in the town as a civilian. Julius was in touch with the maquis. He knew the escape routes and I believed he could hire a guide who would be ready to assist Prior out of the country. Reluctantly he agreed to undertake the task.

'M. le Pasteur,' he told me in his grating, fluent, Slavonic French, 'I advise you against this adventure. You should be going home yourself. You do not know what lies ahead. I tell you, we will be lucky if we are alive when another year passes. The Boche grows frightened. At such times he is dangerous to people like us. He seeks victims.'

The words chilled me. Recent weeks, visiting the camps, had kept me busy and action lulls one into a state of confidence. This old soldier was a brave man and my friend. He would not talk in this strain if he was uncertain of the truth of his prophecies.

'Julius, Julius, I can only tell you that if we died helping this man to escape we might be dying to win a battle more important in its consequences than many bigger actions. He is an important person.'

We drank a cup of coffee and my friend walked home with me. Long into the night I lay awake pondering on the problem of my fellow-guests, the Gestapo, in the hotel. How could I divert attention from my room until Prior was safely on the road to England? Sometime in the small hours a plan came to me. The following morning I returned to my routine of visiting members of the church.

It was a pleasant and kindly task. We chatted, discussed church affairs, news of each other's activities, books and the possibilities of returning home before we were old. And in every house I asked my friends, as a favour to me, to visit my hotel room between the hours of 5 and 7.30 p.m. They must spread my invitation quietly and discreetly. It must not be discussed. It was a matter of some importance. If questioned, I was their minister and the call was spiritual, social or dealt with church business. The trick worked marvellously.

As soon as the queue of ladies and gentlemen began streaming through the hotel as evening fell, the Gestapo became interested. On the second night I was amused when a great fat clerkish-looking N.C.O. heaved his bulk upstairs as a party of dear old dowagers proceeded through the hotel lobby, making towards the stairs leading to 'dear Padre Caskie's room.'

The following evening the interrogations began. Selected visitors were halted in the corridors leading to my quarters and taken to the S.S. Office. I wish I could have heard the cross-examinations that went on. The interrogators must have had a lean time for my visitors could not be incriminated. They did not know of my work and had no notion of the reasons which lay behind my urgent invitation. Some of the older ladies, I believe, assumed that I had chosen this way because I was such a hospitable man and was greedy for guests. There was nothing more to the invitation than a desire to keep open house. One reported her interview with the most charming vagueness.

'They are rather rough men, Padre.'

'In what way rough, dear lady?'

'Brusque, you know, and they breathe so heavily.'

'What did they ask you?'

'Oh, I can't remember, the silliest questions I am sure. For example, they kept asking why I was calling on you.

'And what did you tell them?'

'Why, Padre, the truth of course. You know. You are our minister. You invited us to tea, didn't you? I told them of our nice talk about Henley. They are very odd men, the Germans. They seemed quite upset. Very strange. They do dislike us, don't they?'

For about four or five days the interrogation continued and then began to dwindle. The procession of guests continued as the weeks passed into a month and then, at about 6.30 one evening, a quiet double-knock brought me to the door. Commander Prior stood waiting, a smile on his face. He had moved through the hotel without being halted although three S.S. men had followed as he entered. They were entering the corridor as I spoke to him.

'Come right in,' I said. 'Your wife is enjoying a cup of tea.' The Germans passed us as he walked past me.

My eyes ran over the tall, slim figure. Prior was still an emaciated man, but the air of self-possession that had come to him in prison as we talked had increased. There was something almost jaunty in his demeanour. He was going into action.

I did not waste time in talk, but stood listening while he swallowed a hot drink. There was silence in the corridor. I opened the door and looked out.

The coast was clear. 'Redvers,' I said, 'you go out into the black-out, and watch the hotel door. In about five minutes you will see me leaving the hotel. Follow me at a respectable distance, and I will take you to a safe hiding place. The Germans are keeping a close eye on me, and we must make sure that we are not being followed.'

Commander Prior did as I suggested, and in about five minutes I left my room. On the stairs I met two members of the Gestapo, who were then occupying rooms in close proximity to mine. They eyed me rather suspiciously, and then said, 'Bon soir, Herr Pastor.'

I left the hotel and went out into the dark November night. Redvers Prior was standing in a dark corner opposite the hotel. He followed me at a distance through the winding streets of Grenoble, until I was perfectly sure that we were not being followed. We made contact, and I conducted him to a house on the outskirts of Grenoble, the home of Harris Rudowitch of Jewish extraction, born in London, whom I knew I could trust, and who had often proved himself a friend in need during my sojourn in Grenoble. Having explained the situation Harris and his wife were delighted to be of service. They hid the Commander in their home, and gave him the best meal he had had since he left England.

'Padre,' Redvers kept saying, 'you must get me away as soon as you can, and if possible tonight. I know that they are after me, and I must get home. I am needed for the great landing on the coast of France.'

'Redvers,' I replied, 'it is rather difficult at the moment, but believe me I shall do my very best to get you away tonight.'

Leaving Redvers Prior in the safe custody of my good friends, Mr and Mrs Harris Rudowitch, I went to see my Polish Colonel friend. I asked him if he would help me to get an English soldier across the Spanish frontier, adding that it was most urgent, that he must leave that night. The Colonel nearly exploded.

'Impossible, M. le Pasteur. It is known that an escapee is somewhere in the district. Grenoble is cordoned off. Patrols are everywhere. Dogs, Boches, militia. No guide will dare move. Prior must wait two or three days.'

This was bad news for in my view the Commander's condition made it unlikely that he would endure the strain of hiding out for days. At the moment his spirit was high and he was keyed up for the adventure. If we allowed him to slacken off into anxiety again the effects might be fatal. The man had suffered, physically and mentally, too much. He must not be made to endure more or he would crack. Roughly I spoke to Julius.

'It must be tonight. I want no mistake about that; tonight without delay. I will pay you anything.'

He stopped his pacing up and down and looked at me coldly.

'Do you think I was joking, M. le Pasteur?'

'I know you are serious,' I answered. 'But this man must go tonight. I'll pay anything. Understand?'

He flushed and quickly I continued.

'Listen, Julius. I know that money does not influence you. But it will help you to get a guide for Prior. That is what I want, tonight. You want it too for you have accepted my word that our friend has such information for London that any delay might wreck the second front.'

Like all in Grenoble, Julius thought the second front was imminent. Under the influence of Commander Prior I believed his information was so important that I did not consciously exaggerate its value. I spoke out of deeply stirred emotions and my words struck home.

Julius shrugged his shoulders.

'You will excuse me, M. le Pasteur,' Julius said, and he left.

Two hours later he returned breathing heavily. He had not wasted time.

'One man has volunteered, Pasteur. At a price—£75.'

The sum amounted to all I had in the world but money did not mean much to me in those days. More would come. 'I'll find the money,' I said as I left the Colonel, and I returned in about ten minutes with £75 which I handed to him.

It was a cold night and the stars were out as I slowly and sadly walked back to the hotel. I had little hope of Prior's escape. It was true that the expensive guide was a good man, good at his job, brave and honest and if the pair won through to the point where they could join the escape route, Prior would be safe. But I could not forget the tortured, tired man, sick almost unto death, of La Turbie. If they were challenged I feared he would collapse again as, exhausted beyond endurance, he had collapsed on the road into Marseilles. He was a supremely brave man but there is a point beyond which the bravest must break. Slowly I walked across the hotel lobby. The manager, whom I detested, watched me. A Gestapo agent sat, with a drink before him, smoking at a filthy table. I took my key and walked upstairs. A door opened and the fat N.C.O. stuck his head out. In my room I lay down. It was barely four hours since Redvers Prior had come to me. Before I slept I prayed for him.

When I awakened in the morning I lay for a few moments with fear soaking through me like water pouring into a tank. I had come to like the Commander very much. His courage, intelligence, high moral standards, pristine patriotism and heroism, when seriously wounded and in agony, would arouse any man's deepest feelings. His fanatical determination to return home and place all he had learned before his superior officer and then go out again to fight on the second front made him seem like a hero of antiquity. But his physical condition at the internment camp at Chambarran, the long worn face, yellowing complexion, and red-rimmed eyes, heightened the effect of absolute self-sacrificing courage. I despaired for him throughout that first day, when news of patrols came to me, when the Germans were angrily excited, and I knew the reason for their mood. When men with rifles on their shoulders and with dogs straining and howling on long leashes sped through the city on lorries out into the country, I despaired for him. He was so ill and there were so many obstacles he and the guide must pass before safety was reached. I found myself praying as I went about my duties, walking on the streets, halting as I ate. When I went to bed late in the night I fell into a troubled sleep with a prayer on my lips.

I felt better when morning brought no news of Prior. No news was good news when one of our men was on the run to freedom. The authorities knew that each man who got clear away to England raised the morale of his still-imprisoned comrades. Others were inspired to follow his example. When a refugee was captured, guards boasted of his folly in all the prisons and he was paraded past his comrades before being punished. When no news reached us we knew our man was still at liberty and most likely moving towards the last frontier between Gestapo-dominated Europe and freedom.

The days merged into a week, during which I was particularly irritated by the peering eyes of the hotel manager. I was convinced in my heart that Prior had reached England.

And then I had a visitor.

He was a slim, youngish, Jewish-looking gentleman, dressed with the quiet good taste of an extremely successful business executive. Without ado, indeed bluntly, he said as he removed fine grey leather gloves from manicured hands:

'I believe you have been of great service to my dear friend and business associate Commander Redvers Prior. I am told you spent all your cash upon the arrangements for sending him home. I wish to repay you on his behalf for the money you expended. Such is my gratitude, so great the service you have rendered to his friends, that debt I cannot ever repay. Now, how much do we owe you, M. le Pasteur?'

He was an extremely confident man. Looking straight into my eyes, in the most friendly way, he smiled.

'Commander Prior?' I said. 'I have heard of Commander Prior. I ministered to him in prison about a month ago. You say he has escaped. I shall make enquiries. Come back and see me in a few days. I never discuss the movements of my imprisoned compatriots with strangers.'

His jaw dropped. I was too old a hand to admit anything to a stranger; with the Gestapo as my fellow lodgers in the hotel I was more keenly suspicious than I had been in Marseilles.

'If you have not helped him,' said my visitor, 'may I ask if there is another Scottish pastor in the city? My information is that the Scottish minister helped my friend. My name is Kolhmann. I am not of your religion. I am Jewish. You can trust me, I hope, not to work for the Germans. Prior is my partner in a shipping business. I must help the man who helped him.'

I asked the now excited Israelite to visit me on the following day. That evening I conducted an investigation. I found that he lived with his father-in-law, a distinguished old gentleman of the Hebrew race and the whole family were above reproach. Their home on the outskirts of Grenoble was a resort for intellectuals of all religions; they were liberal, kindly and good. In better times Mr Kolhmann had been engaged in the shipping business with an English friend who was his partner.

Next morning, over coffee in my room, I confessed to him my duplicity of the previous day. It had worried him, he told me, but he agreed that caution was necessary in my position. He invited me to his father-in-law's home for dinner.

'You will find there, I believe and hope, M. le Pasteur, congenial company.' I accepted his offer. He rose to leave, handing me an envelope.

'You must accept this on behalf of my friend and as a small token of my gratitude. He is a dear friend.'

I opened the envelope when he left. It contained a sum

amounting to a little more than £100. Kolhmann and I
listening to the radio broadcasting from London about a
month later heard that Prior had reached home and been
elected M.P. for Aston. He had made a startling speech in
the House of Commons. We drank to him. We had returned
our member and I had not forfeited my deposit.

CHAPTER THIRTEEN

The Ladies of Chamonix

GRENOBLE BECAME an inferno of wanton cruelty and violence
as the Allies intensified their air attacks on the Reich. The
enemy became more and more dominated by hatred. The
milice, his French collaborators, were diabolical in their conscienceless brutality. M. Hullier, the manager of the Hôtel de
l'Europe, was one of that unsavoury band. I knew the time
would come when he and his accomplices would strike at
me.

In January, 1943, they committed one of their most evil
crimes against a friend, not one of my congregation, a gentle
Jewish lady, Mrs Jessie Cohen, whose husband came from
Dundee.

Twice Mrs Cohen was arrested and brutally questioned about
my activities and released when she could not answer. I had
not asked her to help me for obvious reasons. My Jewish
friends had a greater burden to carry than any of us. A crime
against them was an active good deed to the Nazis. I should
not have dreamed of employing this lady whose need for pru-
dence was great.

Cohen had been sent to a concentration camp in Germany.
His wife lived in a neat little house in Grenoble near the
River Isere with her two children and her mother. She was
a quiet little soul, eternally preoccupied in worry for her
husband. The end came savagely and quickly. The *milice*
burst in on the family about two o'clock one morning. Grandmother, mother and children were bound and taken on a

lorry to a bridge over the Isere. Neighbours heard the women screaming. There they were dumped in the river to drown. Agents of the maquis, hiding nearby, watched helplessly. Jessie, her mother and children were as innocent as newly born children. Apart from the pure evil in the hearts of those who committed it their murder was motiveless. The *milice*, if anything, were more depraved than the Gestapo.

They are a strange people, the Germans. There was a night-mare quality in their attitude to life. One night Mrs Harrison Dulles, sister-in-law of the American diplomat, living at Villars de Lans near Grenoble with her son, then a child, who was ill with pneumonia, was disturbed by loud knocking on the front door of her villa. Mrs Harrison Dulles is not easily intimidated. When she found a German patrol in the garden she imperiously demanded their reasons for intruding. Roughly an officer interrupted, ordering her to dress, while upstairs her child gasped and moaned. The mother protested again, and told them the boy was in a dangerous condition. No one answered her.

'What does all this mean?' she asked. 'What have I done? Do you accuse me of some crime?'

Still there was no answer and then:

'Get your clothes on,' rapped out the officer. 'And dress the child too if you do not want him to be naked when we take both of you from this place.'

Mrs Harrison Dulles went upstairs and dressed while the soldiers waited in the corridor outside her room, shouting through the door to her to hurry. In all the extra clothes she could find she dressed little Billy and then wrapped the sick child in a blanket and opened the door. Downstairs she carried the boy and out on to the road where a lorry waited. There were feet of snow on the ground, the sky was clear with millions of stars, keeping sentinel in the night sky.

With soldiers sitting around her, Mrs Dulles held on to the child as the lorry drove for some distance towards the mountain. It stopped on a road between the slopes and she was ordered to get down with the child. No one offered to help her. The party began to struggle through the snow on the outer slopes of the vast hill.

Staggering, praying, her head bursting, the brave woman lurched on, clutching the heavy boy, bearing him up until she had to let him slide to his feet and walk beside her.

' Halt.'

The word rang out harshly. They had come to a hut under the mountainside. Snow began to fall again as they stood there

The officer drew out a pistol. He waved it, waving to the lady to stand against the hut wall. She obeyed.

' Take the boy with you. Stand up straight. Do not move. Silently the patrol lined up opposite the mother and child The officer passed in front of them. Mrs Dulles cried to him:

' Have you no children of your own? I beg you to free the boy. We are both innocent but he is a mere child. You cannot do this.'

' I have children. What does that matter?'

The officer was looking at her as he spoke. There was no enmity in his eyes. His features were calm, grave, courteous in expression. His words came out brutally.

' Now stand up straight.'

He turned away from the couple in the direction of the riflemen. As the man moved, the child, his head protruding from the bundle of blankets, said:

' Mother. look up at the lovely stars. God is not asleep yet. He is watching us.'

Their persecutor halted, listened intently, stood motionless in silence for about sixty seconds, and then yelled an order that shattered the night. The rifles were lowered. Another order was yelped out and the men began to file away from the hut. down the hillside to the lorry. Stupefied by shock, Mrs Dulles watched. The officer spoke to her.

' Yes, I too have children,' he muttered quickly. ' You are free.'

A few minutes later the vehicle moved off and she began the march through the snow back to her villa. The child Billy recovered from his illness and now is a healthy young Etonian. Neither he nor his mother were troubled by Wehrmacht patrols again. Why she was taken to the mountain for execution, she never discovered. Why she was set free. she knew only so far as any sane person can follow the general behaviour of our former enemies. Was that execution just part of a night's sport for the German troops? Very often I have wondered. The blend of anarchistic killer and sentimental father in that German officer is to me, as it is to that lady, inexplicable. But it was one of the facets of the German character.

Evil breeds fear and through fear, which is lack of faith, more evil is born. Looking back on those days I realise that the only fears that were in the hearts of my friends in the organisation were for others. We trembled when we thought of torture, not for ourselves but because it might wreck our powers of self-control. We then might incriminate those whom we had come to love, our comrades. Thus we avoided all information except that essential to our tasks.

In the early spring of 1943 with the Allies coming closer to Italy, the landings made in North Africa, the enemy became more and more like an evil beast. On impulse he struck, blindly but fatally I suppose the strain began to tell upon me when I was banned again from the camps. My fight against the authorities irritated them: and exhausted me. A message came from London that the escape route through Spain was becoming so difficult that we must try to find another way. The agent who brought it advised me to go to Chamonix, the winter sports resort which lies at the foot of Mont Blanc. My health was poor and when I applied for a permit to visit this innocuous place I was granted one without fuss. The medical certificate enabled my friends in the Sûreté at Grenoble to grant the visa quickly.

Chamonix is a very beautiful little town at any time of the year, an international meeting place of climbers and other sportsmen. I came to it on a Saturday and wandered through its streets drinking in the beauty of the country, spiritually relaxing in its peaceful atmosphere and revelling in the cheerful voices of the men and women walking its streets on shopping forays. I strolled to the graveyard attached to the Anglican church and stood before the statue which has been raised to British climbers lost on the lovely but dangerous mountains. I was very tired. During the nine hours' journey from Grenoble the train had been boarded repeatedly by examining officials, stupid, pompous and selfish men who had asked us the same questions more than once, varying their form each time. A man with the most extraordinary squint travelling in my compartment was, I knew, shadowing me. He had booked in at the Hôtel de la Gare where I had taken a room and the atmosphere of that pleasant place was now marred by his unsavoury presence. The climbers' statue stood above the snow. I remember the exalted beauty of the Alps around the town that day. I felt grateful for it all. It was with reluctance that I dragged my feet back to the hotel, ate a very small meal and went to bed. I did not awake until eight o'clock had struck next morning, and the sleep and the air of Chamonix had revived me. Feeling a new man I set off for the little Anglican church.

The building was crowded with the townsfolk. None of my countrymen or women seemed to be present and I felt disappointed, at the same time chiding myself ironically with the thought that in Britain the winter sports season had been postponed for a few years. I lost myself in prayer until the singing began and I heard voices, singing in French, but unmistakably English voices. I did not manage to isolate them from the rest of the singers until we were crowding into the centre aisle after the service. Two neat little English ladies, precise, delicate and as sure of themselves as miniature guardsmen were walking with their fellow worshippers. I was sure they were English. When I reached the entrance of the church I waited. They returned my bow in a dignified way.

'Pardon me, ladies. May I ask are you English?'

'We are, Monsieur.'

'Then may I introduce myself. I am the Rev. Donald Caskie, Minister of the Scottish Kirk in the Rue Bayard, in Paris, presently chaplain to the British people in the city of Grenoble.'

They bowed again, almost curtseying. Their right hands advanced and I shook them, watching the ladies all the time in a way that must have seemed rude. They were so English. The hats, the little veils, handbags, longish tweed coats, the blouses with beads embroidered up to the necks, the frills, the determined little chins, might pass anywhere at home unnoticed. They spoke French with the fluency of old residents.

'My name is Miss Forrest,' said the smaller of the two. 'This is Miss Wood. We, of course, have heard of you and your work, dear Mr Caskie. Alas, we are the only English persons remaining in Chamonix, but we are safe and contented. M. le Maire is our friend and most kind to us. We have nothing but friends in the town. May I invite you to our mission this evening?'

'Your mission, Miss Forrest?'

'Yes, dear friend. We were trained to be missionaries by the Faith Mission in Edinburgh. I do not need to tell a student of Edinburgh what that means. We shall never forget the excellent training we received from J. G. Govan who founded the Faith Mission. But perhaps you will join us for a meal this evening.'

They smiled at me with that curiously strong, paradoxically frail, charm of old ladies who have seen much of life and surmounted all its difficulties doing the work they believe to be sacred.

'I know your Mission very well, dear lady. I shall be happy to come to you this evening and enjoy your hospitality. But please do not expend much on my entertainment. You must have big demands made upon you.'

My remark seemed witty to them for they looked at each other and giggled aloud.

'Yes, we have uncommonly big demands made upon our stock of food at present. But to entertain you will be a great pleasure to us. We warn you we shall insist upon you eating a good meal.

The moon was up when I plodded through the snow towards their Mission that evening. The valley was that wonderful stainless white which stretches like a lunar landscape in Switzerland in winter, challenging, awe-inspiring, its whiteness tinged with blue under the evening sky and the white globe of the moon. One feels close to God in the moonlight on such a night, in such a place, and I thought of the Faith Missioners. They had been founded in Edinburgh by J. G.

Govan; their motto was 'Seek Ye First the Kingdom of God.' By it they lived. Their little mission halls were built in the most unexpected places but surely Chamonix, centre of cosmopolitan society in the season, world-famous as a climbers testing place under the most invulnerable of Europe's Alps, was their strangest mission. Did Miss Forrest and Miss Wood expect to convert the local people to their branch of faith? They were so English, so self-assured in their modest way. I could find no answer.

The mission hall at the foot of the mountain could have been set down anywhere in the world from Manchester to Bombay and it would have looked as odd. Practical, unadorned, strong; hundreds of buildings of the kind are to be found in the U.K. From the interior I heard the sound of a harmonium. Respectfully I opened the door and timorously gazed into the hall.

'Come in, Mr Caskie. Do come in.'

Miss Forrest, a Bible held confidently in her hands, confronted me from the far end of the room. Miss Wood, seated at the organ bowed, and continued playing. The congregation filled the seats, men and women, all local people who turned and gazed at me with the expectant look of a congregation of established church members contemplating a new boy.

'Please sit down, Mr Caskie.' Miss Forrest was firmly and courteously in control. I wasted no time in taking a front seat which obviously she had reserved for me. The service began.

The sermon was concise and practical, its message, perhaps the most important in Christianity, that we exist by God's love, are brought to life, sustained and saved by it. Miss Forrest's French was lucid and fluent and her delightful Northern English accent gave it a flavour which made one conscious of each word she enunciated. She halted after making a point and gazed at us, allowing it to sink into our minds, as automatically she adjusted the frills on her blouse. She did not speak for more than a quarter of an hour; the congregation listened raptly, hanging on her every word. When she ended, she raised her hands, looked at me and then steadfastly at her flock.

'And now,' she said, 'let us pray for our poor brother, Dr Donald Caskie, here present, a servant of God who has been working so very hard for British lads imprisoned by our enemies and who has been himself unwell in health.'

They prayed and then Miss Wood's organ pealed out, Sankey's hymns filled the little hall there on the side of the mountain so remote from the places where they had first been sung. Not far away the armies of the Nazis surrounded the humble hut where the old ladies carried on their work and across the seas men and metal assembled from all the four corners of the world, were gathering for the greatest battle of all time. Unafraid, unconcerned Miss Forrest and Miss Wood in that Swiss enclave sought first the Kingdom of God. I know all things were added unto them.

The Sankey hymns, even rendered into French, filled me with nostalgia; as the little organ pealed out and the rough peasant voices blended into their fervour, my mind strayed to city square, street corners in working-class tenements, the spaces in public parks, all those open-air meeting places where simple people pray and sing to their God on Sunday throughout our island. The singing stopped; the organ lingered for a moment and there was silence in the hall. We stood up and I joined the ladies in the porch where they bade the members of their congregation farewell until the next meeting. We walked slowly back to their little house adjoining the hall.

A fire burned brightly in their kitchen-dining-sitting-room. The table was neatly laid, the modest silver glittering by the sides of shining blue plates. We might have been in Huddersfield.

'We hope you are hungry, Mr Caskie?' Miss Wood was smiling with that good humour which is the mark of a born hostess.

'Ladies, I am so hungry, I shudder to think of it in these times.'

'Do not speak of it,' Miss Forrest broke in. 'We always have a few tins set apart for emergencies. Tonight we shall have a feast.'

They gave me a splendid meal, a feast indeed, although I suspect that in better times few families would have con-

sidered it more than a makeshift repast. A soup made from
stock they had hoarded, laced with a small tin of broth, a
hotpot made from canned meat and potatoes, with lots of
gravy, and a sweet created from cake, dried fruit, saccharine
and cream, whipped from milk that had stood for a day,
and then a good piece of Swiss cheese. We finished with the
greatest luxury of all, two cups of tea each. And then we
sat back and smiled at each other.

'Alas, in better times it would have been roast beef and
Yorkshire pudding,' said one of the good ladies.

Miss Wood's hands rose in mock sorrow and dropped to
her lap again. 'But we do hope you found our poor hospitality
appetising.'

'May I give thanks for the table, ladies?' I asked. 'I
am grateful for a delightful meal, beautifully cooked and for
your kindness to me.'

We stood up and my eyes wandered around the homely
room, the brass gleaming before the fireplace and on the
walls, the fire reflecting in its sheen, the photographs of
family and friends, I suppose, the pictures, mostly Bible studies,
the books, china, the dear knick-knacks old ladies assemble
in every town in Britain. I said our thanksgiving with great
fervour.

'Tell us, brother, about your work.'

Miss Wood was leaning towards me and I began describing
to her the work of the church in Grenoble and our order of
services. I spoke of the social side, the meetings, concerts,
tea-parties I arranged and the work we were trying to do for
the aged.

'And then,' I continued, 'there are the soldiers in prison.
I visit them as you know. But sometimes they visit me.'

Miss Forrest looked at her friend and both smiled. Miss
Wood spoke.

'You mean you help prisoners-of-war to escape?'

'Yes, ladies. I'm afraid I am considered a dangerous man.
I help prisoners-of-war to escape.'

'So do we. Don't we, Elizabeth? That is why we laughed
so rudely at church when you spoke of demands on our food.

Boys come to us and we send them across the mountains to freedom. Not as many as come to you, but some.'

The room was swinging around my head. Miss Forrest had given me the biggest surprise I had received since war began. Hands on lap they gazed, sweetly smiling, into my face.

' You send them across these mountains.'

' Oh, we don't send them all by themselves. The best guides work for us. This is Chamonix, you know. We have quite a reputation here for our guides. Haven't we, Charlotte?'

' You know the guides?'

' Why, of course we know the guides. We know everyone in Chamonix. They are our friends. We often have them to tea.'

During the next few days I met those friends and Miss Forrest and Miss Wood agreed to become a regular link in the underground escape route. Until then, bravely and haphazardly, they had helped the stragglers who came to them. They saved many lives. From that day forward the traffic on their line became a steady flow. They handled it with workmanlike efficiency. Selfless in their attitude to life, profoundly intelligent, shrewd in their estimation of character, there could not have been better agents in all France or Europe, nor more unexpected. They were without vainglory and when, after the war, those of us who knew their work tried to ensure that they were honoured for it, we ran into one and only one insurmountable difficulty. Neither Miss Wood nor Miss Forrest would hear of it. In peace-time they preserved a united front of modesty as they had done during the dangerous years.

My remaining days at Chamonix were pleasant when I was working with these ladies. But the man who had travelled from Grenoble in my compartment revealed himself more obviously to be a spy. A medium-sized, fat fellow with a yellowish face, oddly red on the cheek-bones as if touched with rouge, his terrific squint coupled with big, broken, nicotine-stained teeth, constantly bared in what I assume was meant to be an ingratiating smile made him a disturbing object to confront at every turn.

A few moments after I sat down for breakfast each morning he would enter the dining-room, bow smoothly, his head coming down and forward to greet me so that he looked like a duck about to dive. More than once as I opened my bedroom door to retire for the evening, he passed me in the corridor. I never saw him in the street except reflected in shop windows or mirrors. He had a gift for disappearing. He never spoke to me except in greeting. The squinting eyes were unsmiling and, darting about above the flabby smiles, created a hideously sinister effect.

In the evenings when I set out for the Faith Mission I knew he followed me. Somewhere along the route he hovered waiting to pick up my tracks when I returned to the hotel. I have mused often on that peculiar agent's possible reactions if he came close enough to the mission hall to hear us singing, in French, *Hold the Fort for I am Coming* and *There is a Gate that Stands Ajar*.

On the morning of my return to Grenoble I moved quickly out of the hotel. My bag was packed. I paid my bill and reached the station with only a few moments to spare before the train moved out. In my pocket I carried a map of the new link in the escape route. Before the first stop was reached I saw my friend M. Squint-Eyes as I called him, move along the corridor. Quickly he turned his head away from me and hurried onwards. But I was not mistaken. When the train halted at the next stop I saw him dismount further along the platform and scuttle across it into a refreshment room which was filling with travellers. The engine started up. Within a few minutes a tall, quietly dressed man sat down opposite me. I tried to read but whenever I raised my eyes I saw this newcomer carefully scrutinising me. He was one of the Deuxième Bureau, the French Scotland Yard. I was under observation, I was sure, by the French as well as the Gestapo. The map in my pocket began to feel heavy. Before we reached the next stop I hurried to the toilette and there I memorised it carefully. Fortunately the document was drawn on very thin cartridge paper. Carefully I chewed it up into pulp. One became absurdly careful, reacting I suppose against the heady risks we had to take from day to day, in tasks of that kind.

Piece by piece I flushed the pulp down through the lavatory pan. Slowly I walked back to my compartment.

Before I reached Grenoble I was searched three times on that journey, methodically, politely and each time by the French.

The ending was in sight but I was curiously confident. Julius's prophecy was coming true and while with a half of my mind I knew that capture was imminent, another part was aware only of the tasks to hand and oblivious of the dangers that loomed before me. My friends among the young men in Grenoble were being thinned out by arrest, deportation and death. When I moved from the hotel I was always followed. I kept on working at my task because I thought that only one thing was inevitable, that I should not return home until France was freed and my fellow-countrymen and women in France and my dear neighbours the French all liberated.

Before the end it would have been easy to go. One night an agent from England arrived and sent an urgent message ordering me to meet him in the home of a friend. He was one of those anonymous men, thin, tough, friendly, rationing his breath and his words to the minimum.

'Caskie, you are going to be arrested.'

'I think you may be wrong about that.'

'I know I am right. You've had it as far as work is concerned in this part of the world. You've had a good innings, Padre.'

I remember feeling mildly irritated by his confidence and yet smiling at it. There is something comic about a man who blithely prophesies another man's ending as all part of the day's work, and something charming when the speaker accepts probable death as his own wage.

'I hope you are wrong about that.'

'Caskie, you must go home.'

'Can you arrange it?'

'Yes.'

The answer, I confess, staggered me but I knew I could not agree to accept his offer. The road into Bithynia still stretched out before me and, unlike that day in Bayonne when I was tempted to return to Scotland, I had no doubts whatsoever in that dark room in Grenoble. I thought of the prisoners and of the old people, who needed coal and food and a minister in Grenoble. But it seemed discourteous to refuse the offer without discussing it.

'You are kind. What do you suggest?'

'I am not kind. I have my orders. A plane is landing above the town tonight. We must move quickly. We leave now. You will be in England before breakfast.'

'I am afraid I won't, my friend. Forgive me for wasting your time. I shall not be a passenger on that plane. I must remain where I am needed. Grenoble is my parish until someone arrives to take my place.'

He smiled at me and shrugged his shoulders.

'Good luck, Padre. I hope we meet again.'

I left him and went back to the hotel. As I moved through the foyer Germans stood around calmly watching me. They did not hide their interest. Even the fat corporal did not bid me good night.

CHAPTER FOURTEEN

The Feast of the Passover

I WAS AWAKENED by a quiet knocking on my door. It was so quiet that I lay for a moment thinking I imagined it. Hesitantly the tapping began again. I turned back the bedclothes and reached for my dressing-gown.

'A moment, please. I am coming.'

Outside the doorway one of the older servants stood. His eyes were cast down so that I could not see them.

'M. le Pasteur. . . .'

'Yes, Pierre. Is something wrong?'

'M. le Patron demands to see you as soon as possible.'

'Is that all? But he must be in a great hurry.'

'We are sorry, M. le Pasteur. We are your friends.'

Before I could speak he turned on his heel and shambled

off, moving with all the speed his old bones could muster until he disappeared out of sight.

I dressed without delay and made my way to Hullier's office. He was seated at a desk littered with papers and he swung round on a swivel seat as I knocked and entered. Without greeting, he began:

'M. Caskie, you have abused the hospitality of this hotel. You will pay your bill and leave immediately. We do not wish your kind here. I do not wish to discuss the matter further.'

He swung away from me and picked up a newspaper. I gazed at the broad glistening black back of his waistcoat.

'What does this ridiculous behaviour mean?' I began. 'How dare you speak like——'

'Get out.'

The monosyllables were measured. I think the man was afraid and, on reflection, he had much to fear whether the Germans were victorious or not. In a terrible way the French were to take vengeance upon their traitors. The maquis lived for that day of revenge—but even if the Allies had lost the war the wages paid by the Nazis were seldom to the taste of their quislings. One needs a long spoon to sup with Satan. Hullier was trembling. Resolutely he kept his face turned away from me.

'Get out.' Intensely he whispered the words. 'Get out. Get out. Get out.'

'Give me my bill.'

A hand reached into a pigeon-hole above his head. Over his shoulder a sheet of paper was passed to me.

I counted out the money I owed him and flung the notes on to the table.

'I'd be obliged if you would give the change to my friends in your employment. I expect you know them.'

The sun was shining as I walked out on to the pavements of Grenoble and strolled through the avenues to a café where I ate breakfast under the trees. Spring had come again and the two years I had spent in the city had made me one of its citizens. I came to love that graceful centre of learning, know-

ing that here were cradled honest scholars and brave men who
longed to live for learning and when the time came were ready
to die for freedom. I ate slowly wondering what the future
had in store for me.

After breakfast I telephoned my friend Harris Rudowitch
and told him that I was homeless. Immediately he gave me the
name of de Verger, a boarding-house in the suburb of La
Tronche. Before lunch-time I was settled in a pleasant room.
I then set out to collect my few belongings and inform all
my friends and contacts of my new address. Throughout the
afternoon I was shadowed but in the evening I gave the sleuth
the slip and made my way to a secret meeting place where I
encountered an escaped prisoner-of-war who will always have a
special place in my memories. William Nash of Whitburn was
his name. William was the last ' tourist' I helped escape to
Britain.

The farce of neutrality was over in France. William was
one of those who used his intelligence to make the most of
an opportunity the new dispensation presented to him. Cham
barran on the Isere near Grenoble where he was imprisoned
was, until the Italians and Germans invaded Vichy France,
not a bad camp. True, the lads were held behind barbed wire,
the French kept them prisoners and went through the motions
of strict discipline; but they gave their charges an easy time.
Live and let live was their motto. Their attitude to the Ger
mans was cynically correct.

We had one extremely good friend in Chambarran, the
French interpreter whom I shall call Jacques. Jacques' grand
father was a Methodist clergyman in England. The lad was
reared a staunch Christian. When I conducted divine service
for the prisoners he accompanied the singers on the har
monium. A witty man, with a sparkling and generous sense
of humour, Jacques helped me on numerous occasions in ways
which might have led to his death had he been detected.
He was a great morale-builder among the prisoners. Through
him I knew all that went on in Chambarran and he kept us
informed as to the moods of the officials in charge. Jacques
was a favourite among the men.

There were 1,000 men interned in the camp when the

news spread that Italians were coming to transport them to captivity in Italy. The British did not like the prospect, but most of them had to reconcile themselves to it when Italian lorries, guarded by men armed with tommy-guns, arrived to escort them to their new homes. William refused to reconcile himself to the journey and planned his escape with a nice sense of timing and a shrewd knowledge of the lay-out of the medieval château in which he was held. Early on the morning of the day the prisoners were to leave, he crawled from his bunk, dashed across a court and into stables which adjoined the house. There he climbed as high as he could into a loft and covered himself with hay. Though buried in that comfortable substance, he still could watch the court through an open window. His compatriots lined up for inspection by the Italians. Approvingly William noted that they moved very smartly.

A roll was called. His name was unanswered and he lay very quiet in his hiding place expecting a search to begin. There was much excitement down below. Roars of rage from a stout Italian officer, much rushing about on the part of N.C.O.s and then, in the midst of this upheaval, the officer consulted his watch. Transporting 1,000 men is not a simple task. Trains are scheduled and must run to time-tables. A whole operation can be drastically delayed by even a brief pause, and officers consequently censured, if a general hold-up ensues. William deduced that Fatty had to get his contingent to the train so quickly that he could not halt and form a party to search for the missing man. Fatty began to issue brisk orders.

The prisoners marched out of the camp. William watched until the courtyard was empty. Stealthily he crept to the window stuck his head out and looked all around him. The place seemed deserted. And then Jacques strolled out of a doorway, a cigarette in hand and a blithe song on his lips. William gave him a low whistle. The interpreter looked up, laughed and said:

'Why, there you are. Naughty, naughty boy. And all your friends gone to sunny Italy worrying about you being missing. They were heartbroken. Naughty boy.'

William hurried down to the court, clapped his friend on the shoulder and the little man continued, 'But why don' you go to Italy? Don't you like spaghetti? It is very pretty.'

William knew exactly what he wanted. His tastes were chauvinistic. He came from West Lothian.

'No, I don't like spaghetti. I want a good plate of broth Scotch broth if you want to know, Jacques, my lad. None of your fancy French or Eytie stuff. And that's why I remained behind.'

'Mon Dieu,' said Jacques. 'You, Ecossais. All you think of is bagpipes, broth and whisky. I don't blame you, either Maybe I too am Scotch, eh?'

'Maybe you are, Jacques. But you can help me?'

'Come with me.'

Jacques took William by an arm and led him down into a cellar under the château.

'Stay there until I come for you.'

The Scottish lad waited, crouched against a stone wall, peering at an aperture until the daylight faded. When eventually Jacques whistled and he crawled forth to see the irrepressible organist grinning down at him, he was famished by hunger and cold.

'Would you like a bowl of spaghetti now, Scotch boy? Here are sandwiches. Drink this.'

William took a bowl of broth, French broth and very good in his hands and gulped it down. The sandwiches disappeared under his coat.

'The nice Italian mans are all gone home. Now listen to me, William.'

His face now serious, Jacques described the route to Grenoble and when he finished he handed the lad a few hundred francs. He had told him where and how to contact me in the city.

'Go to M. Donald, William.' With a broad smile, 'Is he not a Scotch boy too. He is a good mans and will see that you go straight home to your Scotch broth. Good luck, my dear friend.'

William was outside the prison and on the road to Grenoble Rain drizzled down and dusk had spread a blanket across the land. Next day we met and I saw him safely on our branch of the underground. I hope the broth was ready when he reached the end of the line.

My commission as an underground conductor ended with him, although I did not know the future when we said good-bye. My next few days were preoccupied with a project to speed up the delivery of food to be parcelled for our old people, and in visiting the sick. Then one of the wickedest acts of the Gestapo was attempted, a blow directed at these aged and physically failing invalids.

As a security measure the Germans who now controlled Grenoble announced that all British and alien subjects and known Gaullists in the city would be shipped to the Reich for internment. I knew what this meant and so, God help them, did the threatened innocents. They would be sent to the horror camps, to the gas chambers, for many of them were too old to be used as the beasts of burden that the Nazis made of their physically strong prisoners. I dropped all other work to fight this hideous measure.

From morning until night I waged a one-man war against the authorities. Before I slept each night I beseeched God to help us and I thanked Him for the guidance that stopped me accepting the offer to return to England made by the London agents. Here I could do something to defend the poor from the miseries that the Godless new order was heaping upon them.

I wrote letters to friends abroad and had them smuggled across the Swiss frontier. I bombarded, through the same channel, the Red Cross and our own Government with pleas and protests. I charged into every relevant office in town threatening the day of justice and, I now realise, taking the most appalling risks. Most of these offices were controlled by that time, with cowards and craven place-seekers. The Gestapo had rooted out the better Frenchmen. Those who survived were keeping quiet, waiting for the liberation. The traitors sat in the chairs of authority. One of them had me kicked out into the street. I realised then that I must take a final chance. I went to see the new commandant of the city who was an Italian.

Signor Commandante was a self-important man, beautifully groomed, good-looking in a plump way and like most vain men incorrigibly stupid. Left to himself, he would have been, I believe, a harmless sort of creature, efficient enough as a small tradesman and skilful enough on a suburban bowling green. Left to himself he wouldn't have made a big mark in the smallest parish in the world. But he had taken the Duce's nonsense about Cæsar's Rome surviving in the new Rome of the twentieth century, the façade raised by Mussolini himself, very seriously. Signor Commandante, I could see, had a prophetic vision of himself wearing a laurel wreath and returning to the Eternal City to burn sacrifices before gods that died with Constantine. He had flattered his way to success. He struck attitudes. He brooded. He looked magnanimous. He looked stern and pompous, and ever so often he looked in the mirror. He was very handsome and quite ridiculous.

'Signor, these people are innocent!'

'M. le Pasteur, they are enemies of the Italian Empire and dangerous.'

'Dangerous to you, Signor Commandante! Forgive me, it is ridiculous.'

The manicured hand ran over the thick, shining black hair. He was thoughtful and clement. He smiled.

'You do not understand, M. le Pasteur. We fight a total war. All enemies are dangerous until they are subdued.'

'Life had subdued these people, Signor. They are old. They are ailing They are women. Does Italy fight the aged and sick? Do your soldiers war on women?' and, taking a risk, 'Such battles make the Italians look ridiculous before the world.'

'You forget yourself, Pasteur. Our allies, the Germans, have investigated these people. Our allies wished them removed to the Reich. They will go.'

Leaning back in my chair, I grinned as offensively as I could, reached for a cigarette and when he stared at my effrontery I said with as near a leer as I could manage:

'I understand, Signor Commandante. You take orders from the Gestapo. I have been wasting your time, and my own. Forgive me. I'll see your commanding officer at S.S. Headquarters this evening. And I'll put a kind word in to him for you. You have been generous.'

I stood up to go. He jumped to his feet, pulling at his collar. Here it comes, I thought, now is the end. He pointed a shaking finger at me.

'Sit down,' he shouted. 'How dare you talk to me in that way. You forget yourself. If you were not a priest I'd have you shot. I'd have you shot now, this instant.'

'Forgive me, Signor,' I apologised. 'I know you are a humane man and I feel that only under duress would you agree to the brutish treatment that my poor compatriots are receiving. They will be killed in Germany. Now, if they were being sent to Italy, they would be happy. The Germans are not a cultured people, like your compatriots. These people, believe me, are too weak to menace anyone.'

'My information is that they are dangerous elements.' He was composed again, hand brushing the sleek hair. 'I shall investigate tonight. They do not leave until the morning. If there is truth in what you say, they will remain in Grenoble. The Germans, as you have noted M. le Pasteur, are not civilised in the high Roman manner.'

With a flick of the hand he dismissed me. I left the office in low spirits. The poor silly man meant well, but I did not doubt that he would forget the matter or succumb to the bullying of some German, and my friends would be lost in a death camp.

Early next morning, I watched as they were herded out of the prison and on to lorries which had no coverings and looked filthy. Each of them carried a suitcase which was all the luggage permitted by their persecutors. They brightened when they saw me and called out. I spoke with each, offering words of good cheer that sounded hollow in my ears. The lorry filled and pulled a few yards up the street. As it started one or two shouted in despair:

'Good-bye, Padre.' The others waved their hands and wan faces struggled to break into smiles. Tears ran down my cheeks. I heard sobbing from French men and women who had come to watch their friends taken away. They had no doubt that they would never return. The scene was heart-

breaking. But there was a respite when the lorry halted a
few yards up the street and another drew in to the pavement
opposite the entrance to the gaol. Immediately another party
of victims filed out and again the good-byes began. I clasped
their hands and told them I would keep on fighting on their
behalf which, to me at least, seemed poor consolation to them.
But even those few words of kindly intention pierced their
sorrow and they brightened a little. The S.S. Commandant
looked on. His face unmoving. He was silent except for an
occasional quiet instruction to a roaring sergeant of the
Gestapo.

Four lorries filled and were lined up in the sunlit street
and the fifth was drawing in when I heard the screech of a
motor siren, the sort of thing that is used for dramatic effect
in the more violent types of cinema entertainment. The screech
turned into an agonised squeal of brakes as a luxurious Italian
saloon car pulled in before the lorry. A young officer jumped
out and shouted to the driver of that shoddy vehicle to with-
draw. The German driver roared back until a second, less
ornate car pulled in behind the limousine and a huge Italian
N.C.O. leapt out, followed by a platoon, each bearing a tommy-
gun. The young officer spoke to the giant very quickly. The
latter turned round, focused his eyes on the Aryan lorry
driver and yelled so loudly that the old ladies on the lorries
started with fright. Another Italian car arrived at that moment.
Another platoon was disgorged from it. The lorry withdrew.
Then and only then Signor Commandante stepped out from the
limousine. With a wave of his hand he called over the S.S.
Commandant who stepped forward briskly and saluted.

With rapid, florid gestures the Signor Commandante began
to speak to his ally. The latter seemed to answer sharply.
The Italian patiently listened and began again. The German
answered as sharply and there was a roar of anger from the
Signor. His arm shot out like a railway signal; and obviously
he was ordering his racially pure friend indoors. There was
going to be trouble and to a man in his position, he may
have felt that a fish-wives' squabble on the street of Grenoble
would not bring prestige. The laurel leaves might have wilted

He spoke to the young officer who in turn addressed the sergeant and then followed his master indoors.

The Italian men-at-arms moved along the pavements, stringing themselves out beside the lorries. The German guards eyed them dubiously.

Nearly a half-hour passed before Signor Commandante emerged with his lieutenant. Again the latter spoke to the sergeant. Their car drove off and the S.S. Commandant appeared. Italians and Germans sprang to attention as he gave orders. Then, to my relief, they started to clear our people from the lorries. Those exhausted victims of more than three years of war descended and again filed into prison. There still was hope. That evening some returned to their homes, again on parole; within three days all were freed. I sent a letter of thanks, full of operatic praise for a noble enemy, to the Signor. God bless him wherever he is. The poor man was just a victim of the sort of nationalist superstition that irreligious dictators can fasten on simple people.

April, 1943, was a month of sunshine, a golden month of heat cooled by pleasant breezes from the north. During the week after my friends escaped from the German transportation plan, I constantly visited them and tried to readjust the older and the ill to the sense of security which had been rudely disturbed by the threat of removal from Grenoble. I wrote letters and with my assistants parcelled up into generous rations consignments of food that came to us from the Red Cross. I was elated by the victory won with God's help over the Germans and began to feel that the fears of my friends about the future were exaggerated. My confidence was strengthened by a visit from some of the more active members of my flock.

' Padre,' they said, ' we have arranged a social meeting of all your friends to take place on April 17th. We wish to make a small presentation to you as a token of our respect and gratitude for all you have done for us, especially your intervention when so many of us were about to be transported last week. You saved our lives.'

So long as a Minister of the Gospel has a congregation he has a home. I listened to those good folk that day and felt

I might be in Scotland. I forgot for the time being that thei
lives had been endangered just a few days earlier; and it wa
release from that danger that had inspired their gesture o
affection. I felt secure in their love and even now I knov
that the feeling was not misleading. A man exists by th
love of God and he lives out his existence best when tha
greatest love of all is reflected into his heart by his fellov
men and women.

I told them that I was grateful and that truthfully I wa
more indebted to them than they to me. We were all in
finitely indebted to our Redeemer, the Master who save
all of us from wicked men and I agreed to come to thei
celebration. The tree-lined streets of Grenoble were alive i
the sun that April day and I was happy going from Britis
home to British home in the city, seeing love blossom agai
with fear cast out and watching our French neighbours' relie
from the agony, knowing now that their allies and friend
were safe again and next door to them. So the days passed awa
until April 16th, the day before the presentation. That evenin
I was invited to the home of a friend Harris Rudowitc
which he shared with his father-in-law, Abraham Korn.
was the feast of the Passover and I rejoiced that I was goin
to be a guest of the Jews and would pray with them.

Condemning the anti-Semitic laws of the Nazis, outrage
by them, a famous churchman once said that we Christians a
all, in our Faith, Semitic. I pray that someday all of us wi
come to understand exactly what he meant. Until we do s
we cannot be wholly Christian. Our God when He chose
walk the earth as a man, became a Jewish man and so th
promise made to Adam was fulfilled. The Jewish scriptures a
part of our Bible. The psalms we sing are Hebrew, as a
the lessons we read and the texts of so many of our sermon
The Cross was raised over the world after the Feast of tl
Passover. The time is holy.

In that Jewish home on that April evening I was prese
and broke bread with my friends, representatives of the pere
nially victimised race, in a ritual older than the Europe whic
is Christian; Europeans had gone to their land as conquero

t was Jews, the Apostles, who invading Europe, brought us, n return for persecution, Christianity. There is an infinite enderness in Jewish family relationships. The patriarch Abraham presiding, the neat ritual caps giving authority to he occasion, curiously isolating this family, strong in its faith, rom the warring nations beyond the walls, had the atmosphere of eternity.

I listened to the ancient words and was moved by the simple undemonstrative way I was brought into the family circle as part of it. These people were intellectuals of the finest and most sensitive type in Europe and they had survived partly because France provided pockets of silence where a man might find a retreat and wait for better times. But at any moment now jack-boots might strike echoes from the road outside and father, grandfather, his children, their children might be consciencelessly taken away and blotted from existence, liquidated as if they were worthless and malignant things. They simply were good. They were masters in the arts of elaborated goodness. They gave to the poor, the sick, the dispossessed; to unhappy Christians who had fallen victims to political persecution they gave friendship and compassion. They kept open house for all who came to their door.

As their guest on that blessed evening I found myself caught up in the old ritual, passed down from generation to generation, prayers elaborated and refined to a point of wonderful complexity yet so simple when offered by these men and women who spoke from their hearts.

When the time came for us to part I took the two hands of each member of the family in mine and wrung them warmly. I walked from their door in the state of high exaltation that close communion with God brings to a man, the words of the scriptures recurring in my mind as I made my way home. I thought of my own flock who would gather tomorrow to show their love for me and I felt grateful. They had part of their Bible in common with my Jewish friends and they had suffered in common with them for the same things.

When I reached the boarding-house it was in darkness.

The whole world seemed asleep. The garden was silent with that whispering silence which comes on a warm spring night. My mind steeped in prayer found the world infinitely beautiful. I opened the front door with my latch key and tiptoed upstairs to my room, halted on the landing for no reason at all and then opened the door and walked toward my dressing-table to switch on a bedside lamp. Behind me a switch clicked over. The room was full of light. I turned around and found myself looking at five pointing revolvers.

I could have laughed aloud but surprise mingled with shock and I was silent. Five armed men had come to arrest the little Minister as some of the Scottish lads called me. I must have made a considerable reputation. I must be reckoned a desperate character. The faces behind the guns were stern and unsmiling, solemn as only the faces of those who have the temerity to point guns at a man can be. It seemed ridiculous.

'Pastor Caskie, you are under arrest. You must come with us. Now.'

I asked for a few minutes and collected my Bible, a cigarette case, a pen and a razor. I put on a coat and they put handcuffs on my wrists. The manacles were too small and cut me. I winced and held them out.

'They'll do for you,' I was told.

As I walked downstairs between my captives I realised that I would miss the presentation party on the following afternoon. But already that part of my life seemed very far away. I hoped the old people would not miss me too much.

CHAPTER FIFTEEN

Voices in the Villa Lynwood

THE CASERNE HOCHE in Grenoble is not the best of prisons.
The cell into which I was flung was filthy. The wall against
which I fell was hard, the guards violent. My face was bruised.
On the floor, the bedding, a bundle of rancid straw, gave
off a poisonous smell. Brutally the guards twisted me around
until I faced them. They removed my braces, tie and shoelaces.
The Italians were not as efficient as the Germans but they were
more cruel. Their prisoners have been known to hang themselves with accessories of the kind that they took from me.
They treat prisoners like vicious cats playing with mice; but
they lack the final savagery of cats. They do not kill without
orders. Their absentminded vindictiveness degrades the
prisoner.

For two weeks I was held in the Caserne Hoche, adjusting
myself to a new small world of darkness bound by damp
stone and uninhabited by anyone who saw me as a human
being. I asked to see the Commandante and the guards did
not answer. I asked for a trial and they guffawed. I asked
them to tell me the nature of the crime I was accused of
committing. They told me to 'shut up.' It was a strange,
isolating experience, desperately humiliating, in which a man
might have collapsed into despair. But my knowledge of
the Scriptures saved me, and my recollections of the imprison-
ments of the Apostles and later Christian martyrs gave me
a rule by which I lived during those weeks and the months
that followed. I existed in memories of good days, and in
prayer.

They took my Bible from me and the few possessions I
had brought from de Verger. When I protested, an official
answered with a sneer. 'You are a priest. You should have
this book in your head.' I had it in my heart and head and
it preserved my faith and sanity. Each day I was given a

small crust of bread and a flat tin containing less than a
half pint of water. After the second day I felt no hunger
for food. Imprisonment was my torture. During the first
long hours I wandered around the cell like a mouse on a
tiny tread-mill, but I was a man and I hated the limitations
of the place and the frustrating bounds it set upon me. I
thought of my family in Scotland and I resented the misfortune
that had halted my work. I worried about my friends
in Grenoble and wondered if I had left evidence that might
compromise them. The Italians did not interrogate me and
this led me to suspect that I might be only one victim of
a wholesale round-up. But when despair threatened to engulf
my soul the voice of Christian reason asserted itself and I
prayed. The knowledge came back to me that I and my
persecutors were in God's hands. In His time he would make
everything just again and I was consoled. In the darkness
my heart lifted and joy surged through me.

Years later I learned that I was the only person arrested
that day. My imprisonment was not a signal for an out-
burst of persecution. When I did not arrive for the presentation party my friends, British and French, investigated my
absence and were told of my imprisonment. They asked for
permission to visit me and this was refused. They were told,
in the words of the Italians, that M. Caskie was ' being treated
with all the honours of his rank as a Protestant clergyman.'
My rooms were searched and two friends, Miss Ethel Davidson
from Aberdeen and Mlle. Suzanne Creton of l'Ecole de la
Legion d'Honneur were visited by the Gestapo and interrogated, but not arrested. They were faithful friends and
brave women. They both helped me, encouraged me, and
inspired me in my work. Sometime before my arrest they
agreed to hide documents of considerable importance to the
organisation. These were secreted in a wooden box in the
toilet of their flat when the Germans came. Fortunately for
the ladies, no search was made, but the danger did not pass
immediately. Later when I had become a memory in Grenoble
an epidemic broke out in the school and the Gestapo transported pupils and teachers to the Château des Combres near
Voiron. The ladies were not searched on the journey. The

epidemic may have done them good service in this respect for they were not even approached by officials. A very cursory inspection of the travellers would have revealed that Miss Davidson carried the documents on her lap under the travelling rug she held about her knees to keep her warm in June. Caught with that evidence, I cannot but believe that those two courageous women Ethel and Suzanne would have been shot or sent to a death camp in the Reich.

At the end of April, I was taken from the Caserne Hoche and transferred to Cuneo in Italy where I remained for a couple of nights sitting on a stone floor without bedding of any kind in complete darkness nursing raw and bleeding wrists. The handcuffs used on the journeys were again so tight that I cried out when they were forced on to my wrists. Rusted, crudely finished, dirty, I thought at first they had crushed the wrists to pulp and I would be crippled when the implements were removed. But when blood forced its way back into the blanched hands that were hanging limply by my side I knew that soon I would be able to use them again.

The prison at Cuneo was an evil place. During my few nights there I heard screams coming from neighbouring cells and, not for the last time, I prayed in the darkness for patriots who might, even as I lay there, be dying like beasts without the consolations of family and religion. There was no bedding in the cell and no light penetrated its walls. Time was one long unending night and when they came to take me to the Villa Lynwood at Nice I blinked like an owl as the door opened and light struck my eyes. The guards sniggered as they dragged me outside. They did not use handcuffs that time but wound heavy iron chains around my wrists, leaving the ends hanging so that they struck against my heels as I walked. Thrust upstairs and, with carabinieri walking behind me carrying rifles with naked bayonets attached, I reeled into a courtyard where a lorry stood. The sun hurt my eyes. I fell to my knees and struggled to my feet again. Shuddering with shame at my condition, dirty, unkempt, weak from starvation, I rocked on my heels. I ate no food at Cuneo. They did not give me any. The guards heaved me on to a lorry and during most of the journey to Nice kept me standing. Light-headed, half delirious, I gazed sickly about me, seeing nothing and aching to scratch my face where my beard, under the hot sun, was itching in a painful way. Sweat ran down my face and nausea nearly overcame me. Before we reached the villa in the evening, after numerous halts, during one of which I was given a crust and a pannikin of water, I was allowed to sit. When the lorry pulled into the avenue leading to the big house, I was barely conscious.

The Villa Lynwood, in peaceful days on that beautiful coast, had been the property of an English lady. It was large and beautifully proportioned, standing in about an acre of ground. The gardens had been cultivated with the good taste in gardening for which the English are justly famous. Happy sunlit holidays had been spent in it by the English lady and her friends and they must have taken grateful memories home. In May, 1943, it was a house of torture isolated in a garden that had degenerated into a wilderness. Barbed wire enclosed it. An air of sadness and the sordid hung about its walls. Heavily armed men guarded every entrance; dogs wandered loose in the garden through the night. Many prisoners suffered torture in the Villa Lynwood and the maquis believe that many murders were committed in its dark and gloomy cellars.

When the lorry jerked to a halt that evening I lay still upon the floor; my face pressed against its rough boards. Suddenly my mind was feverishly active. My limbs remained leaden. Two carabinieri caught me by the heels and dragged me to the ground, catching me as I fell and thrusting me on to my feet. With hands under my armpits they heaved me through the house, down into the basement and along a corridor. We passed a door of bars leading into a cell and I saw a woman gazing out, on her face a look of desolation that spoke of suffering and privation. It was Odette Churchill, the heroic woman who was the centre of one of the epics in the annals of the Resistance. I forced my head up and tried to smile at her and I saw her face light up before a heavy blow drove me onwards to the end of the corridor. I never saw Odette again and, indeed, it was later when one of her comrades was imprisoned with me, that I learned the identity of the lady in the cell in the Villa, but her tired bravery impressed me during those few seconds outside her cell.

A door clanged behind me and I sank on to the floor into a deep sleep or coma from which I did not waken until early morning when hideous and sustained screaming seemed to fill the house. Indescribable acts were being committed and I writhed helplessly in the cell below. I grasped my ears, shutting out the cries, and began my first day in the villa by lying with my face pressed against a rancid wall praying with violent fervour for the poor soul whose body was being degraded into a pitiful death nearby.

When the screaming petered out I collected myself and tried to recreate in my mind the writings of St Paul on his imprisonment. His God was the God of the poor tortured soul above. His God was tortured by men unto death. His God was mine and I struggled upwards to him begging for strength to endure what might come my way. It still was dark when I fell asleep again. When I wakened the morning was advanced and a broad shaft of light lay across the cell. Above my head was a window on ground level and by standing on a bucket which had been left to supply sanitary conveniences I could see out into the deserted courtyard. About noon, as I reckoned—it may have been later—a piece of very hard bread and a pan of water were thrust through the bars at me. By dipping the bread in the water I was able to eat it. The Italians, I realised, had attained a certain efficiency in their arrangement for dieting penal establishments. They simplified it.

During that day I saw no one but a silent patrolling guard who gazed through the bars every hour as if checking on a peculiar, voiceless beast. When I spoke to him he did not answer. He did not so much look at me as through me, as if I were part of the not very lavish furnishings of the place. When evening came he opened the door and took out the sanitary pail. My food he always put through the bars. Another day passed during which I lost myself in a world of memories, separating myself from the cell, recreating my own life. I meditated upon the Scriptures and found that while gaol lacked the amenities penal reformers in my country took for granted, it offered wonderful opportunities for meditation upon the mysteries of my religion. When the hours of torture began I prayed quietly, stilling my angry and enraged compassion for the bodies and souls in hazard in the rooms above. I came to think that maybe my vocation lay there in the villa, offering prayers for the lost ones of the patriot organisations. The padre to the prisoners had been chosen by God to follow those whom he could not conduct in other days and live with them on the brink of death.

In my cell there was evidence that the Villa Lynwood had become a projection of hell upon earth. The plastered walls were covered with the names of men and women who had halted there on the road to death or the camps. Among them I found signatures of old comrades of mine who had disappeared. Some I knew were dead, others had just vanished.

The sound of feet dragging in the corridor beyond my door brought me away from my meditations on the second day and a few minutes later a man came into view marching blindly. I rushed to the bars and gazed out at him. A guard carrying a rifle and bayonet marched behind. The victim did not raise his eyes but staggered the few yards to the outside walls and leaned against them. The naked bayonet prodded him. He did not cry out but turned heavily on his feet and moved away out of sight again, passing my door. I saw he was young. The dark face gaunt, unshaven, sagged. He staggered as he walked. A few minutes passed and again I heard the dragging feet and saw him move towards the wall at the corridor's end. The guard now carried the rifle resting in his armpit and again he prodded the poor body that automatically rested against the stone. This ghastly patrol continued all through the day. Whenever I stood by the door the rifle bayonet was turned towards me significantly. I lay awake throughout the night praying but all through the next day the march went on. It continued for four days and for most of the time I lay on the floor watching that body propelling itself, staggering, falling, being prodded until the back of the ragged shirt was soaked in blood. The guards changed. The torture was unending. On the third day the marcher fell against the bars of my cell, his head pressed between them, his mouth open. Frantically I crushed a few crumbs of my bread into a pellet and dropped it into his mouth before the guard hurled him to the floor and opened my door. Swinging his bayonet above his head he screeched:

'Sale Anglais, I'm going to kill you.'

He drew the weapon above his head and then let it sink to his side.

'I shall kill you if you look out of the door again at this filthy Frenchman. Remember.'

He left the cell and kicked the body on the floor of the corridor until, miraculously, the poor man heaved himself on to his hands and knees, crawled to the wall and pushed himself upright. All through the night and late into the following morning, the awful torture continued. Then it suddenly stopped and I heard no more of the man who marched.

For hours I sank in misery, praying for him who had gone and feeling miserably futile, realising as never before the bonds that can be put upon a man's soul when his body is held in prison. My every instinct, all my training for the ministry, all my service to God and His flock urged me to help that shambling broken man. A bayonet held between us stayed me. When the guards rattled the bars of my cell and I went forward to take my crust and pan of water, I saw in the latter a fly scrambling to get out. I picked it out and set it on the floor where its legs flickered like tiny thin black lines. I watched it begin to move. It crawled across the floor and I followed it to one of the walls where former prisoners had inscribed the honours roll of those who had passed through the Gethsemane of the Villa Lynwood. I was one of them. My nails were long and uncut and I recall the irony that filled my heart as I considered the claw on my right thumb. Carefully I inscribed my name and rank in the Church of Scotland in the hard plaster. The task finished, I observed my handiwork. It was, I flattered myself, quite a neat job. The roll was up-to-date. But I was the padre. Choosing a largish space on the plaster untouched by names, I wrote:

'Thus saith the Lord. . . . Fear not for I have redeemed thee . . . I have called them by name. Thou art mine When thou passeth through the waters, I will be with thee, and through the rivers, they shall not overflow thee When thou walketh through the fire, thou shalt not be burned, neither shall the flame kindle upon thee . . .'

The light had changed when I completed my task. Slowly I had prayed the words as I cut into the plaster, sending them out to the man whose tired soul maybe was at peace as I wrote. I stood back to study the verse and heard noises outside the window. Climbing on the bucket, I pulled myself up and gazed through the misty pane. The light was still good enough for me to see a figure that was familiar standing outside, his hands bound behind him. He turned his head and I recognised Gerald Hakim who had been an agent in the South of France when I was more actively engaged with the organisation. He bent and peered at my window and then I knew he had recognised me. With an effort I managed to hold on with one hand while I placed a finger on my lips to silence any demonstration from him. The effort was too much for me and I tumbled backwards into the cell, banging my head against the hard floor.

Long into the night I lay thinking of Gerald. The slightest disturbance of prison routine, I discovered in gaol, unleashes all sorts of memories and associations in the mind of a human being who is a prisoner. The figure in the garden outside my window brought to mind events that led me back to my experiences. I wondered how the enemy had captured Hakim and if he had been submitted to torture; if he was fit and what they would do with him. At last as sleep was coming I composed myself for the final prayer of the day and then a hideous scream coming from a cell in the corridor brought my nerves taut as a bow. It died into a whimper and I indistinctly heard a guttural voice utter a few words. For a moment there was silence and then the scream tore through me again. The whimpering followed and a burst of guttural oaths. On my stomach I crawled, propelling myself along the floor, using my arms as legs, dragging my stockinged feet, to the door, and listened.

It was an interrogation. The prisoner, I gathered, was young, French and an agent of the Resistance. His group must have been a good one for the inquisitors were determined to wring from him the names of his fellow maquis. The questions relentlessly continued. He screamed and whimpered like a man tortured beyond endurance but he was a brave man for he endured. They did not get a word from him. The only sounds that came from his lips were great sobs rising to high pitch like a demented, diabolic violin as the guards applied their trade of cruelty to his body. It went on for about an hour and a half and then they left him, posting a sentry outside his cell. I could hear the guard shuffle his boots. When the coast was clear and his superiors well out of the way, a match scratched and there was a momentary lessening of the darkness; I heard his rifle being settled against the wall. And then the victim in the cell began to weep helplessly and weirdly. As the sobs racked his body I could hear him trying to sing. Louder and louder the words came through the voice of his agony. Intently I listened and the words came more clearly to me. He was intoning Bach's *Passion Chorale*. Within the sobs stronger and stronger it emerged:

> *O Sacred Head sore wounded*
> *With grief and shame weighed down*
> *O kingly head surrounded*
> *With thorns Thine only crown*
> *How pale are thou with anguish*
> *With sore abuse and scorn*
> *How does that visage languish*
> *Which once was bright as morn*

The verse which, God help him and his persecutors, he sang in their original language is ' O Haupt Voll Blud und Wunden.' The chorale of the gentle Bach was giving heart to a victim of the musician's own race and their Italian ally

in this little hell secluded in a garden on the most beautiful
coast that God has created for the joy of man. Over and
over again, he sang until the voice died to a whisper, and we
both slept. They must have taken him away early in the
morning. Throughout the next day there was silence.

I returned to my routine of meditation, my heart bowed
down by a feeling of inadequacy to help my fellow prisoners.
When in the night screaming echoed again, waking me from
a deep sleep and overpowering me with its horror, I shouted
for the guard but no answer came. I felt that even God had
deserted us in the Villa Lynwood. My head reeled and I
thought, ' this must be Hell! There is no escape, this horror
will go on for ever.' The words of our Saviour came to my
mind and I whispered into the darkness, ' My God, my God,
why hast Thou forsaken me?' In the most curious way that
despairing whisper brought me some hours of tranquillity.
Often the words had been read to me by my mother while
we sat around listening as she pored over the Bible in my
home in Bowmore, Islay, the peat fire glowing on the hearth,
spreading its light on the young faces of the family, the
brothers and sisters to whom my thoughts reverted during
that time of sorrow. I saw them as children again and I was
a child. My memories of them grew big in my mind and
like the peat fire cast a glow around my chilled heart. Clearly
I heard the soft tones of my mother as she spoke her favourite
paraphrase, which I later learned was the favourite of Mar-
garet Ogilvie, mother of my famous countryman, J. M. Barrie.
In a cracked and tired voice I sang it to myself in the cell.

> ' Why pour'st thou forth thine anxious plaint,
> Despairing of relief,
> As if the Lord o'erlooked thy cause,
> And did not heed thy grief?
>
> Art thou afraid His power shall fail,
> When comes thy evil day?
> And can an all-creating arm
> Grow weary or decay?'

Each time I sang those words I felt His arm grow stronger around me and I knew that even my agonies listening to my brothers in the Villa as they were dragged towards death by our enemies were justified so long as I did not lose faith. Each of us carried his own cross in the Villa Lynwood. To be restrained from helping the needy, suffering and dying is the final test that is put on a Christian man. He must suffer with those who are enduring the bitterest agony and suffer for them and learn to endure his own limitations and leave them to God. That was my burden and God helped me bear it. He taught me to pray for freedom and the opportunity to work for the Christian cause, part of which is to strive that such things will never be repeated.

Thinking of my mother I fell asleep. When I awoke, two guards were standing over me. They took me to a cell on the other side of the house where one of them motioned to me to enter. I was very tired as I walked mechanically through the door. One develops in gaol an instinct for obedience to guards. I looked around me. The place was just another cell, but a man was in it. It was my friend Gerald Hakim. Trembling I held out my hands and he grasped them.

'Padre, Padre, what are you doing in this place?'

At first I did not answer but just looked at him. To measure the joy I felt seeing Gerald and hearing his friendly voice I should have to recapture the feeling of having escaped from that dreadful vacuum of pain again. He clapped my back gently and put an arm around my shoulder. We sat upon the floor and talked throughout the day. I told him of my arrest and the events that followed but neither of us lingered upon our experiences in the villa. I spoke of Scotland and he of England and we compared notes on our memories of home. We spoke of our wartime professions. He told me his story and revealed that the woman I saw on my first night in the villa was Odette Churchill.

Gerald was one of those amiable men who undertake perilous duties with the absentminded *savoir-faire* of a clerk going about routine tasks. The Intelligence Service employed him to travel around the South of France collecting information and he knew the terrain well, was a brilliant linguist and well-trained to exploit a talent for recognising every relevant movement of traffic, troops, supplies and people. Using no disguise and the minimum of forged papers, he toured France on a push-bike. He cycled into towns and villages, spent a night or so observing and drifted on his way, all the time gathering details of enemy activities which formed parts of a vast jig-saw puzzle which, at Whitehall, was being constantly assembled into a moving picture of Europe under the Nazis and Fascists. When Odette was arrested at Sevrier on the lovely lake of Annecy in the Savoy, the Gestapo knew of Gerald's work with her. They sought him too but he was gone and they arrested all the inhabitants of the little village, herded them together and drove them through the interrogating rooms they had established in a little villa Gerald had occupied in 1939. He had escaped on his push-bike and his work continued. They did not betray him.

A traitor betrayed him in the Nice district. This man was an old friend, Carlo Monferrino by name, whose treachery puzzled Gerald. They had been close to each other for nearly twenty-five years and had shared a common passion for ski-ing and rock climbing. They had endured much as comrades in the latter sport. The betrayal seemed inexplicable to Gerald but it was a fact. He was a prize the Gestapo reasonably sought. His apparently absentminded progress on that push-bike had brought him to places and people a more conservative agent would not have attempted to reach.

His 'star turn' as he called it, deserves a note, at least, in the annals of those years. Pierre Laval's secretary was stopping at Thonon-les-bains in the Haute Savoie and Gerald decided to call upon him. The secretary was a busy man and by collecting a little information about his background, Gerald casually convinced him that his caller was an old friend of his family. They drank coffee together and talked for more than an hour. M. Hakim departed with his head crammed with valuable information. He chuckled like a boy when he told this story. It was a hard blow to me when the door of the cell opened again and I was taken out and escorted back to my first cell. But I felt happier in soul and body when I lay down to sleep. My day with Gerald Hakim restored to me a feeling of human companionship, and I knew that I was not alone.

Early on that first morning of my return to the private cell I scrutinised the wall. Another name had been inscribed upon it. It had been occupied in my absence by another guest. I looked at the verse I had cut with my thumbnail and began to cut it deeper into the plaster. I became engrossed in the task. 'The rivers shall not overflow thee . . .' When I reached these words I was interrupted by guards dangling handcuffs. They told me to come with them.

They had come to take me to the fortress of St Remo in Italy.

CHAPTER SIXTEEN

The Fortress by the Sea

LIKE A great sprawling rock the prison at St Remo was almost surrounded by water, from some angles it resembled a man-made island. When clouds obscured the sunlight it loomed darkly like a charnel house of the living.

Many centuries have passed since it was built. A multitude of men and women have lived in chains within its massive walls, never feeling the ocean breeze on their whitened skin and never the touch of the blessed Italian sun. A mournful heritage of age-old cruelty gives the place an atmosphere of doom. For centuries there was no hope for those held in its black, remorseless bowels. It is an ante-chamber of hell, a place Dante might have imagined. Water drips from the four-feet thick cell walls as though the sea beyond, in beating against it, had turned malignant and slowly penetrated to play its part in the tortured isolation of the inmates. The dungeons are foul, encrusted with the filth of centuries. I believe they have never been properly cleaned at any time since the place was heaved into existence. Poor sanitation is part of the Italian tradition and no attempts were made during World War II to improve it. A bucket was left in each cell. Sometimes it was not emptied for a week or more; even then it was slopped out and not rinsed with clean water. Sometimes it was taken away for a few days and returned still stinking to the prisoner. The stench of St Remo symbolised the moral evil done within its ancient walls. But the diet did not leave material for nausea to exploit and the sickened body writhed in physical frustration.

I was brought to the fortress on a May evening when the sun was sinking and the Mediterranean winds were fresh. The gates closed with the ponderous movement that prisoners had heard from ancient days. The guards awaiting grasped me as if I had been a dangerous beast or a lunatic likely to attack them in a homicidal way. They were of the Neapolitan breed of prison attendants and, I believe, the worst in the world.

There is common anonymity in conditioned human brutes. They live by persecuting the bodies of their victims and using their own bodies for pleasure. Sensuality deadens the brain and kills the soul. Such a man becomes an animal, joyless and unthinking, a carcass lazily going through a life that surely will bring a corrupt death to him. Redemption he is offered and, refusing it, he is one of the legion of the damned who court Satan so assiduously that the mark of hell is on them. They look alike. Hating God, hating men, they kill their own hearts. The Gestapo was manned by intellectuals of a perverted breed. Each in his way was an artist and had his own refinements of cruelty. Belsen is their war memorial. The Italians were in a tradition of evil, shabby, sin-eaten beasts, unreflecting and stupid. They shunted us about as if we were senseless objects, unaware apparently that we had minds. They had an age-old system with prisoners. Without comment they immediately applied it to me. It was the initiation to St Remo.

Through narrow winding passages I was shoved, downwards on uneven stairways and along passages until it seemed we must be approaching the pit. All around us was darkness. We halted and a torch was flashed. Its beam steadied on a narrow iron doorway, rusted into the deep stone. Laboriously it was opened outwards, creaking with age and I was pushed inside.

I found myself in a medieval 'bottle' cell. There are, I suppose, special chapters in the history of penology treating of these diabolical apartments. I do not wish to read them. The 'bottle' cell in my experience is ingenious, easy for the torturer to operate and guaranteed in time to drive the strongest victim insane. Shaped like a man, it is a bottle-shaped cell of stone big enough to contain one human being but short enough not to permit him to stand upright and narrow enough to restrain him from lying down. It tapers at the top so that the face is never more than two inches from the walls that encase his head. If a man's stomach is full when he is enclosed in it, his vomit pours back over his body. He cannot move his knees more than a few inches. If he rests on his shoulders the strain on his legs becomes agonising. The flow of his blood and cramp will deprive him of consciousness so that he hangs in stone bonds; his body deformed by them, until consciousness wrests him into pain again. His own stench fills his lungs for there are no facilities for physical relief in the 'bottle.' It is, I conjecture, the most vile instrument of torture ever devised by men. When it became unbearable a man might scream or shout and the iron door fitted deep into the walls holds the noise of his screaming from those outside. The sound beats back through the passages of his ears, to the centre of his brain where it is orchestrated in the most fantastic noises, weeping, laughter and a final crescendo of blaring cacophanies until he sinks again into the unfeeling grasp of the stone and oblivion.

They left me for only twenty-four hours in the 'bottle.' Then I was picked out and taken to a cell where I was flung upon the floor. When my wits were assembled I found bread and water lying beside me. I drank the water and fell asleep.

When I awakened I was exhausted, so tired that the flesh seemed to hang upon my bones with a dead weight, the bones felt curiously dry. I have never felt so conscious of my body. There seemed to be thin sand in my veins and life was draining away There was no sound in the place, no light. I might have been entombed. How long I lay there I cannot tell. In absolute darkness and silence time is immeasurable. Sometimes I crawled on the floor, perhaps a few yards, until

my head found a wall. After a moment of rest I stood up with
a movement between a push and a crawl. Erect I leaned my
head against the stone which was wet. My fingers moved
across its rough surface and found water trickling in the
crevices. How long I stood there I do not know. I must have
slipped to the floor again and dropped into sleep. For the
second time I awakened, but now I was slightly refreshed and
my mind began to work, my eyes became accustomed to
the darkness. Dimly I saw that the dungeon was bigger than
the cell at the Villa Lynwood but the iron door was solid.
Beside it a bucket stood and there was a plate on which some
crusts of bread lay and two pans of water. Without interest
I gazed at the objects and saw there were two plates and two
pans of water. I was hungry and thirsty. Ravenously I rent
the crusts with my teeth. They had the texture of charcoal
and were tasteless. I dipped them in water and they tasted
good. One pan I drained, the other sipped and with a little
water I rubbed my eyelids. Again I slept.

I do not know how long this state of mind and body continued but I remember awakening and lying watching the
door and hearing it squeak, softly like a frightened mouse.
I watched, there was a fumbling noise and it opened. My
eyes moved downwards and I saw a plate slide in and a
gloved hand being withdrawn. And then I knew I was in
solitary confinement. I was weak and I did not mind being
alone. I lay back and rested, unthinking, unworried, barely
alive. I began to pray.

The hours became long and I waited for the hand at the
door to reassure me that I was not dead and walled-up, that
they had not entombed me and left me to die, my flesh to
rot and then my bones swept out into the sunlight, anonymous,
forgotten by all save those who loved me and were praying even
then in Islay, Paris, Grenoble, Marseilles and beyond the sea.
Thinking of my loved ones steadied me and I remembered the
religion we held in common and thus after an unending night
of darkness and brooding I began to live again. I yearned
for my Bible and the words of the Apostles filled my head.
I began to murmur whole chapters of the Bible aloud to myself,
not chanting but whispering and reflecting, my mind moving

over the words as it did in peace-time, and as it still does when I work on sermons or seek advice or solace in sorrow. The book might have been open before me. I saw its pages in my mind's eye. Strangely this vision came to me as I meditated on the blessings of recollection and I thought of my school in Islay and the schoolmistress who taught me French and was in charge of our Sunday school.

Miss Jessie Marshall is one of the persons to whom I shall be indebted throughout life and eternity for she gave me the language which was the means of my work in Paris, and she was one of those, next to my dear mother who taught me to pray. I was not an easy pupil, sometimes lazy like all healthy boys who wish to be off in the heather when they should be at their books. Oh, those French verbs! In the dungeons of St Remo I thought of her in my distress and found myself smiling, for Miss Marshall has become one of the legends of the school at Islay and I, her recalcitrant pupil, am part of the legend. Carefully I led my mind into the past. I had rebelled one day when she chided me for not working as hard as she would have wished.

'Why must I study this wretched language,' I stormed. 'It's no use to a Scotsman. I hate it.'

'French is a great and wonderful language and you will be grateful for it some day, Donald,' she answered.

Reluctantly I took her instruction and thus she made me a citizen of Europe and enabled me to contribute a little of Scotland and our religion to life in Paris. When I was called to church in the Rue Bayard she was overwhelmed with joy. Our Scottish people hold the ministry in great honour; for one of Jessie's boys to achieve the pulpit in the Rue Bayard was an achievement crowning her teaching. In the years that followed whenever a boy or girl was absentminded about homework, she would raise her fingers and say:

'Once I had a pupil who, like you, asked why he should learn this foreign tongue and today that boy. . . .'

She told the story so often that there came a time when the class chorused to her:

'We know, Miss Marshall, the Reverend Donald Caskie, the Minister in the Paris Kirk.'

Jessie smiled then because, like all good teachers, she used examples to teach a lesson, and lessons should be learned by heart as they say. So one of her unworthy pupils shares a little of her fame in the school at Islay. I thought of her, lived again my schooldays and to my surprise, found that my cheeks were wet with silent tears. During my waking hours I marched the length of the dungeon and its breadth, so that my limbs knit again and I felt stronger. Courage came back to me and I even began to feel hungry. Resolutely I pushed my mind out of St Remo back to Scotland again and my childhood.

More than a month passed before I saw a human being apart from the silent guard. The dungeon I made a world of memory and prayer. For hours I continued to recite the Scriptures. Whole days would pass while in reverie I reconstructed my past life. I would end a Bible session with a thought of my family and my mind would drift to Islay. The dungeon walls would disappear and I would see again the Paps of Jura, the view across the water, the blue hills and green fields, the lapping water on the beach. I heard the voice of my mother call me at seven-fifteen on a winter's morning and I smiled as I remembered driving my grumbling body from between the blankets. As memories filled my mind I stretched out on the stone floor and luxuriated in them.

I have six brothers and one sister, Kate, Mrs MacIntyre of Bogside, Inverkip, Scotland, who, with her husband Sandy, have been a tower of strength and encouragement to me all my life. As it so often happens in a family of the kind, my sister was the boss. As a child she was our counsellor and into manhood I relied on her advice. She was our mother's lieutenant and she drove, encouraged and goaded us out to school in the morning. And so I summoned her to St Remo to stay my spirit when it seemed to fail. I thought of schooldays and university, of the winding braes and broad streets of Edinburgh, of the prairie parish where I served my kin in Canada, of work in Egypt, Gretna and Paris. I prayed for the lads I had helped from Marseilles and those who had fallen into the hands of the Germans, and for my friends in Grenoble and comrades of the organisation. The days

stretched behind me. I lost count of time. I felt reconciled
to my fate, I was relatively happy but physically I had weakened considerably although I was then unaware of it. A daily
crust of bread and pan of water were rather less than the diet
my body had been accustomed to absorb.

Days, weeks, more than a month passed. On the Sundays
I devised for myself, I projected my soul to Islay and the mid-
morning Gaelic service when the blessed words are spoken
in our native language and then at another service at noon
in English. I attended both. I thought of us, six brothers,
helping with the little family tasks after lunch. I re-lived
the Caskies going off to church in the evening, and the singing
at the organ when we returned, with the neighbours' children
clustering around my mother. 'Trust in God always,' my
mother had told me when I left home and my father, speaking in the old tongue, elaborated the advice. 'Never be dis-
couraged, lad. Have faith in God and your feet on terra
firma.'

So I lived out my solitary days filling the dungeon with
the laughter of my family and friends until the day came when
the dungeon door opened and a figure was hurtled through
to fall beside me. Almost timorously I touched him and
then helped him to his feet. One can live almost too long in
a world of one's own devising. The prisoner was dazed and
bruised, but he was real.

'Vallet's the name,' he murmured. 'Captain Vallet. Je
suis Français. I'm glad to see you, Monsieur. I've been in
solitary. Nearly killed myself. It was at Nice, in the Villa
Lynwood.'

His eyes were red-rimmed. His whole body trembled. After
he had spoken he lay down and slept while I sat by his side.

Captain Vallet had been wounded and crippled for life
in the 1914-18 War. In 1940 he became a soldier of the
Free French Army. In St Remo he became my friend for
life. He was not young, but he was a singularly brave man.
I confess that when, in retrospect, I think of the engagements
in which he and many of my friends took part during those
years I wonder any of them survive today, to sit and talk
over old times after dinner in the manse with me.

T.P.   G

'I was terror-stricken when they took me,' he said. 'I know too much. Under torture I might have betrayed some of our friends.'

His task, I learned, had been supremely important to the organisation. He had been in control of the despatch of officers of very high rank escaping from the Boche. Their route, I was startled to hear, ended at Cap d'Antibes where a submarine surfaced at certain specified times and the V.I.P.s were taken aboard for transport home. Fortunately Vallet had been free of company and papers when he was taken. It seems uncertain that the Italians knew how important and useful his work had been to the Allied cause. They flung him into the Villa Lynwood at Nice and there his experiences weighed on his mind to such an extent that he contemplated suicide. All this he told me and he added the words that bind us in friendship to this day:

'I was on the point of cutting a vein and killing myself when I looked at the wall of my cell and saw words that stayed my hand and brought me comfort, consolation and strength. I am no longer afraid. I'll never forget those words.'

He relapsed into silence for a moment and then slowly he quoted the text from Isaiah I had carved into the wall of the cell at the Villa Lynwood.

'I am Donald Caskie,' I told him, 'I wrote those words on that wall.'

He did not speak and both of us sat quietly. I looked at him and saw tears running down his face. He took my hands in his and then we ate our bread together and talked until we were exhausted. During the days that followed, my friendship with Vallet deepened by our exchange of common memories, opinions, ideas, hopes and fears. I had learned the worst of the prison at St Remo and although weeks of discomfort and starvation lay ahead of me I was not left alone again for more than a few days.

Vallet remained in the cell for about a week before his transfer to another camp. Some days passed and then I was joined by Pierrugues of the Brigade of St Jean. Pierrugues was an old soldier of the maquis who would have been at home in the Grand Armée of Napoleon. Soldiering was a trade to him. He would work out plans and maps in the dust on the floor and use the plates and pans on which our food and water were delivered as objects illustrating his themes. He had no doubt of victory. To this day he continues to be my friend, still the staunch lover of France.

He was a liaison officer of the underground; one of the men who distributed orders and intelligence to units scattered through France. When he first told me of his duties, he smiled a little crooked smile as he said:

'I was compelled to take Holy Orders, Monsieur Donald, to carry out my task. I got myself a cassock from the curé of our village, a good man who did not like his parishioners to go without clothing fitting to their day's work.'

Pierrugues' term of duty before his capture had been long. He worked for over two years without detection and his disguise as a priest was more than adequate. He could tour the villages without arousing anyone's suspicion. Late in the evening he would come to a village church, he told me, and install himself in a confessional apartment. There the local maquis lieutenant would meet him and receive his briefing.

'But, my friend,' I said, with a shudder. 'Supposing a true penitent came first. What did you do?'

The brown face broke into a broad grin. Prison pallor had not taken the sun out of Pierrugues' skin.

'Pasteur, Pasteur, it was simple. I merely said that he or she must see M. le Curé since I was using the "box" to shrive certain people who were all known to us. No one questioned my reply. No sacrilege was done and God forgave us, I am certain, when we used the Church as part of our plan, for He knows we did not invite the Boche to invade our country. Let the Germans get back where they belong and you will be able to return to your place in the pulpit and I to my job during the day, the café in the evening and my church on Sunday. That is where we belong.'

I learned much from Pierrugues and Vallet as I talked with them and the two men who followed them, Raphael and Ribout, a Jewish father and son who had fought tenaciously and relentlessly before they, like Pierrugues, were betrayed by the one Judas who occurs in a thousand patriots, on whose head may be laid the guilt of betraying hundreds.

Thin, wiry men, in appearance a curious blend of the purely Hebrew and the French townsman, they were strikingly alike, like an old and newer version of the same man. Radicals of an old, tough and honest kind, they knew nothing of their own religion. Their Jewishness and native good taste, I suspect, kept them from the excesses of anti-clericalism that have marred and distorted the Radical movement in France. Perturbed to find themselves gaoled with a *clerc,* not out of distaste for the cloth, but because to see one in prison affronted their very Gallic ideas of dignity, they soon engaged me in discussion of the Idea of God, the Jewish and Christian religions and the Churches in general. Their approach to these subjects began with inessentials, continued with the repetition of anti-clerical gossip and ended with rather inflated ideas of the advantages ' the revolution ' would bring to the poor. It was easy to dispose of their rather obvious assertion of the truism that all priests and pastors were not saints and the extraordinary deduction they made from this fact, that there is no God and consequently all churches are frauds perpetrated upon the simpletons of this life. I reminded them that all revolutionaries were not loyal. They were in gaol because of a traitor who certainly was anything but a priest. But what absorbed me most was taking them through the Bible and explaining the theological arguments upon which we base our faith. They would listen, question me, agree or disagree, argue and so our days passed. I began to feel almost at home in St Remo. When the morning came that I left I was sorry to say good-bye.

The brute-guard who brought us food opened the door of our dungeon and motioned me to get out. Raphael and Ribout had lightened the burden of my days. I think I had taught them something of my religion and their ancestral Judaism. They were good companions, those Jewish comrades, father and son and, like Good Samaritans, they gave comfort to at least one Christian. I grasped their hands and left them, so touched by their kindness that I did not know where I was until the guard led me into the cammandante's office.

Brusquely the Italian officer behind the large desk told me to stand up straight. I was weak and my sudden release, after months of incarceration in the dungeon, disconcerted me. My wits did not so much wander, as fly in all directions. What was going to happen now? The officer issued quick orders to an N.C.O. sitting at a smaller desk and this man went to the door and called in a middle-aged sergeant who snapped handcuffs on to my right wrist, leaving one cuff dangling at my side. An envelope was handed to him and he motioned me to the door. Outside in the courtyard I was helped into a truck and there the other cuff, with me attached, was locked on to a pallid young man who sat on the floor. The lorry moved out of the prison precincts and that was the last I saw of St Remo. I sat on the rumbling lorry and did not attempt to look back at the place. It was the worst prison I ever entered.

It was July, 1943. All round the world the armies of the free world were being marshalled. In Asia, Europe, from West to East, millions of people were slowly dying in camps. In peace-time this would have been the height of the season on the Mediterranean. The sun was high and the air from the sea was fresh in the truck. My companion was silent and the miles were quickly covered, past beaches, villas, casinos and wayfarers.

At last the young man chained to my wrist spoke to me. Another underground fighter, he was on his way to possible death and torture. I tried to comfort him until the road became familiar and I knew we were approaching the Villa Lynwood. I said good-bye to my travelling companion when we reached the sinister building. I prepared myself for the worst. In my cell I prayed for strength to face the morrow.

I was awakened early and without formality brought to the courtyard and placed on another truck. We drove off and Italy receded. I was being returned to France. The villa behind us, my heart lightened. It is good to go home and France is my home—even in chains. We reached Toulon and

I was handed over to a German corporal with another soldier in attendance. Both were very solemn in their attitude to the Italians and very 'regimental' in their attitude to me until we reached the station and I heard the older one mention Marseilles. He winked when he spoke and handed me a bundle of sandwiches.

'Prisoner's rations, sir,' he said. 'Hope they are up to Italian standards.'

When we settled down on our seats in a train compartment the corporal was smiling. Blandly he stuck a 'reserved' notice on the door. He leaned towards me and took my hands. The handcuff clicked and came off.

'We'll forget about these things in the meantime, Pastor,' he observed. 'So this is the way they treat the clergy in Italy. Now make yourself comfortable. You can feel at home with us. I go to church, your church I think. My name is Hans and that's what our pastor calls me.'

The square face, under a thinning thatch of hay-coloured hair with white streaks in it, broke into a wider grin and in my weakened condition I could have wept. It was a decent, working man's face. It would not have been out of place taking a parade of recruits at Maryhill Barracks at Glasgow, the Gordon Barracks at Brig o' Don or the Black Watch Barracks in Perth. I had helped many men who might have been his brothers to escape from Marseilles. Hans noticed that I was emotionally moved.

'Tell me, Pastor, are you English still singing that song —now, how does it go?' He had loosened the collar of his tunic; his legs in the jack-boots stretched out across the floor. In a raddled baritone he sang:

> 'We're going to hang out the washing on the
>   Siegfried line,
> Have you any dirty washing Mutti dear . . .?'

The heavenly choirs, if I am blessed to hear them sing will sing no sweeter than Hans sounded in my ears in that shabby compartment. I found myself joining in and when the chorus ended we laughed aloud, he, I and the solemn young soldier who was his comrade.

'Pastor, it looks as if they will hang out that washing before much time passes.'

Hans was looking at me very seriously. Throughout the journey to Marseilles he brought me up-to-date with news of the war and I was heartened. The tide of war was running our way. German soldiers, I learned, like the French civilians, were devoted listeners to the B.B.C. 'We are *kaput*, Pastor.' When we reached my old parish I was primed with encouraging information.

Outside the station Hans took me to a café and there he and his comrade ordered the best meal the place could provide and I ate it while we talked. Over coffee he said that I must prepare to be handcuffed again.

'It is our orders, Pastor, and it will not help you if we arrive at St Pierre without the bracelets.'

I held out my hands when the meal ended, thanked both men and received their good wishes. I parted from them in the orderly room of the Prison of St Pierre at Marseilles which was thronged with arriving prisoners. Part of a long queue, I stood in a corridor and listened for four hours as the others filed into a doorway beyond which lay an interrogation room. The door was never closed and my heart sank during those hours. The inquisitors were not gentle. They stormed at their prisoners. I heard the sound of blows being struck and men crying out in agony, and then I was pushed through that door.

CHAPTER SEVENTEEN

Holiday Camp

THE GESTAPO officer was tall, his uniform fitting sleekly to his slim, unbelted waist. The boots gleaming black. In his mouth he held a thin brown cheroot as he stood over the desk, scrutinising the papers which had been placed before him. About a dozen members of the corps stood around or sat on chairs. There was only one desk. All the subordinates wore gloves. A prisoner was hustled half-conscious from the room as I entered.

The officer found the papers interesting. He read very carefully, taking the cheroot from his mouth, absentmindedly picking a piece of tobacco from his lips with finely manicured hands. He was very handsome; the fair hair shampooed to a fluffiness, the long tanned face with that finished shaven look that only a valet can impart. On his wrist a gold watch shone, held in place by a thin tracery of gold threads woven into a strap. I stood for about five minutes waiting. He put the papers aside and motioned to a sergeant. A chair was placed behind me. I was told to sit down and the officer sat down also, laid his elbows on the desk top, bent his head forward, smiled in the most kindly way and burst into song:

> ' My heart's in the Highlands
> My heart is not here.
> My heart's in the Highlands
> A-chasing the deer.
> A-chasing the wild deer and following the roe,
> My heart's in the Highlands, wherever I go.'

Around the room the underlings sat up in their chairs, admiration on every face. I gazed stupidly, fearing at first that he was mad and then thinking this was one of the famous Gestapo novel approaches to torture. He continued until the ending:

> *'My heart's in the Highlands,*
> *Wherever I go. . . .'*

Applause broke through the room. He waved it down with a magnaminous hand.

'Alas, M. Caskie. I am saddened to see you here in this place. It grieves me to hold you under arrest. I have orders, but you will find that here in St Pierre you will receive treatment worthy of your position. But what do you think of my knowledge of your folksongs? You are surprised, I expect.'

'You are a very fine tenor, Herr Commandant,' I stammered, truthfully. 'And I know your people often have knowledge of our Scottish music. I have heard it sung, and sung it myself in Germany for friends, in happier times.'

'Ah, you have visited the Reich. But of course. All men of education know our country. Let me tell you I know England and Scotland well—very well, especially Clydebank and Coventry.'

He arose from his desk and began to pace up and down the room, blowing thin columns of smoke from his pursed lips. I could not forget the treatment I had heard meted out to my unfortunate French fellow-prisoners. I watched an interesting and uncommon type of monster.

'I, Pastor, am an engineer. I mentioned Coventry and Clydebank because they were some of the many places I visited just before September 1939 in England and Scotland. Coventry and Clydebank! Alas, so many fine engineering plants. Those machine-tool manufacturers. All gone, you know. Such a pity but it was necessary. The Luftwaffe is ruthless and it must be so. But I know all those former great centres of engineering. And now they are no more. I expect you knew the magnificent Clyde shipyards. Alas, you will never see them again. War is ruthless and we were forced to act. It grieved us, you know, and none more than the Fuehrer.'

The thought of the Clyde destroyed sickened me; I had no means of knowing that he lied or was a victim of Goebbels' lies. I remained silent, utterly sickened. He continued, diverting on to folk songs. His knowledge of the subject would have been remarkable in a Scotsman. Even I, a man with a lifetime of study in music, given to a great extent to the folk music of Scotland, had to keep my mind alert as he touched on aspects of the subject, traditional and contemporary. Burns set to music seemed to fascinate him. He quoted the lyrics, sang them, hummed Gaelic airs and obviously enjoyed himself. He stopped his singing abruptly.

'Alas, we must stop this interesting conversation, Pastor. I hope you will be comfortable here. I shudder to think what you must have endured in the hands of our vulgar Italian allies. Here you have nothing to fear. But I must warn you. Accept discipline. Do not attempt to escape. Keep to our orders and we will be kind. Good afternoon.'

The blue eyes contemplated me almost tenderly. It would hurt him to discipline me. A package was pushed across the table.

'Take this, Pastor. It is yours.'

As I followed two members of the corps to a cell, I opened the little parcel and inside found the cigarette case, Bible and other things commandeered by the Italians in Grenoble months earlier. In the cell a little shopkeeper from Toulon greeted me with a question about the commandant.

'He was polite,' I said. 'But isn't he a strange man? Before I was called into him I heard the sound of beatings and torture. They were treating the other prisoners like cattle. All he spoke of to me was music.'

The thickset figure was hunched on the floor, resting. The fleshy, red face suddenly emitted a spittle which shot across the cell.

'Music. Sale Boche. Music. He is the most cruel swine I have ever met. He kills by the centimetre and is polite as he does it. But they are vain, my friend. They are vain. He found in you an audience and tried to impress you. The flattery of the fools under his command he knows is worthless.

But you are a foreigner and a man of education. Besides, we will win the war and your people and the Americans will be here. He fears the French and thinks you British and the Yanks, who are sentimental, will protect his fancy skin.'

He helped me as he spoke to arrange the meagre bedding provided, which was clean, and I thought over his words. Later experience and conversations with other prisoners were to convince me that he was a good judge of the prison O.C.'s character. My first fears were reasonable. The dandy engineer was a professional torturer of skill, a man who gloried in the terrible trade. It was reasonable for him to fear the French; for they had vowed vengeance for the wrongs done to them, wrongs outside the experience and beyond the range of the imagination of the British and American forces which were commanded by humanitarian soldiers. Eisenhower, Montgomery, etc., represented a unique breed of officers to the Germans. But the O.C. kept his word in one important respect. After the Villa Lynwood and St Remo, St Pierre was like a holiday camp to me. There I met other prisoners at exercise in the prison courtyard, talked with them and exchanged ideas and opinions with a French pastor to whom I lent my Bible. I managed to throw a message over the wall into the garden of a man who had been a well-wisher of the organisation when we worked in the Rue Forbin.

I was worried about my mother. When I sent letters home to Islay from Grenoble I was always uncertain that they would reach their destination. For the past four months I had been gaoled and without contact of any kind with the Christian organisations which might have kept my family informed that I was alive, at least. Word of my arrest, I was certain, had been sent home and mother would fear the worst and perhaps, as time passed, come to believe I was dead. Adjacent to St Pierre there was a house and garden which, two years earlier, had been the property of a man known to Henri Thebault. I had a stub of pencil and just enough paper to wrap round a stone. We were not under surveillance all the time. I wrote the words: 'Inform mother I am safe and well, Donald,' addressed the paper to Henri and in the yard

wrapped it round the stone. Watching for an opportunit
I waited and then quickly flung the little object over the wa
towards the friendly house.

Throughout the next day I worried, feeling that I ha
taken a foolish risk, but as nearly a week passed and I wa
not challenged, I assumed that the paper had either bee
found or had now been washed or blown away from th
prison walls. The truth was that I had been extremely lucky
The paper was delivered to Henri Thebault and he wrot
to a colleague in his firm who was stationed in North Africa
This kindly man sent a message to a mythical personage h
described as Monsieur le Lord Maire de Bowmore, Islay
Ecosse, asking him to inform Madame Caskie that her sor
Donald, was alive and well in Marseilles. So by a strang
chance the message flung over the prison walls of St Pierr
in Marseilles was transmitted to an unknown friend in Casa
blanca, from there to the Highlands of Scotland and on
mother's worries were stilled.

My heart lifted in St Pierre for more than one reason
After the nightmare months in St Remo the companionship
of Christian men brought me back into something like norma
human society, even if we were gaoled. The Germans watche
us closely; but their very efficiency was protective after th
brutal medieval methods of the Italians. All was order and whil
the food was sparce it was clean and the sanitary arrangement
seemed luxurious. I was given the use of a razor and my fac
assumed its more normal clerical appearance. I sympathis
with my fellow-men who cultivate beards but when con
ditions force a man to grow hair on his face and at the sam
time forego washing, the consequences are not to be recom
mended.

Some days before I was removed in mid-August I received
food parcels, a consequence of my surreptitious correspondence
with Henri Thebault. They were addressed to me and ir
themselves were evidence that someone knew I was alive
I was to find out later that my friends had been unremitting
in their enquiries and unsuccessful. One lady, Mrs Schroeder
of Schroeder's Bank, London and Dunlossit Castle, Islay, hac
approached the Vatican Commission which did admirable

service on behalf of prisoners-of-war and their dependents and the Roman Catholic authorities in Rome set out to find me. But they met a blank wall. Donald Caskie was unknown to the Italian War Department. My message to Henri brought those parcels.

Henri's life had been difficult since my departure from Marseilles. His friendship with me had been a mixed blessing. It led to his arrest and then, by one of those odd ironies of life, his release by the Germans. They accused him of complicity with a British agent, the notorious Donald Caskie. Under interrogation he denied this and insisted that he knew Donald Caskie only as a clergyman of his religion. His association with him was slight in Marseilles. It stemmed from a closer friendship formed before the war. In support of this statement he produced my wedding gift to himself and his wife, the Bible I gave them when I married them in the Scottish Kirk on the Rue Bayard, Paris. The Germans accepted this explanation of his crime in knowing me and Henri was released.

Cheerfully I distributed the contents of the parcels delivered to me by the German guards and the cigarettes, tins of food, magazines and soap were accepted by my fellow alumni of St Pierre. I felt happier when I was taken under guard to a railway station in Marseilles for despatch to the prison of Fresnes on the southern outskirts of Paris.

The train journey was long and, I suppose, hazardous, but to a Scot abroad in time of war the danger was invigorating. The Allied air forces were, almost literally, making hay of the French railway system. For days we were diverted, shunted, held up for hours. Although I encountered no raids on the way, I was told all about them for I had company, the nicest kind of companions, poor soldiers, Germans who had been ' crimed ' and were travelling under light escort to the Reich's equivalent of our ' glass-house.'

My own guards, the customary corporal and one other rank, were easy-going old soldiers, if not so talkative as Hans and his companion of my journey from Toulon. We settled comfortably into our compartment and when, a few moments after the train moved, a young soldier put his head through

the door and asked if he and his fellow-travellers might joi
us, the corporal agreed. I was, he observed, a chaplain an
could do only good to the criminals in the next compartmen

There were about six of them nondescript, happy, nea
scruffy, talkative and silent, a pretty ordinary lot of recruit
They tumbled beside us singing, their guards standing bac
in the corridor laughing at them. Their crimes too were un
original. Some had been caught 'flogging' stores to civilians
others had been drunk; another had taken French leav
which in the German Army I gathered savours of high treaso
and one, more original in his misdemeanours, if entirel
normal in other ways, had been old-fashioned enough to fa
in love with an English girl. The latter apparently was
faithful swain and he took up arms against his lady's peopl
with reluctance. Instead of cherishing a marshal's baton i
his knapsack he kept Sally's image on a snapshot taken whe
she was on holiday in the Reich in 1938. As the war progresse
his attachment to her deepened. It infected his attitude t
her people to such an extent that his affection for the Fuehre
waned. Fortunately this had led him no further than expressin
his scepticism of certain propaganda reports on the German
war effort which were being addressed to his unit. He had tol
an N.C.O. that he found them hard to swallow and he was o
his way to the place where his type was disciplined. From hi
companions I gathered that his scepticism, if specially inspired
was now the general condition of the Wehrmacht.

The six prisoners, their guards and mine, I learned ha
accepted defeat. The invasion of the Reich they expecte
would come within one year. Hamburg had been destroyed,
was told, and the British and U.S. Air Forces were devastating
German war factories. The Italians had collapsed. Germany
was at the end of its tether—'kaput'—and still new armie
were massing against her. They and all their comrades knew
that victory was a dream which would not be fulfilled. The
Fuehrer went in terror of his life and only the most fanatica
members of the 'party' believed he could save the country
I listened and felt happy. Whatever lay ahead of me I knew
that the efforts of every man who had died in 1940 and those
who lived to fight on had not been in vain. The dead ones

who gave their lives and the traitors' victims were justified. In that noisy compartment surrounded by happy prisoners I rejoiced and sent up grateful prayers. Through nights when we lay in sidings and moved cautiously along side-lines I sat awake feeling exalted.

We sang together during the hours of daylight and shared our rations. I did not want for cigarettes on that journey. The young soldiers, I learned, longed for defeat. Years of inactivity had killed the illusory zeal for soldiering instilled in them by the Nazi propaganda machine. The facts of Germany's devastation could not be hidden from them. I parted from my German friends when we reached Paris and came to Fresnes in good spirits, my hopes aroused by their information of the Allied victories and their prophecies of future defeat for their country. Nearly four years had passed since I locked the church in the Rue Bayard and left the manse in the Rue Piccini. Even in handcuffs it was good to be back so close to my parish.

The Prison of Fresnes lies about five miles south of the centre of the capital. Fifty years ago the ground on which it stands was a pleasant place of rolling green fields marked off by tall chestnut trees, their colours changing with the seasons, their tones as subtle as music. The young Impressionists must have found inspiration there. One can imagine them on their picnics and week-end excursions, visualising the masterpieces they painted and which now are treasured throughout the civilised world. The fields on which the *maison de correction* is built are not far away from the main road. Often they have been invaded by the rollicking trippers from the Left Bank. Today they offer a grim and forbidding aspect to the passer-by.

Fresnes is the biggest and most spacious prison in Europe. Much younger than St Remo its history, in its time, has been sorrowful. In its half-century of existence hundreds of thousands of men and women have been incarcerated within its walls. There have been hundreds of suicides in its cells. Fresnes was one of the first places commandeered by the German S.S., after their triumphal march down the Avenue des Champs Elysées and under their command the dark and dismal building became still more dark and more dismal. Most of the British residents in the city were rounded-up, arrested and brought to this gaol before being taken to the Caserne de St Denis, north-east of Paris, for internment. I, being a criminal, was brought to Fresnes.

I was exhausted when I lay down in my cell that evening, travel-sore and hungry, dispirited by recollections of the stories I had heard of the *maison de correction* and apprehensive of the morrow. There was a dreadful silence in the great building, I yearned for company, and it came to me from an adjoining cell occupied by someone who was, I assume, for I never met him, Scottish. He began to sing and I listened:

> *'Maxwellton's braes are bonnie*
> *Where early fa's the dew*
> *And it's there that Annie Laurie*
> *Gave me her promise true.'*

The familiar words were clear in the silence and they filled my heart with solace. In a measured, cheerful way he sang the ballad right through and then began again. I joined in with him. We sang it to the last note and were silent and then, with a joyful note of irony, I heard him begin:

> *'Should Auld Acquaintance*
> *Be forgot*
> *And never brought to mind*
> *Should Auld Acquaintance be forgot*
> *For the days of Auld Lang Syne. . . .'*

The duet continued and again we sang the song twice, were silent for a few moments, and my unknown companion closed the recital with the National Anthem to which I stood to attention and added my quota.

We slept on straw in Fresnes. The floors were stone. Before I rested that first night I thought of Luke's story in the Acts of the Apostles relating how Paul and Silas imprisoned in Philippi sang together in a cell and the other prisoners hearing them felt happier. I was the prisoner in the cell. I thanked

my Master for the ministry of song and praise. My spirits rose
slightly and I slept soundly.

The tramp of jack-boots through the corridors wakened me
one day at 5 a.m. and the roaring voices of the S.S. sergeants:

'Raus! Raus!'

My eyes still filled with sleep I forced myself to the alert.
They passed my door and I did not see anyone until a guard
brought bread and water. He did not speak when he entered.
Plates were put on the floor. The days of solitary confinement
were over and I received cell-mates but I returned to my St
Remo meditations, relying on my Bible and my past life to
further populate my cell. I had become a gaolbird-contem-
plative. When at last I was taken to exercise I was steady on
my feet. My spirit, I am grateful to write, was serene in that
dreadful place.

Fresnes was not, like the Villa Lynwood, a house of torture,
nor like St Remo a place where men and women were left
to rot. It was a slaughter-house. It was crammed with Gaullists,
maquis of all colours and the perpetual victims of the Nazis,
Jews.

At five o'clock each morning the silence of the great gaol
was broken by those shouts I had heard on my first awakening
and the thud of the jack-boots. It was part of the S.S. routine
of death. Paris is a free city, and the tyrants devised a system
for keeping it at bay while they prepared to kill the free
world. In 1943-44 when they were fighting off the friends of
France they applied their system ruthlessly. They took a
batch of ten men from each district and imprisoned them.
If any German was attacked in the area from which these
men were taken the hostages were shot out of hand. There
were no trials and vengeance was taken on the innocent for
the actions of the men who fought to liberate them. They were
freedom's scapegoats.

My remaining physical strength began to ebb away in
Fresnes and though my spirit remained serene I think I came
to accept death as inevitable. I knew that our armies would
be victorious but I thought that we in the *maison de correction*
would be butchered before the S.S. took flight. I ate my meagre
food and prayed and lived apart. Under the tuition of my cell-

mates I learned how to use the prisoners' grape-vine, to tap out messages on my walls and receive them from the inmates of nearby cells. It was always the same report we received, death, death, death, and always the innocent.

One evening, it must have been late in November, there was silence in the next cell—the answering taps did not come —and when morning came I heard a slight commotion in the corridor. That evening the grape-vine told me of a suicide. Our neighbour, a young maquis, had killed himself. He was a daring youth who had been caught setting a fuse which led to a mine under a railway line a few minutes before a German troop train was due. Taken by the Gestapo, he was sentenced to death. They brought him to Fresnes and held him there for a few weeks. The thought of death at their hands had unnerved him, but I did not know he had a razor-blade smuggled into the gaol in the front seam of his shirt. As we tapped on his wall that last night he was cutting the veins on his wrists. His blood was seeping over the cell floor.

I prayed for him and when they came for me on November 26th at the customary hour, I was ready.

'Pastor Donald Caskie?'

'Ja.'

'Folgenden.'

I followed them down the corridor and waited while they brought me a companion from another cell. He was a thin-faced, very young man, stricken with fear and trembling. We were led out and ordered into a Black Maria.

'They're going to shoot you, Monsieur?'

'I do not know,' I answered. 'We must be of good heart and pray. All will be well with us. We have done no evil and war was forced on our people.'

'They have told me I shall die today, Monsieur. Pray with me.'

I had come to the end of hope that morning. I was resigned to death. He spoke of his wife and children. They were young and my heart ached for him and that girl and those babies. When the van stopped, he tried to leave it ahead of me but the guard motioned him back.

'Not you. The pastor dismounts here. You are for the

Rue des Saussaies, Pastor. The other one is for Mt Valerien!'

'May I say good-bye to him?'

'You have two minutes.'

The pale face turned to me blankly. It was deadened by despair. I put my hands on his shoulders and spoke to him, telling him that his children would be safe and soon the Allies would be here and peace would come. His children would be protected. Tears streamed down his cheeks. I told him to remember the One who died on the Cross for love of him and for his children.

'He is with you now, mon cher. It is He who has brought us together this morning. He has sent me to tell you this. You die in His company. You are secure in His care, and you must pray for all of us who remain.'

The young face was serene and at peace before he took my hand and I jumped from the Black Maria. The door closed and the engine started. I knew my own destination now. The Court of the Gestapo, in a building in the Rue des Saussaies, was strangely enough a few hundred yards from the British Embassy in Paris.

CHAPTER EIGHTEEN

The Rue des Saussaies

A CLOCK HUNG on the wall over the long table where the judges sat. It was eight o'clock to the minute. I was marched to a chair opposite the table and told to face the court. There was no other furniture in the room which was big, oblong in shape, with low ceilings, the walls painted a drab colour. The place was bleakly institutional. My judges gazed at me without interest.

There were a dozen of them, ten men and two women. The latter were blonde, heavy-faced German types, one seemed about forty years of age, the other a little older. The younger woman had a strong jaw, a good forehead, thin mouth and cold hard eyes. Her colleague peered out of shrewd, vicious eyes, blue and small. The mouth was curiously curving as if ready to spit. The men were strong and brutish, thick-set in their uniforms, on first glance seeming exactly alike in physical appearance. The President was thin and tall, his face and eyes oddly bright. A bundle of documents lay on the table. These were carefully separated and passed from hand to hand. The silence in the room was broken by the ticking of the clock which seemed to grow louder as the seconds passed. In a leisurely way they read the papers. One of the men achieved identity by turning his eyes towards me with a blank stare and adjusting gold-rimmed glasses as he read. About ten minutes passed and an awful tiredness began to fill my veins. Suddenly an apoplectically red face turned to me and barked words.

'Your name is Donald Caskie. You are English.'

'I am British, by nationality Scottish.'

My interrogator waved a grey-gloved hand. I remember wondering: why do they always wear gloves? Answering the question in my head, I thought, they want to keep their hands clean, and I formed a picture in my mind of Pilate to meditate upon.

'You are a civilian, a clergyman.'

'I am a minister of the Church of Scotland, formerly incumbent of the Scottish Kirk in the Rue Bayard in this city. In recent years I have ministered to my own folk in various parts of France.'

'You are a spy, agitator, agent for escaping soldiers, prisoners-of-war, and friendly disposed towards that hated race the Jews.'

The last accusation brought me out of my exhaustion.

'May I ask you to be a little more explicit,' I said.

'You are an ally of the Jews. You are their friend. We have the evidence.'

Anger drained out of me, and my tiredness went with it. The classical Nazi accusation had been brought. I had committed their favourite crime. I smiled and knew that there was now no hope. I was quite prepared for death and I wished only that it would be soon.

'I do not know what you mean by being an ally of the

Jewish people, sir,' I answered. 'So far as I know they are at war with no one. But then I have been in gaol awaiting some sort of trial for many many months. If you mean I have Jewish friends, of course I have. Every civilised man in Europe has friends among the Jewish people. Are we all going to be tried for our friendships?'

'You have aided Jews against the Reich.'

'I have aided Jews because they are human beings and because of your country's policy they are in need of help. But I never have aided them *against* anyone!'

My questioner leaned back in his chair and spoke in German to his colleagues. The trial was in French and I had noticed bewilderment on most of the faces lined up across from me while I spoke. In my years in France I have become as close to a native speaker of the language as any man who is not a native can come and I love the French tongue. In friendlier atmospheres I had used it as an instrument of debate. Debate is a Franco-British sport. It had no place in the *kultur* of the Third Reich.

As the day progressed I knew that much of the meaning of what I said was lost on the verbal butchers I confronted. My German was not as good as my French and their private conversations eluded me. Voices were dropped. Accents were varied. Deliveries were quick between them and they deliberately excluded me from their colloquies.

The President spoke:

'You deny being a corrupter of youth! Did you not conduct systematic agitation among the students at Grenoble during your term at the University? Did you not infuriate them against the Reich, abusing the hospitality of the professors?'

'I taught the students to make tea,' I answered. 'And I instructed them in English literature. If you wish to know my methods, they were simple. I chose good books, masterpieces of the English written word that I knew would appeal to young people and lead them to more complex works.'

While I spoke one of the men was watching me closely, his pasty face flushing.

'You lie.' The voice was screaming.

' I am telling the truth.'

Another voice ripped out of the silence. It was one of the blonde women, the older one.

' You deluded the professors at Grenoble who gave you hospitality because they are fools. You organised the students into bands of murderers.'

She was a hard, merciless creature. The little eyes screwed themselves back in the blotched face.

' This accusation would be silly if it were not wicked,' I answered. ' I ask you to bring one person from Grenoble who will support this hotch-potch of charges. What sort of court is this?'

' Be silent.'

A man at the extreme right of the table shouted at me. The papers were assembled before the President and the *sotto voce* Teutonic deliberations began again. About fifteen minutes passed and then the interrogation, mostly by assertion began. It continued until eleven o'clock, with questions and accusations being fired from all parts of the table. The most vicious of the pack were the women. Their hatred was terrifying. Some years later I was to see those faces again in a news photograph. According to the picture they were being tried as two of the Belsen murderers. That morning they were my judges and from minute to minute and hour to hour hounded me with their poisoned, irrational charges until the big hand on the clock touched twelve. Then the R.A.F. gave me a respite. Across Paris the air-raid warnings sang their moaning song. My judges stood quickly to their feet. Without a word they left the room and I heard the lock on the door click behind them. I stretched my legs and waited, feeling ridiculously elated. ' The good old R.A.F. is on the job,' I said aloud, and waited for explosions praying that a bomb would fall on this place. For about twenty minutes I was left alone, pacing in the silence, waiting. And then the ' all clear ' sounded and I sat down.

They entered again, talking angrily among themselves. The visitors from across the Channel had not amused them. The younger woman reopened the inquisition. With something

of the air of a schoolmistress giving a good impression of
Judge Jeffries, she began:

'You consorted with the notorious spy Picault. You met
him in a café in Marseilles on December 18th, 1940. The
following night a dozen British spies escaped across the mountains to Spain.'

'I do not remember what happened on the date you mention.
I know Picault but was not aware that he was a spy or notorious, I have never met a dozen spies in my life nor consciously seen so many, outside a moving picture.'

'You lie.'

The lady's method of cross-examination was simple. It left
no opportunity for discussion. A charge was delivered with
cold, arrogant deliberation. The answer was heard impassively.
The subject was closed with the phrase, 'You lie.'

I watched the clock move around as I sat there under the
endless barrage of questions. Its round white face seemed the
only contact with the realities outside the courtroom. When
the clock was tinkling out the stroke of the hour, I heard the
President give an order to one of the men who rose from his
place, went to a side door which he opened and I found
myself for a moment gazing into the face of Pierre, a guide
used during my days in the Rue Forbin in Marseilles. Briskly
he stepped into the room and took up a place before the table,
keeping his face averted.

One of the women stood up and pointed to me.

'Do you identify this man as Donald Caskie, a clergyman
who abused his status to act as an agent for the British?'

He glanced at me unsteadily and I tried to look into his
eyes. They flickered over my face avoiding any communication
with the man behind it.

'Yes. This is Pasteur Caskie. He was in charge of a mission
which was a centre of English spying.'

The President directed ferret eyes towards me.

'Do you know this man, Caskie?'

'I know him?' I answered. 'I should think I do know
him. Even before I suspected him of being what he has now
proved himself to be—a double agent—I regret to say I

associated him in my mind with Judas Iscariot. His purse was his god. His every word and action sought to magnify it alone. He had no other aim in life. May I continue?'

Ferret Face nodded.

'He is the first witness brought into this court against me. I suggest he is hardly one that will assist you to be just. In all our dealings he asserted he was pro-British, not pro-French—although he is, in his strange way, a Frenchman. Perhaps his purse predominated over his patriotism. Perhaps he thought the British paid better. He swore allegiance to us and he used to say—I remember the words exactly —he would give his right arm to get the "sale Boche" out of France. You may agree that he is a most interesting witness. Someday he may give evidence against you. He is a professional.'

The President spluttered a mouthful of German oaths as I finished. He brought his fists down with a thump on the table-top, and shouted at Pierre.

'Tell us what you know of the prisoner.'

I forgot the clock as he spoke. His hands grasped the lapels of his heavy jacket and he shuffled his feet. The voice was eager, so quick that he had to be halted from time to time. The accent was rural and some members of the court, I am sure, could not understand more than a few words. But to the Germans he was a faithful servant; I found myself thinking he told a convincing tale.

In detail he explained my methods of despatching parties. One description of how seven lads had been despatched soon after Christmas 1941 aroused moving memories in me, emotion not unmixed with amusement that Judas should touch the heart of his victim while betraying him. He knew, he observed at one point, that I was a British Intelligence officer.

'How do you know?'

Pierre halted and looked around the room in a puzzled way. The tale had been interrupted, something disconcerting to any artist. He began again.

'Yes,' he said. 'Sir Samuel Hoare told me. Sir Samuel is the biggest Englishman in Spain.'

'Sir Samuel Hoare,' the President observed, 'is British Am-

bassador to Spain, as you say the biggest, most important
Englishman there. What did he say to you?'

'I am a guide, Monsieur. And I was told that Sir Samuel
Hoare would help me to find work. I went to him in Madrid.
He told me if I wished to work for the British Intelligence
in France I must go to Monsieur Caskie, the Scottish pastor
in the Seamen's Mission in the Rue Forbin in Marseilles.
Monsieur Caskie would put me into contact with agents who
would employ me.'

The younger woman took over his interrogation. Waspishly
she interrupted each time he strayed from what she con-
ceived to be the point while he expanded his recollections
of my espionage, all of which were pure invention, based
upon the conjectures of a naturally suspicious man of little
education. His stories of the escaping parties were substan-
tially true. The fables he invented about espionage were nonsense and the Germans must have been able to see them
as they were. But he rambled on. He was in court for forty-
five minutes when he was suddenly halted and told to leave
the court. Pierre bowed and let himself out of the room
closing the door very quietly behind him. He did not look at
me.

'You *are* a spy.' The words were roared by the older
woman.

I denied this and the cross-examination began again and
so it continued until the clock registered 2 p.m., when the
court came to a stop like a machine. A fresh-complexioned
member of the junta had begun to harangue me about my
elaborately fancied plots with Jewish monsters, wholly of his
own or some other fabulist's imagining, when suddenly, in-
conclusively, he halted, looked along the table, reached down
to the floor and produced a leather brief-case. His comrades
followed his example and then, *en masse,* they stood up and
solemnly left the room. Again the lock clicked and I was
left pondering this enigmatic exit. It had all taken place so
mechanically that nearly fifteen minutes passed before I realised
they had gone off for something as human as luncheon.

Waiting for food to be brought to me, I patrolled the room
again but I heard nothing until three-thirty when the court

filed in again, this time talking more loudly among themselves, but of matters that did not concern me. French cooking, I was interested to learn, did not agree with one of them and I regretted that he lacked my experience of German and Italian fare.

Throughout the morning they had smoked, cigarettes and cigars, and I, a moderately heavy addict of that amiable vice, occasionally yearned towards the fumes that filled the room. After lunch some chain-smoked, lighting one cigarette after another until the place was rancid with the fumes of nicotine. Now they moved around the court and their questions came at me from all angles, sometimes three of them shouting from different corners with the women interjecting while I tried to listen. They had lists of agents' names and I was glad that I had told my contacts to keep their names from me. I became dizzy as the light faded and although I felt no hunger became light-headed. But still I stuck to my defence.

'I have committed no crime. I have done what any patriotic man would have done in my place. Would a German have abandoned his fellow-countrymen? Your single witness is a knave, a double agent, a professional betrayer. I am a Scot. Would you have me abandon my people?'

'Where did you get the money to run your spy organisation in Marseilles. Did the Americans not help you?'

It was the young virago who spoke. That flat, metallic voice began another story, into which she mingled some facts of my friendship with McFarlane, the American Consul. A black-out screen was placed over the window. The voice continued in its clipped way. Now she spoke more in German than in French and the mongrel monologue filled my ears until the scene confronting me became dreamlike. And then there was silence for a time and I looked about me. The room was empty. The clock showed me that it was a few minutes past five forty-five.

I slumped in the chair, turning myself to rest my head on an arm propped on the chair-back. I was exhausted, the day was ending and I yearned for my own people far away at the blessed hour when they were returning to their homes.

Sweet memories filled my mind in the courtroom and my mind filled with prayer:

> *Be it granted to me to behold you again*
> > *dying*
> *Hills of home! and to hear again the call;*
> *Hear about the graves of the martyrs the*
> > *peewees crying*
> *And hear no more at all.*

The plea of the gentle R. L. Stevenson who died so far away from the land we love was in my heart and in that place of evil farce I forgot my judges. I was prepared to accept my fate whatever that might be. I knew that the whole Nazi conception was doomed. Our God, loving and kind, was watching and His children were safe in His hands. My comrade of the morning journey was dead at Mount Valerien by this time and God's love was being lavished on him. It would be thus with me and with his other children too when their time came. At six-thirty when the court returned, I faced them with pity in my heart.

The young woman began her rambling story of my complicity with the Americans in Marseilles. Now she was refreshed and used little German. I listened. At seven o'clock she sat down and the court conferred. The colloquies were carried on very quietly, in whispers, with intervals during which the members consulted their notes. A half-hour and more passed and the clock was moving away from half-past seven when the President stood up. The ferret face was composed and his words were enunciated with legal precision.

'Have you anything to say for yourself?'

Placing my hands on the sides of the chair I pushed myself to my feet and I think I swayed. I was very tired and hungry. I moved behind the chair and held it tightly to steady myself. A dozen pairs of eyes were turned in my direction.

'Yes,' I said. 'I have one thing to say. Before God I have only done what any true man would do for his country.'

They waited, but I had nothing to add to my statement and

I sat down. The President placed his hands flat on the table
before him and spoke.

'Guilty.'

The words came quietly. He looked along the table to
his right and then to his left. He raised a hand and his fellow-
judges in a rambling way chorused their agreement.

'Guilty.'

He got to his feet.

'The court finds you guilty, Caskie.'

I nodded my head and they began to file out. Within
a few seconds I was alone. It was seven forty-five. The room
was cold now and the light went out. I sat in black darkness
at peace and waited until there was a click from a switch.
The light blinded me as it struck across the room. Two
guards beckoned at the door. I gazed at the clock before I
stood up. The time was eight-three. For more than twelve
hours I had been in court. I was guilty. They had omitted
to tell me what the sentence would be.

Sleet was falling on Paris and my face was wet when I
entered the Black Maria to be driven back to Fresnes. In
my cell I slept heavily. After the five o'clock rally for the
firing squad passed my cell I lay down to sleep again. But
one of my cell-mates wakened me. I learned that it had been
presumed in the gaol that I was dead, shot the previous morning at Mount Valerien.

Carefully, slowly, I gave them my news.

'I was taken to a Gestapo court and tried and found guilty.'

Lying on straw I waited and my neighbour answered.

'What are they going to do with you? Are you to be sent
to Germany?'

'I do not know. They did not say anything about punishment. I think it will be death.'

'It is to be expected.'

It was to be expected, always, and during the morning I
prepared myself for its coming. When the guard brought
me my food I spoke to him. Little time, I felt, was left to
me and I did not wish to die without speaking with another
minister.

'Please tell the commandant that I wish to see a pastor.'

The man looked surprised.

'A pastor?'

'Yes. I am, as you know, a man of religion and I wish to confer before I die, with a pastor.'

I could see that he was puzzled. He scratched his head and then shrugged his shoulders.

'Oh, well I'll tell them.'

When he left me I dipped the bread in water and began to suck it, feeling despondent. It seemed unlikely that my request would be granted. The guard seemed to think it improbable. But finally it saved my life.

Next morning the cell door opened and a gentle little man in the uniform of a German chaplain entered and bowed.

'My name,' he said, 'is Peters, Hans Peters. I have come at your request.'

'Hans Peters?' My memory stirred. The name was familiar. 'But surely, I have heard of you—many a time,' I said.

He took my right hand and smiled.

'I think that is likely,' he answered, 'for we are ministers and I have heard of you, Herr Caskie, very many times. But perhaps our dear friend, Herr Lamb, is the strongest link between us.'

When he mentioned Lamb's name I recollected all I knew of him. Before the war they had been friends in Nice where Peters served the Lutheran community. Later this German had been a pastor in Paris, at the German church in the Rue Blanche.

'Herr Lamb is one of my strongest friends,' he said. 'Alas, this wicked war which involves us men of God. When first I came to Nice, life was very difficult for me. We Germans had no church and I had to wait very long for accommodation of our own. Do you know, Herr Caskie, I should not have had a place to gather our people but for our friend Herr Lamb?'

The earnest grey eyes gazed into mine and I forgot that I was in a death cell in Fresnes. We were two ministers talking of church affairs.

'No. I was not aware that Mr Lamb had helped you, but it does not surprise me. After all, we are Christians.'

'That is true. But I was desperately worried and he saved me much trouble. He gave me the use of his church, the Church of Scotland in Nice. Yes, he placed the building at my disposal and we never wanted a place in which to hold our services.'

'I think,' I told him, 'you would have done the same thing in his place. I know I should not have hesitated.'

He got to his feet and walked across the cell away from me, turned quickly and we stood face to face.

'I know what you would have done, Herr Caskie. To me you might be the Rev. Lamb, here in this cell. What can I do for you? You are in a dreadful place and, I fear, you have yet to learn the worst.'

'It is death?' I said.

'So you know? I shall do all in my power to save you. But we pastors have no power in the Reich today. I shall try with all my strength. I promise it.'

'Will you give me the sacrament, now, Helmut?'

He stood over me and patted my shoulder, his hand falling very gently.

'Yes, Donald, and you must pray while I prepare.'

He went to the door and called a guard and gave him quick orders. He then placed a little wooden cross on the table. He was a Lutheran. Carefully he adjusted the cross in the table's centre, intent upon his task and then with a start he picked it up in his hands.

'I am sorry, Donald. You are of the Reformed Faith. Forgive me. You are unaccustomed to having the cross when you take Communion.'

'Please leave it on the table,' I replied. 'It is the symbol of our common faith.'

With wonderful tenderness he raised his hands and looked at me, a long, gravely gentle look on his face.

'Ah, yes. There are opposing camps and God has placed us, one in each, but the link that binds us, my dear friend, is closer than the tie my nation has on me or yours on you. The cross indeed is the symbol of our common faith.'

The words were infinitely consoling.

'Neither death nor life,' he continued, 'nor principalities

nor powers nor things present nor things to come shall be able to separate us from the Love of God which is in Christ Jesus our Lord.'

With wonderful reverence he conducted the service and gave me the sacrament. Afterwards he left me, promising to return soon and to spare no efforts for a reprieve. I had little faith that he would succeed. But Helmut had strengthened my faith in the more important life. He left me sustained and greatly comforted.

CHAPTER NINETEEN

Silent Bells Ring Out

THE DEATH SENTENCE had been confirmed said Helmut Peters at our next meeting. I must expect to be ordered to the place of execution at any time but Peters had applied for permission to put forward a plea of reprieve. I remained undisturbed for some days when Helmut went to Germany on leave and there he carried the case to Berlin, emphasising that I was a clergyman and that the evidence against me had been largely based upon the testimony of a double-agent, a man who betrayed the Germans with the British and the British with the Gestapo.

How Helmut's plea would have worked out a year earlier it is difficult to say. In 1943 it had the effect of the Berlin authorities sending to Paris for my dossier. I heard that the dossier had been lost. The most likely explanation for its disappearance, I believe, is that it was delivered when the Berlin Gestapo was in process of being reorganised by the butchers who took revenge on Hitler's own minions after the attempt on his life. It is a fact that the Nazi officials who were handling my case disappeared after the unsuccessful assassination plan and were not heard of again.

For about six weeks after the trial I remained in Fresnes, at first anticipating the death call every morning and then as Christmas 1943 approached hoping that there might still be a chance of life for me. Helmut delivered parcels to me and life was easier. News filtered into the prison and passed along the corridors that the Western Allies were ready to leap into France and before the New Year ended the country would again be a battleground. The maquis were organised, planting men and arms in places where the Germans, now on the defensive, could be harried when their retreat began. Hope strengthened and began to warm even despairing hearts. But still the death squads came at 5 a.m. Still new prisoners arrived in batches. Still my neighbours were dragged away to the place of execution. I would pray for them, and with my cell-mates face another day.

Relief came on January 7th, 1944, when the last entry was made on my *carte d'identité*. The death sentence was lifted. That day I was taken to the Caserne St Denis and my future seemed to be assured. I suppose the gateway to St Denis and the barbed wire that enclosed the camp would have looked grim two years earlier. But I never shall forget the unutterable joy that filled my heart when I came to that place which housed over two thousand of my compatriots whose only punishment was to wait and pray for the tramp of friendly feet through the streets of Paris and the sight of the fleeing enemy.

It was like heaven after the black months that lay behind me. I was a prisoner, but no longer a felon. Around me were friends. We had a concert hall, a cinema and, above all, a church. I became again Padre Caskie and divine service was the blessed anchorage around which the routine of my life revolved. Red Cross parcels brought us food, tobacco and books.

The church apart, the greatest satisfaction of my new life came from the knowledge that once every two weeks I was allowed to send a card to my parents to whom I had not been allowed to write for years and who had not heard of me since the friend in Casablanca contacted His Mythical Worship the Lord Mayor of Bowmore. When word came that my cards had been received I was transported to a seventh heaven of happiness. All seemed well when I knew that my mother's prayers, which had sustained me, had been answered and that she too could look forward to our country's victory knowing that it would bring her son home from the wars.

After Fresnes, St Denis brought me the feeling of being resurrected. The place was alive. Men were intensely aware of the outside world and news poured into our enclosure. Naturally, radios were forbidden. Naturally men made radios out of parts smuggled into the place. One was the property of Major Horsford, the extremely capable and versatile medical officer, who to his professional skill wedded a bedside manner that would have given a lunatic the confidence and poise necessary to pass the Bar examination. The major kept his radio secreted in his medical supplies and through this channel came a steady service of Allied news to St Denis. It was amusing and consoling to hear the inmates of my room in the caserne discuss the latest intelligence from the B.B.C., with all the confidence and almost sporting interest of a group of men in a St James's Street club, amusing and consoling. Major Horsford was not the only 'B.B.C.' reporter in the camp. There was a radio, I know, secreted somewhere near the Sanctuary. The great thing about St Denis was that it was a civilised community. A man can be very happy in a barracks surrounded by true comrades.

There were inconveniences. One could hear them. Indeed, they only emphasised the differences between the caserne and Nice, St Remo, Marseilles, Fresnes and that first caserne at Grenoble. There were the radio raids, aiming to find our sets. From the German viewpoint the raids proved useless. They did not find anything. There was the routine of prison life and its inconveniences but I was alive again and living with British men. I found myself planning services, meditating on the conditions I would face when I was free and making my way to the Rue Bayard. I joyfully saw myself setting out on Sunday mornings back to our dear church and those friends I had left nearly four years ago.

There were talks with other clergymen in the caserne and these gently brought me back into the mainstream of life. Scholarly White Fathers of the Roman Catholic Church in France who had ministered to the maquis were among my comrades in gaol. We talked on the common points and the differences we held. And Helmut Peters kept in close contact with me.

He had believed, he told me, in the early days of Nazism that Hitler was truly the saviour of the German people and he, Helmut, a German patriot, had given him his support. He was not a Nazi. Indeed, like many German Christians, and not a few of our own people, he was profoundly ignorant of the realities of Nazism. The Reich had been in a chaotic condition, politically, socially and legally. There were riots, unemployment and moral degeneration. The Fuehrer had brought order, he believed. It was only later that the dreadful truth of the nature of the New Order penetrated his consciousness. Helmut Peters was, and is, a man of God, married, with a good wife and a large family, a pastor who saw his flock as a part of God's family to which he was a religious foster-father. The horror of the world that Nazism had imposed upon God's creation wounded him and he turned to his religion for consolation. The cross became the symbol of his life, and his faith his sole driving power.

Easter 1944 came and with it a card from my German ally on which the Risen Christ was shown still crucified and a message written to me his 'brother under God.' I cherish that card. It is still in my possession—a link with the friend who is now incumbent of a poor parish near Hanover where his lot was lightened during Germany's hungry post-war years by allied soldiers who, sent by the padre Donald Caskie of the church in the Rue Bayard, left him supplies for his family and flock.

Easter passed. Spring ripened into summer. In June the caserne was illuminated by joyful news that sent us into a riot of happy talk that was not to be surpassed even on the day of liberation. The Allied Armies had landed in Normandy.

I had just conducted early morning service in the chapel which was on the top story of the building. About sixty men were present. The singing had been especially lusty. Afterwards I chatted with each of them, listened to the customary stories of what had happened the previous day, the jokes, the hopes, the anticipations of what might happen any day now

and eventually found myself alone and free to go downstairs
and prepare another sermon.

I was descending the stairs when I found myself facing
Major Horsford who had achieved the broadest smile I ever
saw on his face or any other.

'Padre,' he said. 'The great day has arrived.'

'What do you mean, Major?' I answered, my mind far
away.

'I mean that the great day for which we all have been
praying has come. This morning the Allies made a landing on
the beaches of Normandy, not far from Bayeux.'

'Oh, God be praised and God be with them,' was all I could
say.

'God be with them,' he echoed. 'I feel sure they are having
a tough time. We must remember them in prayer.'

Rushing back to the chapel I sent a messenger to gather
the boys who had been at service, to spread word all over the
camp. Quickly the chapel filled and we knelt down in prayer,
raising our hearts to God, begging him to help our comrades
who even as we prayed were fighting and dying as they re-
claimed France inch by inch, foot by foot and mile by mile
from the Boche.

Throughout that day the caserne hummed with joyful, excited discussion of the news and I prayed with fervour for
those who had come to succour all of us and let light, happiness
and God's freedom into Europe again. When darkness fell
we lay awake in our rooms scarcely whispering to each other
but knowing that each of us was awake and the thoughts of
each were enough to keep him wakeful until dawn. Our loved
ones were close to us for the first time in years.

Throughout the following day we prisoners were excited
and I, suddenly conscious that our moment of joy was the
beginning of a campaign in which a multitude of our brothers
would fight their way over roads and fields, prayed and arranged
services of prayer. The camp leaders reminded us that the
battle was still in process of the fighting and while victory
was inevitable men were risking their lives for our country
and for us now helpless and frustrated in the caserne. We
prepared our comrades for freedom and the problems it would

bring, for we were making ready in our hearts to take up our tasks again.

In talk with Helmut I learned that he was making ready to face the perils of retreat. His wife and family were returned to the Reich. German women were being cleared from the city. None knew just what course the great battle soon to gain ferocious momentum would take and the Germans were preparing to salvage what they could from the debris of their imperial dreams. My friend, like my soldier friends of the journeys from Italy and the south, had expected this day for many months. But there was sadness in contrasting the hopes that had stirred his heart in the beginnings of the Third Reich and the evil thing it had become. That sadness, I knew, was minimised by a new hope, that Germany repentant might work out her days of retribution and that his Germany, the Christian Reich, might rise again and play a decent and honourable role in the intercourse of the nations. Our conversations were tinged by joyful anticipation. Soon there would be peace and Sunday morning again would be the culminating point of the week's work when we would lead our flocks to face another week.

June passed into July and the radio kept us close to the fortunes of the fighting men. Our prayers and our hopes increased. And discipline in the camp grew more benevolent.

I longed for the sight of Paris again, my own parish and for my friends in the city, for all the Scots, whether Protestant, Catholic or Jewish, know the church in the Rue Bayard and have an affectionate place in their hearts for our Caledonian social work. Eagerly I discussed church work with Helmut and one day I found him smiling in his gentle way as I halted in talk.

'Donald,' he said. 'How would you like to make a little visit outside the caserne? Come down to the country with me. Not far, to a place near the river where you can talk in your own language with friends?'

My heart leaped. Outside the July sun was beating down on Paris and the recollected beauty of the city poured into my mind.

'What do you mean, Helmut,' I stammered.

'I mean that I have applied for a pass for you to accompany me to Madame Barroux's home close to the Seine. I think I will get it and we may spend a day with your friend.'

Madame Barroux had already been to me a friend in need. She was an American from Virginia married to a Frenchman. Helmut had arranged that she send parcels to me in Fresnes and these had helped to make the burden of that noisome place easier to bear.

'When do we go?' I asked him.

He laughed and answered, 'Soon.'

Chatou-sur-Seine, where Helen Barroux lives is a pleasant place and on that day as the car sped through the streets of the city I was conscious only of change for the better. The soldiers would soon be gone I knew and the streets of the city, the great and noble buildings under the sunlight would remain. The trees beneath them were radiant and the bright light of the town seemed to exude the laughter of France which is high and gay, confident and wise, and young forever.

Helen, who was to become my friend and helper in the months ahead, greeted us with evident pleasure. An American and, like all the women of her country, a born hostess, the prospect of entertaining someone who had been in gaol made her determined that the day would be remembered by the odd assortment of clerics, German and British, that confronted her in the two little men who arrived hungry and ready for lunch.

We ate a meal that had been coaxed with splendid taste and skill from the scanty materials available in the Paris of 1944 and we spoke of Jacques, Helen's husband, a Frenchman who was in gaol for the crime of loving his own country and freedom more than Germany and Nazism. Jacques, her husband, was a brilliant interior decorator. Through his business contacts, he was given the task of changing the décor at what had been the German Embassy in Paris. He did his work well, but when documents began to disappear from the place shortly afterwards, he was arrested. So effectively had he covered his tracks that they could hold him only on suspicion. He escaped death but he endured the torture of Nazi gaols before freedom was won again.

After our meal on my holiday from gaol we went on the river and, under the sun, drifted casually. My friends, aware that the sun, air and the cool surface of the water, the gentle movement of the boat were indescribable luxury to me, were silent. Such moments of happiness are rare in life. They come as rewards against the days of suffering. I was grateful and I remember as we moved on the breast of the Seine thinking sadly of the friends who had died and of the five o'clock departures from Fresnes to the place of execution. Happiness after such experiences is never unmixed with sadness. In my gratitude I prayed for them, that they might be rewarded. My own good fortune seemed a miracle. I watched the insects dance above the flowing water, the sunlight on the trees, heard the birds sing and their song illuminated my soul. The boat's speed gathering momentum jerked me from reveries and I looked up to see Helmut pulling hard upon the oars.

'I am going to have a swim, Donald,' he said. 'Why don't you and Helen join me?'

Before I could answer the lady intervened.

'No, no, Pastor Peters, I have much to discuss with Pastor Caskie. Perhaps another time,' but turning to me, 'please come home and we'll prepare tea while Pastor Peters swims and perhaps you will advise me.'

I agreed, in a rather mystified way, wondering why the young lady should have waited for a minister who was in gaol, and until a few months ago unlikely to be released, to consult on her difficulties. Alas, she had none. It was part of a female plot. We entered her drawing-room and I spoke:

'What can I do for you, Helen?'

'You can forgive me for deceiving Pastor Peters,' she answered, 'and come upstairs. I have something to show you, something that will cheer you very much.'

Even more mystified I followed her to the very top of the house and there, paradoxically, under the slates, I found what must have been one of the few 'underground' sewing circles in France.

'Do not worry, ladies,' I heard Helen's cheerful voice ring out. 'This is the Pastor from the Scottish Church in the

Rue Bayard, presently interned in St Denis and out on a pass. He is a friend.'

I gazed at their work in wonderment. On a big table lay a number of the national flags of Britain, France and America. On the floor were stacked in profusion bundles of those glorious emblems, Union Jacks, Stars and Stripes, Tricolours. Those on the table were in process of completion. Their makers, knowing I was a friend, gazed shyly at me but with pride glowing behind their gentle smiles.

'Glory be, ladies,' I said, 'what does this mean?'

'It means, dear Padre,' answered my hostess, 'that within weeks we shall go out of here to wave these flags in the streets, to hang them from our windows and set them flying on the house-tops. The Allied armies are drawing near and the F.F.I. is organised. Soon there will be a rising in the city. When the Allies come in, the Germans who have not retreated will be imprisoned.'

'So it is as close as that.'

I stood by the table, running the flag through my fingers, in the happiness of the afternoon feeling already the sense of release which must have come to all prisoners at such times. I had known that the time was close, but this made it real. And I loved those good ladies who serenely ran their illegal sewing bee.

'God grant, dear friends,' I said, 'that very soon now you will have the happiness of seeing your work line the streets when our men arrive to free the city.'

There was a hum of pleasure, much raising of hands in agreement, many smiles; when I left they stood up and bowed.

We made tea and soon Helmut joined us to talk of his plans for the future.

'I shall leave soon, Donald,' he said. 'But we will meet when all is quiet again.'

That night as we returned to St Denis, I could not speak. The accumulated experiences of the day, the drive through beloved roads I had thought never to see again, the lunch chez Madame Barroux, the river and the sun, the seamstresses in the attic and the prospect of liberation filled my mind. I bade Helmut good night and thanked him with fervour.

During the following few weeks the atmosphere in St Denis grew joyfully tense. I saw Helmut once or twice and then I did not see him and sensed he had joined the retreat. From the caserne we could see that in the most ironical way the exodus of Paris had been reversed in 1944. Vehicles of all shapes and sizes, tanks, heavy artillery, limousines carrying, presumably, officers of considerable rank, crowded the road. The staff of the caserne began to thin out. We knew that our imprisonment was now a matter of days, and at night we lay, our ears cocked in the silence, waiting, waiting, waiting. Only air-raid warnings had broken that silence during recent years; and for many nights before sleeping we listened for them.

And then one night as I lay on my upper berth in the big barrack-like cell I shared with thirteen others, I heard the far off blessed noise. It was an impossible sound; I doubted my ears. But faint, sweet and clear it came again and I cried out to my cell-mates.

'Listen, listen. They are here. A bell is ringing. It is the sign of liberation.'

From their beds they moved close to the window. Without a sound, in their bare feet they stood listening and waiting. And then far away, the bell rang again and then nearer we heard another. But still we waited in silence. We were afraid we might disturb the music of freedom ringing from the churches of the city.

That first eager tinkle called more and more bell-ringers to their posts and it was drowned in the rising tide of sound. The bells of Notre Dame, St Sulplice and hundreds of other churches in the French metropolis were ringing out the glad news on that memorable August night in 1944 that the Allies had entered the city and that Zion's captivity was at an end.

CHAPTER TWENTY

A Tank on the Champs Elysées

PARIS RESOUNDED with the rejoicing of the free. The music of the bells echoed throughout the air. We waited, our hearts full of gratitude. Then a man in another room began to cheer and like the bells of Paris the prisoners of St Denis followed the leader. A great roar of happiness bubbled from the caserne. One of my comrades rushed to the door of our room, flung it open and ran downstairs. The place was thronged with mèn. There was not a German in sight. Our guards had fled. Offices and German living quarters were deserted and a thorough search was made by the responsible officers for documentation that might prove useful to the incoming command.

We wandered through the caserne, talking freely to each other, rejoicing in the absence of guards. Some of the younger men were restrained with difficulty from rushing out on to the roads. But already fighting was going on in the streets and before many hours passed a thin, tough youth with a tommy-gun in his grasp arrived to instruct us—for our own good—to keep off the streets.

'Messieurs, the temptation is strong to get out of prison, he said with a quick, tense smile in the tanned face, 'but be patient. Far from ensuring your safety, we will only add to your peril, for the military have not quite arrived. This is a Free French rising. We are fighting our way. At any moment the Germans will strike back.'

He hustled out and we were left to wait. He was a wise mentor. Through the night we huddled in our rooms, listening to explosions, the crack of rifle shots, random shouts, the noises of guerrilla warfare. Morning came and we scraped together meals from the supplies that our fleeing hosts had left behind. During that second day we had a few more visitors, each a hardy youth with tommy-gun or rifle and each repeating the warnings to stay off the streets. Towards evening, one of the young men broke under the strain of waiting and flung his life away by disregarding the guerrillas' advice. He slipped from the barracks and was not seen again alive. His body was found later lying in a gutter, the head pierced by a rifle shot.

The second night of freedom from German supervision was spent even more ironically by the liberated guests of the caserne. Sometime soon after ten o'clock shells began to whistle over the building and we retreated to the basement to await death or the dawn, wondering if we had been wise to follow the counsels of the young maquis. Would it have been easier to dodge bullets in the street than shells in the gaol? Better, someone observed, to be brought down on the leg than to be a sitting pigeon. Dust descended on us in clouds, the walls shivered and seemed about to split. The roar of the exploding shells nearly shattered our ear drums, but there were no casualties. The men with the tommy-guns spoke wisely. None died in St Denis after liberation apart from that solitary one who could not wait for the gate to open for him.

Throughout the day and into the night the shelling continued and we remained disagreeably safe in our basement, listening to the shells bursting and gloomily still wondering about the wisdom of the F.F.I. On the fourth day a Red Cross car arrived with supplies and the official in charge invited me to leave with him.

The journey into the centre of the metropolis convinced me of our wisdom in staying put since the night the bells rang. No one who was absent from Paris in those few days can envisage the running fight through the streets, the winding lanes and squares, the rifles firing from high windows and shops, the bodies dropping on the cobbles, the feeling of a myriad of one- and two-man battles that spat from the very pavements. My Red Cross friend had the genius of the French for making a car behave like a greyhound. The vehicle positively leaped through the city. I crouched down close to the floor conscious of the rifle bullets that buzzed about

us on every few crossings. He dropped me by the Place de
la Concorde and for the first time in years I was alone in
freedom. For the first time since 1940 I was back in my
beloved city, free to put my hands in my pockets and stroll
up the Avenue des Champs-Elysées, which is exactly what I
did. I walked through scurrying men bearing rifles, citizens
rushing towards businesses or what passed for business during
the hectic time of liberation until I came to the Rue du
Colisée and there made my way to the Hôtel Avenida, praying
that the patron, a dear friend, had survived the occupation.

As I crossed the threshold I heard a frantic yell of joy.

'Monsieur Donald Caskie. Monsieur le Pasteur, welcome
home to Paris.' Tears were streaming down her face, her
arms around my neck and she was vehemently embracing
me in the French fashion. 'Oh, cher Pasteur, we were told
you were dead.'

Madam was overcome by emotion and I was so moved
to see my old friend in the Avenida that we both collapsed
into chairs and spoke incoherently for a few moments, trying
to express our happiness in a Paris miraculously free of
enemies. The British and the Americans had arrived. The
familiar friendly khaki could be seen from the windows.

'Oh, Monsieur, to see again our friends and to know those
soldiers out there do not menace us. The Americans throw
sweets and chewing-gum to the children. The British bring
food.'

She was half-weeping, half-laughing and not until a servant
brought us real coffee—'A gift from an American visitor'
—and we drank together did she relax and sit watching me
with a twinkle in her eyes.

Suddenly, majestically, she stood up, with an air of mock
pomposity, belied by a smile.

'Follow me, Monsieur Donald and the Scottish Pasteur
will see how his French friend keeps trust.'

She led the way downstairs, deep into the basement, past
the intriguing scents that come from a French hotel kitchen
and into a cellar.

'Voilà, Monsieur Donald. You see the goods you deposited
here for safe custody before the Germans entered Paris.'

Neatly stacked in a corner were books, furniture and other materials from the various offices I had used in my work as a minister in the old days, among them the Toc H lamp, for before the war, as now, I was Toc H padre in Paris.

Proudly Madam looked on and I thanked her. The possessions which surround one in work become precious to a minister; they are not his property but they, as the years pass, become something like helpers. There was and is something personal in that Toc H lamp; it is a material object that is an old friend.

Madam agreed to lodge me in the hotel until I straightened out my affairs and investigated the condition of the church and the manse. I set off across the Avenue des Champs-Elysées to the Rue Bayard which is about ten minutes walk away.

When I turned the corner of the Avenue Montaigne into the Rue Bayard my steps slackened and I began to fear what I might find. Gaston's café came into view; I could see him setting the tables. I hurried past and there it was, our church. Thankfulness filled my heart for it seemed untouched. I stood outside and gazed at it for many minutes my eyes devouring the blessed place which I had not seen for more than four years. And then I returned along the street to find Gaston clearing a table that stood outside his café on the pavement. He threw up his hands in recognition.

'Monsieur le Pasteur, a thousand welcomes. Monsieur le Pasteur, where have you been?'

I took his hand. He chuckled and shouted his pleasure at seeing me. My homecomings were assuming something like gala proportions in their effects on myself and my friends.

'Come in, Monsieur Donald. But wait, I have something for you.'

He disappeared into the rear of the café and a few minutes later appeared holding out the key of the church.

'See, Monsieur. It is here. I did not give it to them. I am a French Catholic but I have kept the key of the Scottish Church safe for you.'

The theological aspects of his charge seemed to give Gaston

tremendous pleasure. He roared with laughter as he spoke the words and dug me in the ribs.

'Perhaps the key has converted me just a little, Monsieur Donald, to your Protestant faith, eh?'

To see his joy was touching and his pride in keeping the key of the church and the building inviolate lifted my heart.

'It may be, indeed, Gaston,' I said. 'But whatever the cause, how can I thank you?'

Gaston had the French feeling for dramatic occasions. The smile faded and he stood straight, a little absurd in his pride and quite wonderful in his generosity.

'You shall not thank me more, Monsieur le Pasteur. Are we not neighbours and friends? Now let us forget the past. Dear friend, they are gone and now'—he laughed aloud— 'it shall be like it was before they came. Will it not be so?'

'We will make it so, dear Gaston,' I told him. 'We will make it better. The good God has kept us, you and me, safe, and we must be happy now for so many have died.'

'You will have coffee and when you have seen the church you must return for luncheon.'

Over our drink he told me that the Germans had asked him for the key of the church and he denied having it.

'But, Messieurs,' he said. 'There is nothing there. It is a church no more and it is closed. Le Pasteur left when you became our guests and no one comes now. They went away and I was not again approached for the key.'

It was exactly as he said. There was no change in the church except that the key was stiff in the lock and when it turned with a grinding click and I flung the door open, dust lay heavily on the interior. Motes danced thickly in the sunshine that flooded into the porch. The sound of my footsteps echoed in the empty building. On the table by the doorway the sprig of white heather I had left behind me in June, 1940, lay withered and welcoming. I was home; my fingers were gentle as I touched that morsel of Scotland. Before I returned to Gaston for luncheon I prayed again in our own church and thanked God for my deliverance. I remember the words of Abraham Lincoln came to my mind and I thought, ' these will be my guide in the days to come. . . .'

'With malice towards none, with charity for all; with firmness in the right as God gives me to see it, let us strive on to finish the work we are in; to bind up the nation's wounds; to care for him who shall have borne the battle and for his widow and his orphans . . .'

And then I moved around the familiar building, opening windows, noting the work that must be commenced immediately to make the building clean for Sunday's service. The air and sunlight touched the dear walls and the happiness of the minister grew until he fancied choirs of angels were singing as he moved about his task.

The days that followed were busy with our late summer cleaning. From my window in the Avenida I watched Paris liberated take revenge on its traitors and celebrate the arrival of the liberators. There were the wretched women who had befriended the Germans. For their punishment they were paraded shaven-headed through the streets. There were the members of the *milice* hunted into corners, and summarily shot by the maquis. There were the Germans who in their turn had become prisoners-of-war being led in pride of conquest by the F.F.I., to places of internment. For a few weeks Paris was berserk but I was busy, first in the Hôtel Avenida preparing to take up my old life and then from the manse in the Rue Piccini.

Before I moved back to my own home I received a visitor from British Intelligence, the customary polite officer, his deferential approach bringing a quick poignant recollection of the nocturnal callers at the Rue Forbin.

'You are Donald Caskie of the Seamen's Mission in Marseilles and later a member of the staff of Grenoble University?'

'I am Donald Caskie, minister at the Scottish Church in the Rue Bayard.'

'I have been instructed to find you, sir. You are required at Intelligence Headquarters. Please come with me.'

He was an agreeable young man and I had no reason to suspect him but the habits I had acquired in war were not easily put aside.

'I cannot accompany you now. Please give me the address of this place and I shall find my way there tomorrow morning.'

He bowed and handed me an envelope and we parted.

I did not wait until morning, but in the later afternoon of the same day went to the place which was a large villa on the edge of the forest of Boulogne west of the city. As I neared the building two British soldiers challenged me.

'I am a padre, lads,' I said. 'Donald Caskie is the name.'

'Come this way, Padre,' one of them answered. 'We have orders to take you to the boss as soon as you arrive.'

I met 'the boss' on the steps leading to the villa and he knew me.

'Donald Caskie, I presume,' he observed using Stanley's words of Livingstone when they met in Africa.

'Yes,' I answered, 'here I am—at least what is left of me after seven prison terms and the internment camp.'

My host was, in the way of the Intelligence Service, just as polite as the junior members of his corps with whom I had worked.

'Do come in, Padre,' he said, 'and please excuse the dreadful aroma of the place. We moved in only yesterday and there are still some German corpses in the cellar. We have been so frightfully busy, just haven't had a moment to spare to bury the fellows. Must get round to it this evening.'

In his office we sat down and he turned and looked hard at me.

'We know all about your war work, Padre. How are you off for cash?'

'I am penniless. At present I am living on—tick—isn't that the word—with old friends in the Hôtel Avenida.'

Automatically, it seemed, his hand flicked open a desk drawer; he extracted a bundle of French notes and handed them to me.

'Take this stuff,' he said. 'It should tide you over your present difficulties.

'Now,' he continued, 'I suppose you want to go home at once and see your family after all these years of separation. That is what any man would wish and I hate asking you to sacrifice your hopes. But the job here is not finished, Padre. Not by any means. A tricky time lies immediately ahead. Will you remain in Paris as an officiating chaplain and help us with your knowledge of the city and, most important, experience over the past four years?'

Without a pang much as I longed for Scotland, I agreed to wait until my services were no longer urgently needed in the city and so I settled into work again. My days were busy; we opened a canteen for the R.A.F. at Le Bourget, the first British canteen in liberated France and when called upon I aided the Intelligence Service. My friends began to appear in the town, arriving at the manse in the Rue Piccini to share a cup of Caskie's tea.

I became visiting chaplain to our men in various camps, and to military offenders in the prison at Port de Lilas, on the outskirts of Paris and one day the camp commandant from the latter establishment sent for me. I was feeling rather low in health at the time and physically was little more than skin and bone. Major Macdonald, the commandant, opened characteristically by warning me to rest more and then continued.

'I've got a new chap here, Padre. I want you to see him. He's British all right, but he was picked up disguised as an American colonel. A tough case. He refuses to talk. We don't know yet just who he is.'

The major went on to tell me about this taciturn prisoner. It was apparent that he was an interesting specimen. For three months, it was known, he had attached himself to a special unit engaged in recovering art treasures that had been sent to Germany. He was a popular and efficient officer. Then an inquisitive man had discovered that he was doing a little private looting on his own account. He was arrested and the Americans, having discovered he was not one of their forces

—something for which they could be thankful—handed him over to the British.

'He is a crook, all right,' said Major Macdonald. 'I'd like you to have a chat with him. We'll find out who he is soon enough, and for his own sake the sooner the better.'

He was Cole. As soon as I entered the cell I recognised him and saw that he knew me. But quickly he pulled himself together.

'Hello, No. 11,' I said. 'We meet in interesting circumstances. So many of our friends have been in gaol, rather worse gaols than this you will understand.'

He had the effrontery of the born confidence man.

'Name of Smith, Padre,' he countered immediately. 'You've made a mistake. What's more, preaching's not wanted here. Get out.'

The brazen falsehood of the man enraged me. Thoughts of Pat—whom I again thought dead—my comrades of Marseilles, the Abbé Carpentier, boiled in my head and I shouted at him.

'You lie. You disgusting traitor. Are you quite without shame? You deserted your country. You sold your friends for money, accepted money from the Nazis—God help you. And you abandoned your wife to——'

'Leave her out of it,' he yelled back across the cell. 'If you are a gentleman and a Christian you'll tell no man's wife of his mistakes. Soon I'll be gone. Leave it at that.'

But he insisted he was not Cole and I was touched by the spark aroused in him by mention of his wife. I left the cell.

Major Macdonald was waiting for me. I reported what I knew of his prisoner. He whistled and told me that I would be summoned later when a check had been put on my information.

I left the prison that day with a heavy heart. Seeing Cole had reminded me of the dead ones, the bright lives extinguished by his treachery. Comradeship in war is such that while one always feels cut off from the friends who die, somehow one always remains part of that fellowship of death. Always they live in one's memories. In the manse that night I prayed as

I had learned in prison, thanking God for those who died that we might live. Next day the authorities sent for me and, in the course of that meeting, I learned news that lifted my spirits again. Pat O'Leary was alive. It was the first news I had heard of him, except that he had been taken by the Gestapo in 1942.

'I have heard nothing better since the night the bells of Paris rang and we listened to them at the Camp at St Denis,' I told my informant and he smiled and clapped me generously on the back.

'Your friend is alive, Padre,' he said, 'and he will survive. He's not the kind that dies easily. But he is in pretty bad shape. At present he is in hospital in Bavaria, where they are trying to put flesh back on his bones. We will have to wait some weeks before we can bring him to Paris where he will check on your identification of Cole.'

'Pat will make no mistake,' I told him. 'But—pardon me for saying—don't you make one! Cole is one of the trickiest scoundrels that have exploited this war. The devil is in the fellow. Watch him night and day.'

They watched him but he escaped. A great hunt began for him. But Paris is a city in which it is easy to hide. Time passed and I was warned not to venture out alone at night for he had sworn to kill me. There is comedy even in evil. Cole apparently believed my identification of him was a betrayal. I am not of the stuff of heroes and I remained home in the evenings, or went out with friends, except when an urgent call came from one of my people who was ill. And then one evening the telephone bell rang in the manse.

Cole had been located in a flat on the Rue de Grenelle. Would I stand by to identify him when he was arrested? The building was surrounded by armed men. It was expected that the traitor would put up a desperate fight for freedom. It is curiously true that those who sell the liberty of their comrades, always cherish their own. If Cole were taken alive, my caller said, I would be summoned immediately. I agreed and hung up.

It was an evening shortly after the heart-warming news that 'Pat O'Leary' had been awarded the George Cross and

I remember walking the floor of the drawing-room thinking on those extraordinary extremes, the Belgian hero with the Irish name, and the Englishman, and the forces each had represented in the European conflict. The Belgian hero, a professional healer in peacetime, who, in his gay and un-egotistical manner—indeed, he deprecated his own efforts—had given his all for freedom. There was the English soldier, in times of peace a policeman, who had consciencelessly sold the lives and freedom of so many good men and women. The chapter was about to end. Pat had emerged on the side of victory and his courage had been recognised by the King of the country whose side he had espoused. The French were closing in on the poor wicked animal who had sent the Abbé to his death, and many other members of the Resistance.

The telephone bell jangled through the quiet house. I picked up the receiver.

'Is that Donald Caskie?'

'Yes.'

'He's dead, Padre.'

'God help him,' I replied. 'May God have mercy on his soul.'

'We sent half a dozen men in after him. The door was locked and they had to break it down. He got two of our men before the others filled him with bullets. Our two chaps are wounded but they'll be all right in a day or two. He's as dead as ever he'll be.'

I hung up the receiver. I suppose if the troops had waited for a few days, keeping Cole under observation, he would have been taken alive. But I think they did the right thing; he would have been executed anyway after a fair trial. But a fair trial would have brought agonies on his innocent family for the story of his sordid treachery would have been revealed to the world. The French have a logic of their own. He was in the Hands of God the omniscient and merciful Judge and his life was over.

My only difficulties now were of a practical nature, for there was much suffering in Paris during that first period after the liberation. Again I found myself distributing to the needy the contents of food parcels from charitable organisations in Britain and America. Even among the newly imprisoned Germans one found work and this had the healing force of charity and was part of that 'binding of wounds' that Lincoln spoke of so many years ago and far across the sea.

One pleasant afternoon when I had an hour to spare from my tasks I sat playing my piano in the manse when I heard German voices in the street outside. Beneath my window a squad of sad-looking lads in enemy uniform were lined up under the supervision of a couple of cheerful British corporals.

'Hullo there, soldiers,' I shouted, 'are you taking a rest period?'

The British lads smiled up at me and one of them answered:

'Yes, Padre. These blokes down here are going to be medically examined but the M.O. is not ready for them yet and they are taking the air with us.'

'Do you think they would like a cup of tea and a sandwich?' I asked.

'I don't know about them, Padre, but we would,' came the answer.

'Let's try them out,' I said.

One of the corporals came upstairs to the manse, which is on the first floor, and we made tea and opened cans of corned beef, sardines and American salmon. In about twenty minutes we had covered a big church tray with slab-like sandwiches and filled a dozen monster mugs I was storing for canteen work.

The atmosphere in the street became that of a school outing. The cheerful corporals dashed among their charges, dishing out the 'treats' laughing at them and saying, 'Come on chaps, eat up. It's our birthday.' I returned to my piano and strummed on the keys, listening to the happy noise below until the doorbell rang.

A young German officer stood on the mat outside, behind him one of the corporals looking very respectful.

'Padre, this bloke would like to thank you.'

I invited them to enter.

'Herr Pastor,' the officer began, very formally, 'it is my duty and great pleasure to thank you for your generosity to the men below and to me, their officer. They, too, ask me to say that they are grateful and much encouraged by your goodness. May I say that I am a Protestant Christian and to meet you means much to me?'

I was in uniform and I turned to the corporal.

'Corporal. May I see this officer alone? Have you time to spare to leave him here? You will call him, of course, as soon as the M.O. is free to see him and the men under your charge.'

'Yes, Padre, of course. And, Padre, he's a nice bloke.'

When we were alone I asked the young man to sit down. I leaned on the piano.

'There's no need to thank me,' I told him. 'As you say we are Christians and, after all, I am a chaplain to the forces and God would have me help all poor soldiers. I also know,' with a smile, 'that the best way to open a conversation on Christian doctrine with a poor soldier in any army is to give him a cup of tea and a good sonsy sandwich.'

I offered him a little cigar, from a box given me by a kindly American officer and we chatted. He was one of those devout young Lutherans, an intellectual Protestant of a kind that Germany produces, intensely alive to the currents and cross-currents of contemporary Christian thought. When I told him of my friendship with Helmut Peters, he jumped up from the chair and slapped his hands.

'But, Doktor, I know Herr Peters. He is my friend. Oh, it is good to see you, his friend, too, and to know that he helped you and now you help us.'

We spoke of music and I played for him, Scottish airs and then some Christian music which is a universal language. When the corporal called I asked to be given details of Captain Wilhelm's place of internment and put it in my book. During his few months in Paris I managed to obtain his release on a few afternoons. He played the piano, and we discussed music and the Church to his heart's content. He was a good young man and became a friend.

It was a strange time and work was complicated by an

incessant need to forage or, in the dry language of soldiers, scrounge. Autumn came. Fuel was a very trying problem. I mentioned this to one of the Intelligence officers in the villa on the edge of the forest. He advised me to approach a certain major in the British Embassy who would, he felt sure, help us at the church. Next day I presented my card at the British Embassy in the Rue du Faubourg St Honoré and asked for this officer. The official at the door was not hopeful that I would be given an interview.

'He is extremely busy, but I will present your card immediately.'

A few minutes later the major appeared and taking my hand drew me into the hallway.

'Donald Caskie,' he said, 'I have been looking forward to meeting you.'

I must have looked as mystified as I felt for he laughed and continued:

'Do you remember X'—using the name of that agent I knew but never by name—'I am he. We were on the same job, you know. You sent our men across into Spain. I arranged the rest when they reached Madrid. Now, what can I do for you?'

'I need coal, Major,' I answered. 'The church is too cold for the old people in the congregation—indeed, in normal times we would consider it cold enough for polar bears.'

He chuckled and answered:

'Coal you shall have, Padre. Can you be at the Rue Bayard by eight tomorrow morning? I'll see the Army brings you four tons which should keep things hot enough for your people for a bit. When you need more come and see me again. You shall have it.'

On the following Sunday the Kirk was cosy and, I know, the most comfortable place my flock had been in for weeks.

Not many weeks later this same officer helped me again. I heard that all the German property in Paris was about to be confiscated by the French, a move which had my complete approval until it dawned upon me that among the German materials were the family possessions of Pastor Helmut Peters, my friend. In desperation I called upon the major and found that he knew all about Helmut's intervention on my behalf; the whole story of how he had striven to protect me was on record in the British Embassy where the authorities agreed that he saved my life.

Major X wrote to the French Minister of the Interior, explained the services Mr Peters had given the British chaplain, and requested that his belongings should remain intact and be placed under British protection. With great courtesy the Minister granted the request and a few weeks later a British lorry delivered Helmut's furniture to the vicarage in a little village near Hanover. With it went a large parcel of flour, tea, sugar, canned goods, powdered milk and cigarettes. So the Christian International continues to work for its members in peace and war.

The church in the Rue Bayard was open again and services had become as regular as in the old days before 1940. But my happiness on the first Sunday after liberation can only be imagined; it cannot be described.

When I looked out on the congregation that morning it seemed that victory had already been achieved. The building was crowded with men in khaki, British soldiers of liberation and members of the Control Commission, among them the remnant of my scattered flock. I was assisted by Professor E. P. Dickie of St Mary's College, St Andrews, who had been my teacher of Greek. The happy faces of the soldiers were turned to us and surely I have never led a more joyful service to Almighty God our Father, Protector and Leader. And never have men more fervently raised their voices in the Psalm which had been sung thousands of years past by others who had known the bitterness of bondage by the rivers of Babylon:

> 'When Zion's bondage God turned back,
> Like men that dreamed were we,
> Then filled with laughter was our mouth,
> Our tongue with melody.'

The service ended and I had my moment of silence after leading my congregation in prayer.

I walked out of the church and was hailed from a tank which stood on the Rue Bayard.

'Jump in, Padre,' a brown-faced man, in the khaki and black beret of the Tank Corps, shouted. 'Cheers for the Seamen's Mission on the Rue Forbin.'

The tall sergeant whose head protruded through the turret was one of the chaps I had sent out of Southern France more than three years earlier and his grin extended from ear to ear. He was laughing at my astonishment. After that happy first service this new and joyful shock brought me near to tears but in a twinkling I was by his side and the tank, crew shouting hilariously, rumbled on its way towards the Avenue des Champs-Elysées. The August sun beat down on us and I stood beside my old comrade and from the pavements of Paris the people shouted greetings and we shouted back to them. Down the long broad, noble avenue we rumbled in triumph towards the Place de la Concorde and I knew in that moment what victory meant, peace, love, happiness and freedom—the luxury of holding one's head upright marching with friends under God's own sun and sky.

Epilogue

In 1957, looking forward to the building of our new Scottish church in Paris and looking back on 1944-45, I see that last winter and spring of the war in Europe as a chaos of memories, some sad, some ineffably happy, and a few comic. Many of my friends and comrades died in the camps. Others, whom I had thought dead, survived by marvellous tenacity and courage. Lieut.-Commander Pat O'Leary, R.N., most daring and brilliant of the underground leaders with whom I served, fought on, even when he was imprisoned in one of the vilest concentration camps, organising a resistance and never despairing of victory. Peace revealed that this hero of the patriotic forces was no more Irish than most of the other maquis but Dr Edmond Guerise, a Brussels medical man. He was awarded the George Cross for his valiant services, a decoration accepted by him with modesty and thought of with pride by those who had the honour of his comradeship.

One had seen the best of human nature during those years in Marseilles, Grenoble and prison. One also saw the worst. The spiritual reward for all the suffering was a sharpened awareness of the range, for good and evil, of the human soul and a more profound compassion for men. Peace brought recognition for the valorous and punishment for the wicked, and I confess, without shame, that when the news was brought to me of the end of Paul Cole, who had brought death and torture to many of my friends, the feeling that justice had been done was mingled with pity for one who had wasted his life and besmirched his soul so wantonly. He might have served as valiantly as the generous leader he betrayed, Pat O'Leary, but instead he chose Judas as his exemplar.

But life continued in wartime Paris and my health improved. Work was a wonderful tonic and each evening, when free from other duties, I went out to Le Bourget to the canteen which the ladies of the Scottish parish were running. I would talk to the lads assembled there, listen to their songs, and greedily gather from them news of the little towns and villages from whence they had come to fight; places that had never figured in the news, but were the Scotland and England that I love. As Christmas approached we arranged a party for the local children of Le Bourget, and, true to that friendly spirit which is a tradition of British servicemen, the lads gave up their weekly rations of sweets and chocolate, to be put aside for the French children in the district. Lord and Lady Tedder honoured us by coming to the party, and the gifts from the airmen were handed out by Lady Tedder. It was the first time that most of these tiny tots had ever tasted chocolate, and it was a delight to see them enjoying it at this festive season of the Nativity.

That party pleasantly terminates my thoughts of war in Europe.

As 1944 was drawing to a close I decided that I must pay a flying visit to the homeland which I had not seen for almost seven years.

I had heard that the camp commandant at Le Bourget was

flying to England after Christmas, and at the canteen one night, I asked him if he would allow me to share the two-seater plane with him. I longed to see my family again, and would like to ' bring in ' the New Year with them.

' Padre,' he said, ' I am very sorry, but you are not coming with me. You are needed here, and I am taking a grave risk by intending to cross the Channel in this thick fog.'

His words proved prophetic. A few minutes after his plane took off from the aerodrome of Le Bourget, it crashed on a hillside north of Paris, and he was killed. Once more the Divine Hand had barred the Bithynian Road, for my work was not yet finished. My appointed time had not yet come.

The thick fog still hung over the French metropolis, and did so for five days. On the fourth day of the fog, I met a young pilot whom I had helped during the war, and he promised to take me with him, after warning me that it would be a risky business, and that I must be prepared to rough it.

Soon after the take-off, I found myself in complete agreement with the pilot when he had said that we were taking risks. I could see the perspiration streaming down his face as he turned towards me and said, ' Padre, keep praying. You've been through a lot during the past few years, and I feel sure that the God in whom we trust, will guide us safely through this thick fog, and land us without hurt or harm on the English shore.'

He had some chewing-gum, and he handed me a piece, saying, ' Donald, chew this. I have always found chewing-gum helpful in an emergency.' The chewing-gum had the desired effect. It released the strain and calmed our nerves in a most amazing way.

After flying for a considerable time which seemed hours to me, the pilot turned to me and said : ' I see land. Thank God, we're safe. We're over England.'

I looked out and down, but it was not England I saw, but the coast of France.

' We're over Le Hâvre,' I said to my pilot friend. ' I know it so well.'

' Impossible,' he said, ' but, nevertheless, I must make a landing. My supply of petrol is running short.'

Three and a half hours had passed since we left Le Bourget, and most of that time we had been flying over the Atlantic. Without wasting time, the pilot—one of the best—made a forced landing, in a dilapidated airfield near Le Hâvre.

Having refuelled we took off again, but our perilous adventures were not yet over. The tail of the plane struck something, and the machine began to lurch and reel like a drunken man. Then one of the engines failed to function. Fortunately for us, the other kept going, until we landed at the aerodrome in Dunsfold in Surrey.

As soon as we landed, I knelt down on the ground—the dear homeland which I had not seen or touched for almost seven years, and I kissed the ground, and gave thanks to God that I was home again, although it was only England, and not my much loved Scotland. I have always loved England, but from the moment when we landed safely on the airfield in Surrey, and when I recall the warm welcome which I received from the ground staff, it will always have second place to my own native Scotland. I recognised one of the ground staff as a young airman whom I had helped to escape during the war. He in his turn recognised the padre of the Seamen's Mission and spread the news of my return to his colleagues in the Service.

I had no British identity card when I landed in England, but the young airman vouched for me; his helpfulness and kindness I shall never forget.

He immediately telephoned to my family to say that I had just arrived in England, and would be travelling home the next day. After the news that night, it was broadcast that Donald Caskie, the Tartan Pimpernel, had just arrived in England.

Following a delicious supper at Dunsfold Airfield, a car was placed at my disposal to take me to London. Accommodation had been arranged for me, and next day I travelled north to Scotland in comfort, thanks to the services of the airman of Dunsfold in Surrey whom I had helped during the war, and his colleagues.

I reached Pennyfern Farm, Greenock, the home of my sister and her husband, Mr and Mrs Alex MacIntyre, half an hour before midnight on New Year's Eve, and the warm welcome I received from both will always remain in my memory.

The first thing I did when I reached Pennyfern Farm was to telephone to my mother and father. It was approaching midnight, and both, with Bibles in hand, were just leaving my old home in Bowmore, Islay, to attend a Watch Night service. My parents were completely overcome with emotion when they heard my voice. Through her sobs I heard mother say, 'Donald, my dear; my prayers are answered. You are home again safe and well, after all you have been through. Your father and I are on our way to the church for the Watch Night service. We shall give thanks to God, for all the goodness and the mercy which have followed you and us. It will be the happiest and most memorable Watch Night service of our lives. Thanks be to God for bringing you back to us in peace and safety.'

Then she added, that dear little 'Mother o' mine,' who used to pray over me, as a babe in her arms, like many a Highland mother, that I might be called to the Christian Ministry: 'Donald, I am going to ask our minister to let us sing the 23rd Psalm tonight to the tune *Crimond*. It will express the feelings which are uppermost in our hearts tonight.'

The minister gave thanks to God for Donald Caskie's safe home-coming, and the Psalm was sung with its lovely closing verse:

> *Goodness and mercy all my life,*
> *Shall surely follow me,*
> *And in God's house for evermore,*
> *My dwelling place shall be.*

Later that year, I visited Fort William without making a hotel reservation. It was summer and I found every hotel booked to the ceiling. Wearily and philosophically I trudged the lovely city, enjoying its beauty and feeling disconsolate about my prospects for the night, thinking it might be a good idea to open hostels for forgetful ministers. Eventually about ten o'clock a kindly hotel manager suggested that he feed me and I go to a private home on the hillside outside the town where he would arrange sleeping-quarters. I agreed, ate, marched out and arrived at the house about the hour of 11 p.m.

The woman of the house, in the Highland way, greeted me with warm dignity.

'Where do you come from, sir?' said she.

'From Paris,' I answered.

'From Paris,' she echoed, 'do you know the Scottish minister there?'

'I think I do,' I answered, rather ruefully bearing in mind the rather tiresome evening I had spent due entirely to that clergyman's naïve approach to lodgings in the towns he visited.

'Oh,' said my hostess, 'I'd like fine to meet him.'

'Donald Caskie's his name, isn't it?' I said. 'A native of Islay.'

'That's him. He helped one of my relatives to escape from the Germans during the war. A lad who is very near and dear to us in this house.'

I could no longer keep up my deception. I told her that I was Caskie and immediately became a guest of honour.

We have a Gaelic saying that 'where there's heart room, there's house room.' The friendship of those I served in wartime enlarged my heart room and their hearts were big with courage and self-sacrifice. I was given sumptuous meals in that Highland home and when I tried to pay I was told:

'Donald Caskie, I owe you very much. You saved a life precious to me. A night's lodging is poor recompense. Whenever you come to Fort William consider this your home.'

Such friendship was part of the rewards I found in peace. I have met them, the lads who fought and escaped at their peril to fight again; in airports, on the streets of English and Scottish cities, and they have come to the manse to talk, renew our friendship and drink the padre's tea. I have sat by the fireside of Hans Helmut Peters in the vicarage at Hanover and he has told me of the British men who came as victorious troops to his country and fed his wife, children and flock and I have called him Titus for he brought me hope and consolation when I lay, like Paul, imprisoned by the enemies of God and man. He calls the British soldiers friends, for they saved from starvation the family and Christians he loves and serves. The German pastor—Titus—and myself have become the closest of friends.

At the moment we are rebuilding the church in the Rue Bayard. The dear building in which our fathers worshipped for nearly a hundred years fell a casualty in the war. On that first morning of my return I had not noticed that the roof had been pierced, apparently with small effect, by shrapnel. But time had allowed the elements to penetrate and dry rot affected the roof. The building became dangerous and had to be demolished. As always good friends came to our aid. The British Ambassador helped us find a temporary shelter in a cinema not far from l'Etoile and I began the minister's task of raising money. The French War Damage Committee was generous to us, and the B.B.C., which I blessed in war as I do in peace for its responsible and honourable attitude to life and religion, permitted me to speak on 'The Week's Good Cause' feature. Over a thousand pounds were added to the rebuilding fund of our Scots Church in Paris, as a result of the B.B.C.'s kindly gesture.

At the moment we have approximately twenty thousand pounds in our rebuilding fund, but we need at least seven or eight thousand pounds more. But I feel confident that friends at home and abroad will rally to our help, and that the new church will rise on the site of the old, free of debt. One purchaser offered us £25,000 for the site of the old church on the Rue Bayard near the Avenue des Champs-Elysées, but we refused the offer. The site is an excellent one in the very heart of the French metropolis, a little bit of Scotland in the great city's centre.

The work of rebuilding the church began on December 26th, 1956. Knowing that her Majesty the Queen was coming to Paris in April to pay her State Visit to France, I decided to petition Her Majesty to lay the foundation stone of our new church. This I did through the British Embassy in Paris.

When I mentioned the matter to my Kirk session they were not very hopeful, nor yet was the British Embassy in

Paris when I was called there, after receipt of my letter of petition. Her Majesty the Queen was the guest of the French. Her programme was very full, and she had only an hour or two to give to her British subjects in Paris.

Nevertheless, the Embassy agreed to send my letter through to the Queen, and in a matter of days, the glad news reached me that the Queen would lay the foundation stone of the new Scots Church in Paris on the morning of April 10th. In his letter, Her Majesty's private secretary added that ' Her Majesty the Queen was particularly pleased at having been asked to lay the foundation stone of the new Scots Church in Paris.'

The 10th of April, 1957, will always remain in my memory as one of the happiest days of my life. On that day Her Majesty the Queen came to the site of our new church in Paris. In brilliant sunshine, and in the presence of a tremendous crowd of people, Her Majesty laid the foundation stone with a silver trowel, and thereafter tapping the corners of the stone, said, ' To the glory of God, I declare this stone well and truly laid.'

The next day I received the following letter from the Queen's private secretary, Major Edward Ford:

Dear Dr Caskie,

I am sending you herewith a photograph of The Queen and the Duke of Edinburgh, which Her Majesty and His Royal Highness have signed for you in memory of the occasion when Her Majesty came and laid the foundation stone of the new Scottish Church. Although The Duke of Edinburgh was not able to accompany Her Majesty, His Royal Highness would like to be associated with this gift.

I am also sending you, under separate cover, two signed portraits of The Queen and The Duke of Edinburgh to be the property of the new church. Her Majesty wishes me, in writing, to thank you for the admirable arrangements which you had made for this brief, but notable ceremony.

Her Majesty the Queen also presented the trowel and mell with which she laid the foundation stone of the church, to be the property of the new church, and added that 'they be kept at the church as a valued souvenir of its foundation.'

The work of rebuilding the church continues, and it is our hope that within a year we shall be back again, worshipping God in the way of our fathers, in the new Scots Church in Paris.

THE END